Department of Economic and Social Affairs
Division for Public Administration and Development Management

UN Global E-Government Readiness Report 2005

From E-government to E-inclusion

United Nations
New York, 2006

DESA

The Department of Economic and Social Affairs of the United Nations Secretariat is a vital interface between global policies in the economic, social and environmental spheres and national action. The Department works in three main interlinked areas: (i) it generates, compiles and analyses a wide range of economic, social and environmental data and information on which Member States of the United Nations draw to review common problems and to take stock of policy options; (ii) it facilitates the negotiations of Member States in many intergovernmental bodies on joint courses of action to address ongoing or emerging global challenges; and (iii) it advises interested governments on the ways and means of translating policy frameworks developed in United Nations conferences and summits into programmes at the country level and, through technical assistance, helps build national capacities.

Notes

ST/ESA/PAD/SER.E/90
United Nations publication
Sales No. E.06.II.H.2
ISBN 92-1-123159-0
Copyright © United Nations, 2006
All rights reserved
Printed by the United Nations, New York

Preface

In reaffirming the vision of a peaceful, prosperous and just world, leaders at the United Nations World Summit in 2005 outlined a vision of "…building a people-centred and inclusive information society, putting the potential of information and communication technologies at the service of development and addressing new challenges of the information society."

Exploring the interlinkages between e-government and development, the *UN Global E-Government Readiness Report 2005: From E-government to E-inclusion,* presents an assessment of the countries according to their state of e-government readiness and the extent of e-participation worldwide. The UN Global E-government Survey 2005, like its predecessors, ranks the 191 Member States of the UN according to a quantitative composite index of e-readiness based on website assessment, telecommunication infrastructure and human resource endowment.

The basic message in this Report is that there are huge disparities in the access and use of information technologies, and that these disparities are not likely to be removed in the near future unless concerted action is taken at national, regional and international levels.

If disparities in "real access" to ICT are to be removed in the collective global march towards an information society, governments have to build an effective use of ICTs in their development plans. The onus lies, collectively, on the national governments, the private sector and the civil society, on the one hand, and the international organizations and the donor community on the other, to come up with new initiatives for ICT-led development, which ensures that everybody, regardless of socio-economic background, has an equitable playing field. An inclusive mode of governance demands that all citizens of a state have equal access to opportunity. The new imperative of development is to employ ICT applications across the board for promoting access and inclusion.

Expanding the concept of "real access" to ICT into e-inclusion, *From E-government to E-inclusion* presents the *Socially Inclusive Governance Framework,* which is a multi-pronged approach to ICT-led real access, with a special focus on the need to promote access and inclusion to the disadvantaged groups in society.

We hope that the findings in this Report will contribute to the thinking among the policy makers, practitioners and academia around the world for further exploration of the issue of the use of ICT for the "inclusion" of all.

We also hope that this Survey will urge the Member States to come up with new and innovative approaches for bridging the prevalent access-divide for the marginalized communities and in ensuring that new technologies become an effective tool in building an inclusive society for all.

GUIDO BERTUCCI
Director
Division for Public Administration and Development Management
Department of Economic and Social Affairs

Acknowledgements

The ***UN Global E-Government Readiness Report 2005: From E-government to E-inclusion*** has been prepared under the leadership of Guido Bertucci, Director of the UNDESA Division for Public Administration and Development Management (DPADM). In this endeavour, Seema Hafeez is the author of the Report, assisted by Sarah Waheed Sher. In the final stages of the Survey, additional support was provided by Haiyan Qian, Chief of the Knowledge Management Branch, Michael Mimicopoulos, and Carla Valle.

Dr. Gregory G. Curtin, Managing Director of the Civic Resource Group and Director of the E-Governance Lab at the University of Southern California, led the senior research team, which included Robert B. McConnachie, co-Managing Director of the Civic Resource Group, Kim J. Andreasson, Christopher J. Walker, and Vera Orloff. The team acknowledges the research assistance and translation provided by Ruben Alonso III, Iva Bozovic, Moustapha El-Assi, Chris Hoble, Mohammed Holil, Laura Hosman, Li Jiang, Takashi Kamishiro, Cecilia Joung Un Kim, Pavel Nikitin, Pho Pham, Eugenia Saloutsi, Jenny Ceylan Sonmez and Hyemin Lee, who did the cover art.

Contents

Tables

Figures

Boxes

Abbreviation Notes

EU	European Union	OECD	Organization for Economic Cooperation and Development
FAO	Food and Agriculture Organization of the UN	PIAP	Public Internet access points
GEM	Gender Empowerment Measure	PWD	People with disability
GDI	Gender Development Index	PPP	Purchasing power parity
GDP	Gross Domestic Product	UNDESA	UN Department of Economic and Social Affairs
GNI	Gross National Income	UNESCO	United Nations Educational, Scientific and Cultural Organization
HDI	Human Development Index		
HP	Hewlett Packard	UNPAN	United Nations Online Network in Public Administration and Finance
IT	Information Technology		
ICT	Information and Communication Technologies	UNDP	United Nations Development Programme
		USPTO	U.S. Patent and Trademark Office
ITU	International Telecommunication Union	W3C	World Wide Web Consortium
KI	Knowledge Index	WAI	Web Accessibility Initiative
NGO	Non-governmental organization	WSIS	World Summit on Information Society
MDG	Millennium Development Goals	WWW	World Wide Web

Executive summary

An imperative of development today is to employ information and communication technologies (ICTs) to level the playing field for all. The cross-cutting nature of technology provides opportunities and enables delivery of much needed economic and social information to remote areas of the world with the promise of leap-frogging traditional development cycles. Access to information and communications is considered crucial for poverty reduction, since it contributes to new sources of income and employment for the poor, improved delivery of health and education services and competitiveness of the economy.

However, harnessing the full potential of the benefits of the global information society is possible only if all nations and peoples of the world share this opportunity equally. Further, the existing spread of information technologies to a select group of people in the world is worsening disparities between the e-haves and the e-have-nots. There is a danger that far from fomenting cohesion through opportunity, unequal diffusion of technology will reinforce traditional inequalities, leading to a further weakening of social bonds and cultural cohesion.

Exploring the interlinkages between e-government and human development, the *UN Global E-Government Readiness Report 2005* presents an assessment of existing disparities in access to, and use of, ICTs around the world. It comprises two parts: Part I presents the UN Global E-Government Readiness Survey 2005, while Part II of the Report delves deeper into the access parameters of disparity.

The UN Global E-Government Readiness Survey 2005

The E-Government Readiness Survey 2005 assesses more than 50,000 features of the e-government websites of the 191 UN Member States to ascertain how ready the governments around the world are in employing the opportunities offered by ICT to improve the access to, and the use of, ICTs in providing basic social services. Employing a statistical model for the measurement of digitized services, the UN E-Government Survey 2005 assesses the public sector e-government initiatives of Member States according to a weighted average composite index of e-readiness based on website assessment, telecommunication infrastructure and human resource endowment.

The UN Global E-government Survey 2005 finds that a large number of countries solidified their online presence further, venturing into higher and more mature areas of e-service delivery. Many introduced further e-participation features. The total number of countries online increased to 179, or around 94 per cent of the United Nations Member States. Twelve countries were not online, compared to thirteen last year.

Most developing country governments around the world are promoting citizen awareness about policies and programmes, approaches and strategies on their websites. They are making an effort to engage multi-stakeholders in participatory

Technology provides opportunities and enables delivery of needed economic and social information to remote areas of the world with the promise of leap-frogging traditional development cycles.

The E-Government Readiness Survey 2005 assesses more than 50,000 features of the e-government websites of the 191 UN Member States to ascertain how ready the governments around the world are in employing the opportunities offered by ICT to improve the access to, and the use of, ICTs in providing basic social services.

decision-making, in some cases through the use of innovative initiatives aimed at greater access and inclusion.

According to the E-government Readiness rankings in 2005, the United States (0.9062) is the world leader, followed by Denmark (0.9058), Sweden (0.8983) and the United Kingdom (0.8777). As in 2004, the Republic of Korea, Singapore, Estonia, Malta and Chile are also among the top 25 e-ready countries.

Steady progress in ICT diffusion, human capital development and Member States' e-government websites in the last three years led to an improvement in the e-government readiness world average to 0.4267 in 2005 compared to 0.4130 in 2004. As a region, Europe followed North America, while South and Central Asia and Africa brought up the rear.

In e-participation, though many countries expanded their participatory services, a few remained limited in their provision of relevant and qualitative tools for user feedback. According to the E-participation Index 2005, the United Kingdom, as in previous years, was the leader, followed by Singapore (0.9841) and then the United States (0.9048). From among the developing countries, Mexico, Chile and Colombia were the world leaders in participation services.

Fifty-five countries, out of 179 which maintained a government website, encouraged citizens to participate in discussing key issues of importance, but only 32 Member States explained what e-consultation was, why it was important and where citizens should provide inputs to the government, while only 28 countries gave the assurance that the government would take citizens' inputs into the decision-making process.

Approaches to e-government programme offerings varied from country to country. The "how" of what countries chose to display on the websites was a function of the "what" they wanted to focus on and "why" they wanted to focus on the issue.

The pattern that emerges is that for effective e-government development, political commitment to harnessing the benefits of ICTs, a well thought-out vision and do-able objectives are important markers for successful e-government development.

E-government appears to have a strong relation with income per capita. Resource availability appears to be a critical factor inhibiting e-government initiatives in many countries. Part of the reason for the high e-readiness in most of the developed economies is past investment in, and development of, infrastructure.

Notwithstanding the progress, there remains wide disparity in access to ICTs, and consequently to e-government offerings between, and among, regions and countries of the world. Governments in the developed countries are far advanced in the provision of services and their outreach and access to citizens.

A serious access-divide exists across the world between the developed and the developing countries. Of particular concern are the countries belonging to the regions of South and Central Asia and Africa which, together, house one-third of humanity. Africa, as a whole, had a mean e-government readiness at two-thirds of the world average and 30 per cent of North America. Many of the 32 least e-ready countries, which belonged to Africa, showed little relative progress in 2005, compared to other countries, many of which were far more advanced than Africa in their outreach and access to citizens.

The need for equal access also stems from the fact that ICTs are not only tools, but also instruments that have the power to inform and shape the modes of communication and the processes of thinking and creativity around the world.[8] Whereas, till recently, information technologies were considered just another factor of production, the recent information technology advances, especially the Internet and the World Wide Web, have made information the key to competitiveness, growth and development. Information technology reduces the costs associated with imperfect information and thus promotes faster and more efficient connections among actors, resources and relationships.[9]

The rapid advance of ICTs presents a unique opportunity for learning and diffusing information resources.

However, harnessing the full potential of the benefits of the global information society will be possible only if all nations and peoples of the world share this opportunity equally. With ICTs being adopted at a rapid pace, citizens with real access—either across the world or within countries—comprise the "e-haves." Countries where the majority of the population has the potential to achieve real access are increasing their opportunities, i.e., for economic gain, social empowerment and societal improvement.

At the same time the distance between the government and those with no access, no skills and no prospects (the "e-have-nots") has increased. Those with no income, access, skills and resources or those who are disadvantaged fall outside the ambit of the benefits of the information society.

The rapidity of the spread of information technologies to a select group of people in the world is worsening disparities between the e-haves and the e-have-nots.

> Harnessing the full potential of the benefits of the global information society will be possible only if all nations and peoples of the world share this opportunity equally.

> The rapidity of the spread of information technologies to a select group of people in the world is worsening disparities between the e-haves and the e-have-nots.

Access inequalities

The "digital divide" has been the subject of increasing policy discourse, academic research and civil society debate around the world in recent years. Concerns have been raised by many, from heads of states to the private sector to citizen groups, about the dangers of a widening disparity between the digital e-haves and e-have-nots. While countries around the world have scrambled to invest in information technology infrastructure, the focus has remained on issues of connectivity. The assumption has been that if developing nations could somehow get to the same infrastructure level as developed nations, the benefits of information technology would flow automatically to citizens, businesses and governments—that indeed, overcoming the digital divide is a matter of connectivity.

Whereas connectivity is a prerequisite for access to the benefits of ICTs, it is not a sufficient condition. A device needs to be supplemented by an adequate network and the requisite education and skills to employ the technology. Besides the level of economic development, the cost of technology, indigenous research & development, technology to overcome language barriers and the availability of relevant cultural content all have a bearing on the diffusion of technology in a country.

The impact of changing global political, economic and social systems is not the same on all. Likewise, though neutral in itself, the impact of information technology is not neutral on men and women, businesses and customers, rural and urban dwellers, or Asians and Africans. Peoples of the world gain advantage from, or react to, systemic shifts in different ways. Recent research suggests that disparities in countries' degrees of information technology broadly mirror their differences in income and other socio-economic factors.[10] In fact, economic factors appear to be the prime determinants of the wide differences across nations in utilization of digital technologies; the patterns of ICT use reflect traditional inequalities of income, education, research & development and other development indicators among countries.[11] According to some research, information technology tools reinforce electronic era trends towards widespread social and cultural differentiation and increasing social stratification among users, whose educational and cultural differences determine levels of influence.[12] Several studies now warn of the growing ICT-led development gap between the world's richer and poorer countries. According to one such study, existing unequal ICT diffusion patterns have resulted from market or social failures and are leading to negative economic, social and political consequences.[13]

Evidence suggests that, till now, information technology has impacted the various regions and countries of the world in an uneven manner. Initial benefits of ICTs accrued to those advanced nations and groups that had a blend of the requisite physical infrastructure and educational skills, as well as a social structure able to innovate and modify systems and structures to conform to emerging economic and social realities. Such countries, and groups within countries, have been few.

Access to, and distribution of, the tools for information and wealth creation are highly skewed among regions and among countries of the world. Even though between 1980 and 2005 the number of fixed and mobile telephones increased over 30 times in developing countries, in these countries a telephone is still only available to one in three persons, compared to the developed world where there are 1.3 telephones for each person![14] Access opportunities are uneven among countries of the same region too. In East Asia, in the Republic of Korea, every 2nd person is an Internet user and has a telephone, while in Cambodia 300 persons share a telephone and only one in 1250 persons ever goes online. In Western Asia, every 6th person is online in Israel, but in neighbouring Syrian Arab Republic, the Internet is available to only one in 286 persons.[15] Masked by these aggregates is the stark reality that many people in developing countries, especially in the rural areas, have zero access to ICTs.

In many countries large swathes of populations remain outside the information society network with an increasing risk of being marginalized. Women in many countries have less access to advanced technologies than men. People with disabilities, the elderly and other fringe groups are at risk of exclusion due to lower levels of education, lower digital skills, lower income or technical barriers that exclude them from accessing information, products and services.

Inequitable diffusion of the benefits of technology is impacting, and in many instances, worsening poverty. The poor and the marginalized, who generally tend to have a lower set of economic and social opportunities, lack the means to be connected to newer technologies. Lack of access, in turn, reduces their opportunities to better income, health and education.[16]

Many poor developing countries face serious obstacles in providing equal access to ICTs. Lack of telecommunication infrastructure, scarcity of human and financial resources, weak regulatory institutions and the lack of market mechanisms impede faster and wider diffusion of modern information technologies.

This disparity in access is likely to become larger at the current rate of technological advancement—and adoption—in a select few countries of the world. Compounding existing disparities in e-readiness is the speed with which technology is changing. As they struggle to keep up programmes, the rapidity of technological advances is leaving many developing countries behind, with the very applications installed rapidly becoming obsolete. The persistence of these trends may contribute to a number of social problems and increase risks of political conflict. Many around the world are already asking if, instead of the technological revolution decreasing the digital divide, it is actually increasing it.

Unless governments aim at consciously removing disparities, the poor, the marginalized and the disadvantaged are likely to be left out, exacerbating existing access inequalities.

This disparity in access is likely to become larger at the current rate of technological advancement—and adoption—in a select few countries of the world.

Unless governments aim at consciously removing disparities, the poor, the marginalized and the disadvantaged are likely to be left out, exacerbating existing access inequalities.

UN's role in promoting access and inclusion

In reaffirming the vision of a peaceful, prosperous and just world, leaders at the United Nations World Summit in 2005 outlined a vision of "…building a people-centred and inclusive information society so as to enhance digital opportunities for all people in order to help bridge the digital divide, putting the potential of information and communication technologies at the service of development and addressing new challenges of the information society…"[17] The world leaders reiterated this resolve to build an inclusive society once again at the World Summit on Information Society (WSIS) held in Tunis in November 2005.

Access to information technologies figures prominently among the means deemed necessary to reach the Millennium Development Goals (MDGs) and is considered important in its own right as well as for the attainment of all of the other goals. To promote access to ICTs and bridge the digital divide, the United Nations agencies have set up several initiatives seeking to exploit the potential of new technologies. Phase I of the WSIS conference, held in Geneva in 2003, set global targets for improving connectivity and access and measuring progress in acceding to the information society. These were endorsed by 175 Member States. The targets included providing basic access to ICTs to more than half the world's population and connecting learning institutions, research centres, hospitals and libraries with ICTs. So as not to exclude remote areas the goals also included establishing community access points to integrate villages into the information network. This UN-led effort has met with much approval around the world. In a survey conducted by the International Telecommunication Union (ITU) an overwhelming 94 per cent of survey takers responded that cyberspace should be declared a resource to be shared by all.[18] When asked how important each WSIS target was to achieving an information society that would benefit all around 85 per cent said that connecting universities, colleges and academic institutions and scientific & research centres was very important. Around half or more of all respondents thought all 10 targets were very important for realizing the benefits of the information society.

The United Nations agencies actively seek to promote access and reduce the digital divide by fostering greater awareness of the potential of new technologies. Through the United Nations Online Network in Public Administration and Finance (UNPAN), the UN Department of Economic and Social Affairs (UNDESA) takes the lead in disseminating information about policy advice and capacity building to assist Member States in reducing digital disparities and promoting e-government for development.

ICTs and access to them also figure prominently in the programmes of UN specialized agencies. The International Telecommunication Union (ITU) launched a drive, *Connect the World,* in 2005 aimed at bringing access to information and communication technologies (ICTs) to the estimated one billion people worldwide for whom making a simple telephone call remains out of reach.[19]

> The United Nations agencies actively seek to promote access and reduce digital divide by fostering greater awareness of the potential of new technologies.

Figure 1.1.
Global support for information technology targets

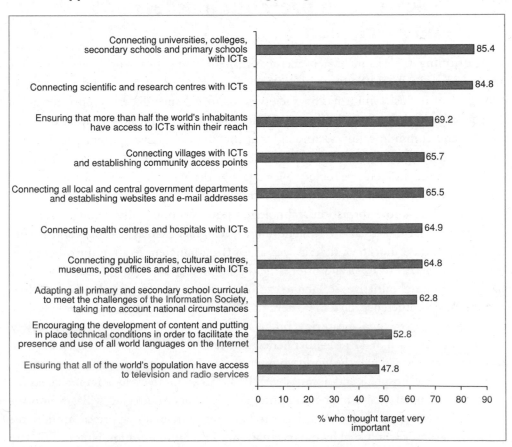

Target	% who thought target very important
Connecting universities, colleges, secondary schools and primary schools with ICTs	85.4
Connecting scientific and research centres with ICTs	84.8
Ensuring that more than half the world's inhabitants have access to ICTs within their reach	69.2
Connecting villages with ICTs and establishing community access points	65.7
Connecting all local and central government departments and establishing websites and e-mail addresses	65.5
Connecting health centres and hospitals with ICTs	64.9
Connecting public libraries, cultural centres, museums, post offices and archives with ICTs	64.8
Adapting all primary and secondary school curricula to meet the challenges of the Information Society, taking into account national circumstances	62.8
Encouraging the development of content and putting in place technical conditions in order to facilitate the presence and use of all world languages on the Internet	52.8
Ensuring that all of the world's population have access to television and radio services	47.8

Source: ITU. http://www.itu.int/newsarchive/press_releases/2004/12.html. Accessed 7 September 2005

Several other UN agencies have taken up the task of promoting the benefits of information technology and incorporating ICT-driven development into national agendas. Among others, the United Nations Educational, Scientific and Cultural Organization (UNESCO) supports actions designed to empower people so that they can access and contribute to information and knowledge flows.[20] As part of this focus UNESCO supports the development of information standards and management tools, strengthening libraries and archives, and fostering access at the community level. Recognizing the importance and role of ICTs in getting timely information to the rural areas, the Food and Agriculture Organization of the UN (FAO) has developed an e-learning initiative known as the Information Management Resource Kit (IMARK). Under its *Access to Global Online Research in Agriculture Register* (AGORA) it provides access to 752 journals from major scientific publishers in the fields of food, agriculture, environmental science and related social sciences. AGORA is available to students and researchers in qualifying not-for-profit institutions in eligible developing countries.[21]

Broadening access to inclusion: a restructured way of thinking

Access-for-all is multi faceted.[22] First, it implies availability of physical infrastructure. The array of baseline tools for end users—such as television, radio and land-line telephones—has expanded to include the personal computer and newer devices such as mobile/handheld computers, mobile phones and hybrid mobile devices (all-in-one phones, personal digital assistants (PDAs). Real access requires some final "connection" for a user: logging on to a computer that connects to the Internet through a dial-up connection, broadband connection, etc.; using a mobile device to connect to the Internet via a wireless connection that depends on a physical network of transponders and routers; or simply having a land line telephone hardwired to a physical system that can be utilized for access.

Along with physical infrastructure, education and skills are a must. These include basic literacy, computer skills and technology training as well as the integration of computers/technology into traditional subject area curricula. Furthermore, with English as the language of the Internet, access becomes related to users' having the relevant language skill and being able to reach content relevant to their needs. For accessibility to be pervasive information technologies must also be affordable. There is a close link between access to technology and the price thereof. Even though costs have gone down substantially, a major cause of low access in developing countries remains the still relatively high price tag. In addition, there are other aspects of access that must now be incorporated into the inclusion model.

The framework of inclusion

The role of government today needs to be advanced beyond public sector management and reform for the development of a competitive market economy to one espousing leadership in providing economic and social equity. Governments need to evolve from providing direction for "an enabling environment" to actively seeking to create equal opportunities for all.

Recognition of the potential of information technologies has led to renewed importance on the value of information in today's economic and social market place. This recognition goes hand-in-hand with a demand for greater participation by citizens in the affairs of government that affect their rights, incomes and social values. Renewed emphasis on peace and security, good governance and transparency, and equity and participation requires evolution of the role of government into one built on a participatory model of governance that, while including the private sector and civil society, also assumes key responsibility in providing a level playing field for the inclusion of all.

In many developing countries millions remain outside the ambit of access to ICTs due to lack of income, literacy and connectivity, as a result of gender bias, or because they live in remote areas. Resource constraints in many developing countries generally lead to prioritizing ICT delivery to elite populations. Continued focus of ICT policies on connectivity or access alone is likely to result in more of the same bypassing of large swathes of populations. Efforts to narrow information technology disparities must begin by recognition of inequalities beyond those of connectivity. The digital divide should be thought of in terms of an access divide.

A new way of thinking which focuses on inclusion is required. This Report broadens the scope of access to the concept of inclusion. It presents a framework for thinking about what it terms "socially inclusive governance." Inclusion as defined in this Report means "to include all." As Figure 1.2 indicates, it stems from connectivity but encompasses access.

The *UN Global E-government Survey 2003* stated that the potential of e-government as a tool for development hinges upon a minimum threshold level of technological infrastructure, human capital, and e-connectivity for all. It maintained that e-government strategies and programmes will be able to be effective and *"include all"* peoples only if, at the very minimum, *all* have functional literacy and education, which includes knowledge of computer and Internet use; *all* are connected to a computer; and if *all* have access to the Internet. It claimed that the benefits—and reach—of e-government programmes were crucially dependant on real access of ICT to all.[23] It was this opportunity of the "inclusion of all" that was the vision of the United Nations.

The *UN Global E-government Readiness Report 2004* furthered the worldwide concept of the digital divide to what it termed an *"access-divide"* encompassing other economic, social, educational and cultural elements. The Model of Access Acceleration it presented stated that physical access to ICT was only the first step towards building real access, which led to economic and social opportunity. Whereas a certain level of physical infrastructure was needed to reach a threshold level for real access to start accelerating, it was necessary for governments to complement it by other access-supporting economic, social, educational and cultural elements.

The *UN Global E-government Readiness Report 2005: From E-government to E-Inclusion* builds upon the messages of the previous UN Global Readiness Reports. First, underscoring the importance of technological advancements, the role of the gov-

Figure 1.2.
A framework of inclusion

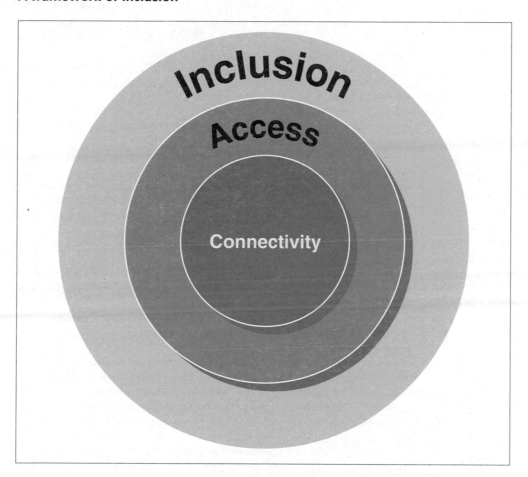

ernment and human development, it presents a vision of the future with technology-led access-for-all. Second, expanding the concept of real access into e-inclusion, it points to the need to place development thinking within what it terms the *"Socially Inclusive Governance Framework,"* which is a multi-pronged approach to promoting ICT-led real access, with a special focus on the benefits of technology to women and the disadvantaged in society. Finally, it draws attention to the risks of the world becoming divided between the e-haves and the e-have-nots. In so doing it presents a comparative ranking of the Member States' e-government readiness in 2005 and a snapshot in time of the extent of access-divides stemming from the current world disparity in information technologies. In this way it contributes to a better understanding of the causes of the unequal diffusion and distribution of the benefits of information technology with the purpose of supporting Member States' efforts for a more inclusive future for all.

Notes

1   Carlos Primo Braga et al. *The Networking Revolution: Opportunities and Challenges for the Developing Countries.* The World Bank, InfoDev Working Paper. Page 3

2   Bangemann Report, *Europe and the Global Information Society (1994)*. http://www.cyber-rights.org/documents/bangemann.htm. Accessed 22 August 2005.

3   http://redmondmag.com/news/article.asp?EditorialsID=6527. Accessed 22 August 2005.

4   International Telecommunication Union. *World Telecommunication Development Report 2003*. Pages 74–76.

5   Ibid. Page 82.

6   Ibid. Page 83.

7   The World Bank. *ICT and Poverty*. http://info.worldbank.org/ict/WSIS/docs/mdg_Poverty.pdf. Accessed 22 August 2005.

8   Kwame Boafo (ed.). *Status of Research on the Information Society*. UNESCO. http://portal.unesco.org/ci/en/file_download.php/ac4662e1f0e63513956927850fa147f6status-1-84.pdf. Accessed 16 September 2005.

9   The World Bank. http://www1.worldbank.org/prem/poverty/scapital/topic/info1.htm. Accessed 15 September 2005.

10   International Telecommunication Union. *Challenges to the Network: Internet for Development*. 1999. Franciso Rodriguez and Ernest Wilson III. *Are Poor Countries Losing the Information Revolution?* May 2000. InfoDev Working Paper http://www.cidcm.umd.edu/library/papers/ewilson/apxc.pdf.

11   Pippa Norris. *Digital Divide, Civic Engagement. Information Poverty and the Internet Worldwide*. 2002.

12   Theory of Manuel Castells as in Mark Warschauer. *Review of the Information Age: economy, society, and culture by Manuel Castells*. http://www.gse.uci.edu/markw/info-age.html. Accessed 7 September 2005.

13   Francisco Rodríguez and Ernest J. Wilson, III. *Are Poor Countries Losing the Information Revolution?* InfoDev Working Paper. May 2000. http://www.cidcm.umd.edu/library/papers/ewilson/apxc.pdf.

14   Based on data from Bjorn Wellenius. *Extending access to communication and information services; guiding principles and practical solutions in The World Bank*. Global Information & Communication Technologies Department. *World Information and Communication for Development 2006:Trends and Policies for the Information Society*. (Forthcoming).

15   *UN Global E-government Readiness Report 2004*. http://www.unpan.org/egovernment4.asp. P. 97.

16   For aspects of access see U.S. Government. *Falling through the Net: Defining the Digital Divide*. http://www.ntia.doc.gov/ntiahome/fttn99/introduction.html. S. Nanthikesan. *Trends in Digital Divide*. 2000; Bridges.Org. *Spanning the Digital Divide*. 2001. Mark Warschauer. *Reconceptualising the Digital Divide*. http://www.gse.uci.edu/markw/papers.html. Accessed 7 September 2005.

17   *2005 World Summit Outcome A/RES/60/1.24* October 2005. P. 18. http://daccessdds.un.org/doc/UNDOC/GEN/N05/487/60/PDF/NO548760.pdf?Open.

18   ITU. Press release. Geneva, 17 May 2004. http://www.itu.int/newsarchive/press_releases/2004/12.html. Accessed 7 September 2005.

19   http://www.itu.int/newsroom/press_releases/2005/07.html. Accessed 16 September 2005.

20   http://portal.unesco.org/ci/en/ev.php-URL_ID=19488&URL_DO=DO_TOPIC&URL_SECTION=201.html. Accessed 16 September 2005.

21   http://www.aginternetwork.org/en/.

22   For aspects of access see U.S. Government. *Falling through the Net: Defining the Digital Divide*. http://www.ntia.doc.gov/ntiahome/fttn99/introduction.html; S. Nanthikesan. *Trends in Digital Divide*. 2000; Bridges.Org. *Spanning the Digital Divide*. 2001.Mark Warschauer; *Reconceptualising the Digital Divide*. http://www.gse.uci.edu/markw/papers.html. Accessed 7 September 2005.

23   *UN Global E-government Survey 2003*. http://www.unpan.org/egovernment3.asp. P. 4.

Part I

UN Global E-Government Readiness Survey 2005

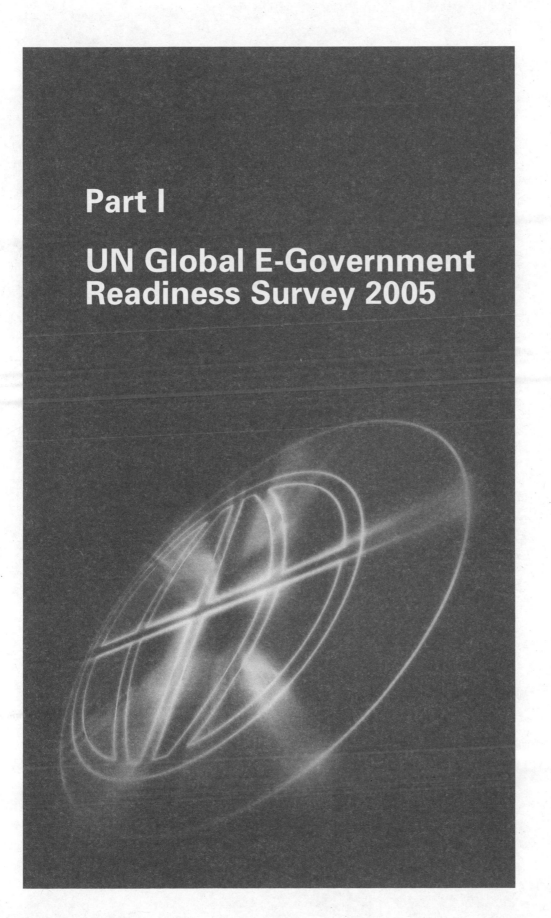

Chapter II
Benchmarking e-government

The *UN Global E-Government Readiness Survey 2005* presents a systemic assessment of how governments use ICTs to provide access and inclusion for all. The Survey offers insights into the different strategies and common themes in e-government development among regions and across them. By studying broad patterns of e-government use, it identifies countries that have taken a leadership role in promoting e-government readiness and those in which the potential of ICTs for development has not yet been exploited.

> The Survey offers insights into the different strategies and common themes in e-government development among regions and across them.

This is the third year in a row that the Survey has tracked the progress of UN Member States globally over time. In doing so it seeks a better understanding of the multifaceted challenges faced by these states in promoting access and inclusion. By identifying strengths and weaknesses the Survey identifies best practices in e-government strategies and policies to overcome the scarcities of manpower and infrastructure, language and content, and income and power. By conveying a better understanding of the emerging patterns of country performance across the world it contributes to the discussion of ICTs' centrality to development

The Survey aims to inform and improve the understanding of policy makers' choices in their e-government programme undertakings. It is a useful tool for government officials, researchers, and the representatives of civil society and the private sector to gain a deeper understanding of the relative position of a country vis-à-vis the rest of the world economies. Thus, it is hoped that the Survey rankings will contribute to the e-government efforts of the Member States' as they move to provide access-for-all.

> It is a useful tool for government officials, researchers, and the representatives of civil society and the private sector to gain a deeper understanding of the relative position of a country vis-à-vis the rest of the world economies.

The conceptual framework, methodology and data measurement

The conceptual framework of the Survey is embedded in the paradigm of human and social development. E-government in this Survey encompasses the capacity and the willingness of the public sector to deploy ICT for improving knowledge and information in the service of the citizen. Capacity espouses financial, infrastructural, human capital, regulatory, administrative and systemic capability of the state. The willingness on the part of the government to provide information and knowledge for the empowerment of the citizen is a testament to the government's commitment.

The UN Global E-government Survey framework encompasses the *economic and social development context* of a country. As the *UN Global E-government Survey 2003* stated, any survey of e-government readiness assessment has to be placed in the context of the overall pattern and the level of development of a country. In a survey which ranks countries, it is vital that the assessment of websites not provide a distorted picture of the progress made and challenges faced by the countries.

E-government readiness is a function not only of the government's e-readiness but also of the country's technological and telecommunication infrastructure and the level of its human resources development, among other factors, and at a minimum it should be based on the level of all three. E-government initiatives, however sophisticated, are unlikely to contribute significantly to development if they reach only the privileged few.

The conceptual question behind the Survey is: how ready are the countries to take advantage of the opportunity provided by advances in information technology? The Survey conceptualizes models of e-government progression and quantitatively measures the relative strengths and weaknesses in e-government for development of countries worldwide. As such it provides a global benchmarking tool for monitoring progress of countries as they consolidate and expand their e-government service delivery programmes. As did the previous surveys, the *UN Global E-Government Survey 2005* presents a comparative ranking of the countries of the world according to a) the state of e-government readiness; and b) the extent of e-participation.

The objectives of the Survey are to provide a:

1. comparative assessment of the willingness and ability of governments in the use of e-government and ICTs as tools in the public delivery of services; and

2. benchmarking tool for monitoring the progress of countries, now three years in a row, as they progress towards higher levels of e-government and e-participation service delivery.

The UN Global E-Government Readiness Index 2005

The UN Global E-Government Readiness Index 2005 presents the state of e-government readiness of the Member States. It is a composite measurement of the capacity and willingness of countries to use e-government for ICT-led development. Along with an assessment of the website development patterns in a country, the e-government readiness index incorporates the access characteristics, such as the infrastructure and educational levels, to reflect how a country is using information technologies to promote access and inclusion of its people. The measurement of e-government is an assessment of a state's use of the Internet and the World Wide Web (WWW) for provision of information, products and services; plus the level of telecommunication and human capital infrastructure development in a country.

The E-government Readiness Index is a composite index comprising the Web measure index, the Telecommunication Infrastructure index and the Human Capital index.

E-government is defined as the use of ICT and its application by the government for the provision of information and public services to the people. The aim of e-government therefore is to provide efficient government management of information to the citizen; better service delivery to citizens; and empowerment of the people through access to information and participation in public policy decision-making.

"Government" comprises the executive, legislative and judiciary organs of the government while the "consumer/citizen" includes any member of the civil society (individuals as well as organizations).

E-government includes electronic interactions of three types: government-to-government (G2G); government-to-business (G2B) and its reverse; and government-to-consumer/citizen (G2C) and its reverse. Not detracting from the importance of government-to-government (G2G), government-to-business (G2B), and citizen to citizen (C2C) and vice versa interactions, as in the past, this Survey limits itself to only government-to-citizen (G2C) and citizen-to-government (C2G) aspects of e-government. However, in the comparative measurement of G2C and C2G services is an implicit assessment of G2G since improvements in G2C and C2G are closely linked to G2G improvements.

The web measure index

As in the past, web measure index 2005 is also based upon a five-stage model, which is ascending in nature and builds upon the previous level of sophistication of a state's online presence. The model defines five stages of e-government readiness according to a scale of progressively sophisticated citizen services. As countries progress, they are ranked higher in the Model according to a numerical classification corresponding to the five stages.

The five stages in the web measure assessment model are reproduced in Box 1.

To eliminate any discretionary rating introduced by a value judgment, by design the E-government Index does not attempt to assess the services qualitatively. In not endeavouring to do so it is different from many other surveys, which combine access to, and delivery of, services/products and quality in one indicator. The purely quantitative nature of the web measure assessment assures minimizing of the bias inherent in combining qualitative assessments with quantitative measures. Furthermore, the Survey adheres to the same set of core features and services assessed in the past. This allows for consistency in benchmarking and measurement of states' e-government progress over time.

The purely quantitative nature of the web measure assessment assures minimizing of the bias inherent in combining qualitative assessments with quantitative measures.

As in the past, all of the 191 Member States of the United Nations were assessed in 2005. The web measure survey assessments are based on a questionnaire, which allows for only a binary value to the indicator based on the presence/absence of specific electronic facilities/services available. The primary site was the National Portal or the official homepage of the government. Where no official portal was available additional government sites were assessed. While not detracting from the importance of local e-government initiatives, the Survey limits itself to central government website assessments alone in order to provide a consistent platform for comparative analysis across the countries. For the countries with decentralized structures of national government such as in education and health, and which had little or nothing online on the central government ministerial/departmental site, numerical scores were adjusted accordingly so as not to penalize them.

Box 1. Web measure model: Stages of e-government evolution

Emerging Presence is Stage I, representing information that is limited and basic. The e-government online presence comprises a web page and/or an official website; links to ministries/departments of education, health, social welfare, labour and finance may/may not exist; links to regional/local government may/may not exist; some archived information such as the head of state's message or a document such as the constitution may be available online; most information remains static with the fewest options for citizens.

   Enhanced presence is Stage II, in which the government provides greater public policy and governance sources of current and archived information, such as policies, laws and regulations, reports, newsletters, and downloadable databases. The user can search for a document and there is a help feature and a site map provided. There is a larger selection of public policy documents, such as an e-government strategy and policy briefs on specific education or health issues. Though more sophisticated, the interaction is still primarily unidirectional with information flowing essentially from government to the citizen.

   Interactive presence is Stage III, in which the online services of the government enter the interactive mode with services to enhance convenience of the consumer such as downloadable forms for tax payment or application for license renewal. Audio and video capability is provided for relevant public information. The government officials can be contacted via e-mail, fax, telephone and post. The site is updated with greater regularity to keep the information current and up to date for the public.

   Transactional presence is Stage IV, which allows for two-way interaction between the citizen and his/her government. It includes options for filing tax forms, applying for ID cards, birth certificates and passports, renewing licenses and other similar C2G interactions by allowing citizens to carry out such transactions online 24/7. The citizens are able to pay taxes, fines for motor vehicle violations and fees for postal services and other relevant public services through their credit, bank or debit cards. Providers of goods and services are able to bid on line for public contacts via secure links.

   Networked presence is Stage V, which represents the most sophisticated level of online e-government initiatives. It can be characterized by an integration of G2G, G2C and C2G (and reverse) interactions. The government encourages participatory deliberative decision-making and is willing and able to involve the society in a two-way open dialogue. Through interactive features such as the web comment form and innovative online consultation mechanisms, the government actively solicits citizens' views on public policy, law making and democratic participatory decision-making. Implicit in this stage of the model is the integration of the public sector agencies with full cooperation and understanding of the concept of collective decision-making, participatory democracy and citizen empowerment as a democratic right.

   The Survey assesses the same number of *functionality same/similar* sites in each country to ensure consistency. In keeping with its conceptual framework of human development these are the Ministries/Departments of Health, Education,

Social Welfare, Labour and Finance, which are representative of the services citizens require most from the government. Each ministerial site was assessed on the basis of the same set of questions.

In total, more than 50,000 online features and services for 179 countries online across six economic and social sectors were measured. Twelve countries were not online.

The assessment of online services was carried out during July–August 2005. It should be noted that, since websites are being continually updated, those of a few countries were under construction or not available during that time. Whereas the sites were checked several times during that period, fresh websites and/or added features on a website may have come online in the months that followed. Since the Survey presents rankings on a comparative basis, reflecting telecommunication and human capital infrastructure developments with a long gestation, this does not detract from the comprehensiveness of the Survey and is unlikely to impact greatly on the results.

It should be noted that each year a number of e-government readiness surveys are undertaken by regional or international organizations, the private sector and/or academia in which the same country may be rated differently. There are several reasons for this. Assessments of the readiness of a country may vary depending on the definition of e-government, the selection of the products and services measured and the statistical methodology employed. The source and the clientele are often reflected in the choice of input indicators and the features and services of the government measured. Furthermore, the definition of e-government may vary from survey to survey. A few define e-government, and measure it, by assessing G2C and some G2B services. Others may focus on sophisticated issues of privacy and/or e-procurement. A few may delve into assessing government provision of state- and local-level services. Almost all allow a qualitative assessment in their numerical scores. As such, a country's rating may not be strictly comparable across all surveys. Comparing rankings across this kaleidoscope of survey methodology would be like comparing apples with oranges.

The *UN Global E-government Survey 2005* assesses Member States only from the perspective of human development and the delivery of basic services to the citizen such as education, health, employment, finance and social welfare. E-government services such as e-procurement, which may be provided as part of a country's e-government initiative and measured elsewhere, are not the focus here.

Each year the Survey captures the year-on-year changes in the e-government readiness of countries as evidenced by their website assessments. The resulting e-government readiness rankings are a measure of the progress of a country *relative to all other countries of the world*. It should be noted that both the e-government index and the web measure index are broad relative indices. As such, they should be read as indicative of the diffusion of e-government in the countries.

The *UN Global E-government Survey* does not suggest that "higher" rankings are necessarily a "better" outcome or even a desirable one. Caution should be exercised in interpreting too finely the change in rankings of a country within a few positions of similarly ranked countries, whether high up or lower down. As was stated in the previous Survey, *each country should decide upon the level and extent of its e-government initiatives in*

Each year the Survey captures the year-on-year changes in the e-government readiness of countries relative to all other countries of the world.

keeping with its own development priorities and its indigenous level of development. Furthermore, the Survey results should be read within the development context and resource endowments of a country. Whereas the indices and rankings measure progress on the e-government programmes of countries and reflect the context of a country's political, economic, technological and cultural development, ranks should not signify a race to e-government proliferation.

Telecommunication infrastructure index

The telecommunication infrastructure index 2005 is a composite weighted average index of six primary indices based on basic infrastructural indicators that define a country's ICT infrastructure capacity. These are: PCs/1000 persons; Internet users/ 1000 persons; Telephone Lines/1000 persons; Online population; Mobile phones/1000 persons; and TVs/1000 persons. Data for the UN Member States was taken primarily from the UN International Telecommunication Union (ITU) and the UN Statistics Division, supplemented by information from the World Bank. Constructing six separate indices for the indicators standardized the data across countries. See Technical Note for details on constructing the indices.

Human capital index

The data for the human capital index 2005 relies on the UNDP "education index," which is a composite of the adult literacy rate and the combined primary, secondary and tertiary gross enrolment ratio, with two thirds weight given to adult literacy and one third to the gross enrolment ratio. See Technical Notes for details.

The e-participation conceptual framework 2005

Promoting participation of the citizen is the cornerstone of socially inclusive governance. The dual goals of e-participation initiatives should be to improve the citizen's access to information and public services; and to promote participation in public decision-making that impacts the well being of society in general and the individual in particular.

E-participation is the sum total of both the government programmes to encourage participation from the citizen and the willingness of the citizen to take part. It encompasses both the demand and the supply sides. For purposes of this Report, however, e-participation limits itself to assessing the G2C aspect of participation at this time. Impact evaluations on the uptake of government e-participatory programmes require a separate inquiry.

The *E-Participation Index* assesses the quality and usefulness of information and services provided by a country for the purpose of engaging its citizens in public policy making through the use of e-government programmes. As such it is indicative of both a) the capacity and the willingness of the state to encourage the citizen by promoting

The *E-Participation Index* assesses the quality and usefulness of information and services provided by a country for the purpose of engaging its citizens in public policy making through the use of e-government programmes.

deliberative, participatory decision making in public policy; and b) the reach of its own socially inclusive governance programme.

E-participation, as defined in this report, aims to achieve these objectives through the means of:

a. Increasing e-information to citizens for decision making;

b. Enhancing e-consultation for deliberative and participatory processes; and

c. Supporting e-decision making by increasing the input of citizens in decision making.

A caveat about the e-participation module is in order. The E-Participation Index and data should be interpreted with caution. The Index is a qualitative assessment of government websites based on the relevancy of participatory and democratic services available on these websites. Whereas all caution is taken, it should be kept in mind that a qualitative assessment may impart a bias in the scores based on the researcher's perspective. As such, the comparative ranking of countries is purely for illustrative purposes and should serve only as indicative of the broad trends in promoting inclusion.

Data and methodology for the E-Participation Index

In total, 21 citizens' informative and participatory services and facilities were assessed across 179 countries which were online and where data was available. Questions were grouped under the three categories of e-information; e-consultation; and e-decision-making. Each country was assessed on a scale of 0–4.[1] The Index was constructed by standardizing the scores.

Box 2. E-participation framework

E-Information
The government website offers information on policies and programmes, budgets, laws and regulations, and other briefs of key public interest. Tools for dissemination of information exist for timely access and use of public information, including web forums, e-mail lists, newsgroups and chat rooms.

E-Consultation
The government website explains e-consultation mechanisms and tools. It offers a choice of public policy topics online for discussion with real time and archived access to audio and video of public meetings. The government encourages citizens to participate in discussions.

E-Decision-making
The government indicates it will take citizen input into decision-making. The government provides actual feedback on the outcome of specific issues.

Country classifications and nomenclature in the survey

Regional groupings are taken from the classification of the United Nations Statistics Division. For details see http://unstats.un.org/unsd/methods/m49/m49regin.htm.

There is no established convention for the designation of "developed" and "developing" countries or areas in the United Nations system. In common practice, Japan in Asia, Canada and the United States in Northern America, Australia and New Zealand in Oceania, and Europe are considered "developed" regions or areas. In international trade statistics, the Southern African Customs Union is also treated as a developed region and Israel as a developed country; countries emerging from the former Yugoslavia are treated as developing countries; and countries of Eastern Europe and of the Commonwealth of Independent States in Europe are not included under either developed or developing regions. For details on geographical groupings see the United Nations Statistics Division website at http://unstats.un.org/unsd/mi/mi_worldmillennium.asp.

The World Bank classifications and data are grouped by low-income and middle-income economies. According to the World Bank "…low-income and middle-income economies are sometimes referred to as developing economies. The use of the term is convenient; it is not intended to imply that all economies in the group are experiencing similar development or that other economies have reached a preferred or final stage of development. Classification by income does not necessarily reflect development status…". See http://www.worldbank.org/data/countryclass/countryclass.html.

This report uses the terminology "developed" and "developing" countries in line with United Nations practice and keeping in mind the familiarity of the average reader with common usage. For example the Republic of Korea, Singapore and Israel are placed in the developing country classification. However, where data and statistics are reported by income groups the report classifies countries according to the World Bank income classification of high-, middle- and low-income groups.

Notes

1   Zero = never; 1 = sometimes; 2 = frequently; 3 = mostly; and 4 = always

Chapter III
Research findings and analysis

Major findings

The broad trends in E-government readiness assessment are presented below.

E-government rankings

1. The UN Global E-government Readiness rankings in 2005 place the countries of **Northern America (0.8744)** and **Europe (0.6012)** in the leadership positions in the world in e-government readiness.

2. In the rest of the world, **South and Eastern Asia (0.4922)** and **South and Central America (0.4643)** had the highest indices, followed by **Western Asia (0.4384)**, the **Caribbean (0.4282)**, **South and Central Asia (0.3448)**, **Oceania (0.2888)** and finally **Africa (0.2642)**.[1]

3. The **United States of America (0.9062)** is the world leader, followed by **Denmark (0.9058)**. **Sweden (0.8983)** has bypassed the **United Kingdom (0.8777)** to arrive at the 3rd global position.

4. Among others, the **Republic of Korea (0.8727)** leads with **Singapore (0.8503)**, **Malta (0.7012)** and **Chile (0.6963)** close behind.

5. The **World** e-government readiness is **0.4267** in 2005.

Global e-government endeavours

6. The majority of countries of the world made gradual but steady progress in e-government readiness in 2005. The total number of countries online increased to 179—or around 94 per cent of the United Nations Member States. Twelve countries were not online in 2005. A large number of countries solidified their online presence, further venturing into higher and more mature areas of e-service delivery. Many introduced more e-participation features.

7. There is no definitive pattern or system to e-government development around the world. Even countries at a similar level of income or development may conduct e-government operations differently. The pattern that emerges is that political commitment

to harnessing the benefits of ICTs, a well-thought-out vision and do-able objectives are important markers for successful e-government development.

8. *Notwithstanding the progress, there is wide disparity in access to ICTs and consequently to e-government offerings between, and among, regions and countries of the world. Governments in the developed countries are far advanced in the provision of services, outreach and access to citizens. Despite their initial efforts, the majority of developing countries are way behind in achieving any meaningful economy-wide benefits of the information society. The bottom 32 countries show limited relative progress.*

9. *Access and inclusion at present is limited to a few in the developing world. Data and analysis indicate that wide swathes of populations are outside the inclusive net of ICT-related socio-economic benefits.*

Global e-government readiness rankings

E-government readiness rankings for the top 25 countries of the world are presented in Table 3.1. As in 2004, 22 of the 25 top e-ready countries are high-income developed economies. All have scores that range from 160 to 210 per cent higher than the world average. Of the 25, 18 are from Northern America and Europe; three from Eastern Asia (Republic of Korea, Singapore and Japan); two from Oceania (Australia and New Zealand); one from Western Asia (Israel); and one from Latin America (Chile).

The **United States of America** leads the 2005 global e-government readiness rankings, as it did in the previous years, with the highest index of **(0.9062)**, followed by **Denmark (0.9058), Sweden (0.8983)** and the **United Kingdom (0.8777).** It is notable that continued progress among the top e-ready countries has resulted in Denmark, Sweden and the United Kingdom, further closing the gap in services with the United States.

The top 25 positions in the global ranking belong to the same set of developed countries as before with only minor reshuffling of ranks in the past year. Sweden has overtaken the United Kingdom to gain the 3rd place and Singapore (7th) and Canada (8th) have swapped rankings. The greatest advancement is in the case of Japan, which improved its ranking from 18th to 14th in 2005. Switzerland and Belgium each slipped two points. Figure 3.1 presents the e-government readiness of the top 25 countries.

The fact that the top 25 positions are occupied by the same set of developed countries as in the last two years indicates that not only are these countries farther advanced than the rest; they have continued to make efforts to further improve and fortify their e-government services so that their relative performance has been maintained. It should be kept in mind that a small relative decline in rankings does not necessarily imply that the losers did less, but that the gainers performed better than some others. Table 3.2 illustrates the ranking changes.

The United States of America leads the 2005 global e-government readiness rankings followed by Denmark, Sweden and the United Kingdom.

The top 25 positions in the global ranking belong to the same set of developed countries as before with only minor reshuffling of ranks in the past one year.

Table 3.1.

E-government readiness index 2005: Top 25 countries

Rank	Country	Index
1	United States	0.9062
2	Denmark	0.9058
3	Sweden	0.8983
4	United Kingdom	0.8777
5	Republic of Korea	0.8727
6	Australia	0.8679
7	Singapore	0.8503
8	Canada	0.8425
9	Finland	0.8231
10	Norway	0.8228
11	Germany	0.8050
12	Netherlands	0.8021
13	New Zealand	0.7987
14	Japan	0.7801
15	Iceland	0.7794
16	Austria	0.7602
17	Switzerland	0.7548
18	Belgium	0.7381
19	Estonia	0.7347
20	Ireland	0.7251
21	Malta	0.7012
22	Chile	0.6963
23	France	0.6925
24	Israel	0.6903
25	Italy	0.6794

Figure 3.1.

E-government readiness of the top 25 countries

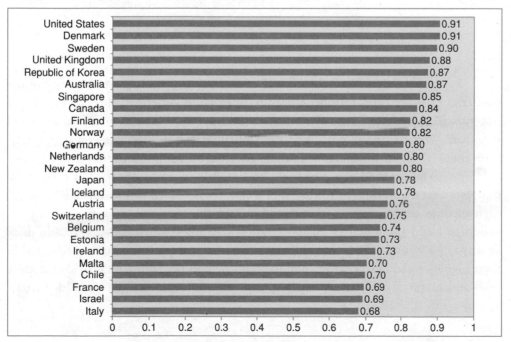

Table 3.2.

E-government readiness index ranking changes 2003–2005: Top 25 countries

Country	2005	2004	2003	Change 2005–2004	Change 2005–2003
United States	1	1	1	0	0
Denmark	2	2	4	0	2
Sweden	3	4	2	1	–1
United Kingdom	4	3	5	–1	1
Republic of Korea	5	5	13	0	8
Australia	6	6	3	0	–3
Singapore	7	8	12	1	5
Canada	8	7	6	–1	–2
Finland	9	9	10	0	1
Norway	10	10	7	0	–3
Germany	11	12	9	1	–2
Netherlands	12	11	11	–1	–1
New Zealand	13	13	14	0	1
Japan	14	18	18	4	4
Iceland	15	14	15	–1	0
Austria	16	17	21	1	5
Switzerland	17	15	8	–2	–9
Belgium	18	16	23	–2	5
Estonia	19	20	16	1	–3
Ireland	20	19	17	–1	–3
Malta	21	21	27	0	6
Chile	22	22	22	0	0
France	23	24	25	1	2
Israel	24	23	24	–1	0
Italy	25	26	17	1	–8

Table 3.3 presents the next 25 countries. In the group the majority of the countries (16) are from Europe; three are from Latin America (Mexico, Brazil and Argentina); three from South-Eastern Asia (Philippines, Malaysia and Thailand) and two from Western Asia (Cyprus and the United Arab Emirates). As Figure 3.2 indicates there is very little difference in the e-government readiness in this group as well.

The preponderance of high- and middle-income countries in the top 50 indicates that e-government readiness in a country is related to income. As expected, high-income countries have the resources and the platform of infrastructure on which to build the potential of information technologies. In the last decade these countries have invested considerable resources in e-government, which is reflected in their higher e-readiness. Further, almost all of the 2nd tier countries provide the same level and maturity of services, which groups their e-readiness index within the narrow range of 0.5329–0.6762.

The preponderance of high- and middle-income countries in the top 50 indicates that e-government readiness in a country is related to income.

Table 3.3.
The next 25 countries

Rank	Country	E-government readiness index
26	Slovenia	0.6762
27	Hungary	0.6536
28	Luxembourg	0.6513
29	Czech Republic	0.6396
30	Portugal	0.6084
31	Mexico	0.6061
32	Latvia	0.6050
33	Brazil	0.5981
34	Argentina	0.5971
35	Greece	0.5921
36	Slovakia	0.5887
37	Cyprus	0.5872
38	Poland	0.5872
39	Spain	0.5847
40	Lithuania	0.5786
41	Philippines	0.5721
42	United Arab Emirates	0.5718
43	Malaysia	0.5706
44	Romania	0.5704
45	Bulgaria	0.5605
46	Thailand	0.5518
47	Croatia	0.5480
48	Ukraine	0.5456
49	Uruguay	0.5387
50	Russian Federation	0.5329

Regional e-government readiness

Steady progress in ICT diffusion, human capital development and Member States' e-government websites in the last three years has led the e-government readiness world average to improve to 0.4267 in 2005, compared to 0.4130 in 2004 (Table 3.4). The regions of Northern America and Europe show the highest e-readiness, followed by South and Eastern Asia. This year countries comprising Western Asia have done very well, pulling up the aggregate index to 0.4384 and surpassing the Caribbean region at 0.4282, which was the fifth highest region in 2004. E-government readiness in Africa, though marginally higher than in 2004, is the lowest in the world.

Oceania is the only region which had a lower average index in 2005 compared to 2004, indicating that the efforts of the majority of the countries of this region have not caught up with the progress in the rest of the world. However it

Steady progress in ICT diffusion, human capital development and Member States' e-government websites in the last three years led to an improvement in the e-government readiness world average to 0.4267 in 2005 compared to 0.4130 in 2004.

Figure 3.2.

E-government readiness in the next 25 countries

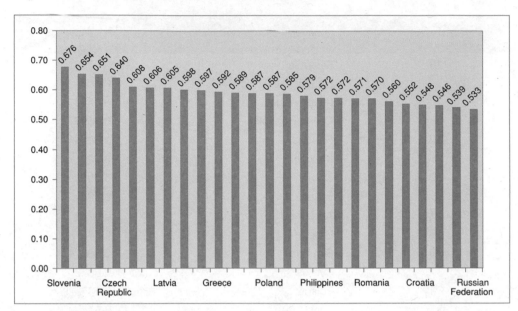

should be noted that the regional e-government readiness indices are *aggregates on a relative scale* and assess the performance of each group of countries relative to that of those in the other regions of the world. A lower average regional index for Oceania this year (0.2888) compared to last does not mean that the region has performed worse than in 2004 but that progress made in other parts of the world was greater. Except for Solomon Islands and Tonga, all countries of Oceania show an improvement in their e-government performance. Moreover, Tuvalu joined the ranks of governments online. For individual country performance see sections below.

Despite steady improvements in the regional means the data show a huge disparity in access to information society parameters. Collectively, Northern America

Table 3.4.

Regional e-government readiness rankings

Country	2005	2004	2003
Northern America	0.8744	0.8751	0.8670
Europe	0.6012	0.5866	0.5580
South and Eastern Asia	0.4922	0.4603	0.4370
South & Central America	0.4643	0.4558	0.4420
Western Asia	0.4384	0.4093	0.4100
Caribbean	0.4282	0.4106	0.4010
South & Central Asia	0.3448	0.3213	0.2920
Oceania	0.2888	0.3006	0.3510
Africa	0.2642	0.2528	0.2460
World Average	0.4267	0.4130	0.4020

and Europe were around 140–330 per cent more e-ready than Africa, the least e-ready region in the world in 2005.

In terms of relative performance some regions did better than others. Again, the regions of Northern America and Europe were leaders in all four indices. Both Northern America and Europe were not only the regional leaders, but also clocked the greatest access to ICT infrastructure, highest level of education and greatest provision of products/services through their national e-government programmes. These disparities are presented in tabular form below.

Despite steady improvements in the regional means the data show a huge disparity in access to information society parameters.

E-government readiness by country

Imputed benefits of information technology have led to massive investments in infrastructure development and strategies and policies to garner the potential of ICTs. The majority of countries are putting in place systems and processes to streamline the public sector, liberalize and reform regulatory regimes, strengthen institutions and provide better service delivery through enhanced e-government initiatives. Each year the E-government Readiness Survey provides a snapshot in time of Member States' efforts. The sections below analyse individual country performance within a regional perspective.

Northern America

The **United States** (0.906) is far in advance of the rest of the world in use and application of ICTs, followed by **Canada** (0.842) in Northern America (Table 3.5).

The United States remains the world leader in e-government readiness as well as in the web measure index. The strength of the online presence of the U.S. is essentially twofold. First, it provides an enormously useful web portal, http://www.firstgov.gov, which gives *enormous amounts of information in one place*. The second strength—and the cornerstone of the United States' approach to e-government—is the *reliance on integrated portals, which collect and consolidate information in one place and thereby increase the effectiveness of finding topic-specific information for citizens in an efficient manner*. Noteworthy examples include the portals for federal government forms, http://www.forms.gov, payments to the government, http://www.pay.gov, and commenting on federal regulations, http://www.regulations.gov. The FirstGov site provides a convenient listing of cross-agency portals "that bring together federal information and services from multiple agencies about a particular topic or for a particular

Table 3.5.
E-government readiness, Northern America

	Index 2005	Global ranking in: 2005	2004	Change
United States	0.9062	1	1	0
Canada	0.8425	8	7	−1
Average	0.8744			

> ## Best Practice
>
> ## Box 3. United States' FirstGov: A true universal portal
>
> The United States FirstGov, http://www.firstgov.gov, is a true universal portal. Its strength lies in its manner and ease of use, accomplished through a search engine that covers 51 million government pages, an incredibly useful "frequently-asked-questions (FAQ)" tool that allows users to ask questions not already in the searchable database, and the targeting of users by group. The convenience of organizing and providing information architecture by audience through a user-friendly "tab" design system enables the U.S. to efficiently channel certain features to those who would be most interested in them. A listing of the "Especially for Specific Audiences" portals and sections is available at http://www.firstgov.gov/Topics/Audiences.shtml. Moreover, demonstrating its commitment to continuous refinement, the U.S. General Services Administration recently announced that new web search and news capabilities will be added to the site in an effort to make it an even more efficient source for locating offerings at all levels of government.[2]

customer group" at http://www.firstgov.gov/Topics/Cross_Agency_Portals.shtml. Added to all this is the incredible amount of information available, all of which lends itself to making the United States the undisputed world leader in e-government.

Overall, therefore, it is the ability to organize this magnitude of information and services effectively for the convenience of the user that is the key to the United States' success.

Also of note is that while English is the apparent *lingua franca* of global e-government, the U.S. promotes language accessibility for Spanish speakers by providing a fairly comprehensive Spanish version: http://www.firstgov.gov/Espanol/index.shtml. Finally, reflecting the commercial podcast interest, another, more recent, cutting-

It is the ability to organize this large magnitude of information and services effectively for the convenience of the user that is the key to the United States' success.

> ## Best Practice
>
> ## Box 4. The U.S. online discussion forum promoting access
>
> In addition to its basic approach, the U.S. is also engaged in a number of interesting initiatives. For example, the Department of Education, http://www.ed.gov, offers a dedicated "Teachers Ask the Secretary" section, http://www.ed.gov/teachers/how/reform/teachersask/index.html, where anyone can ask the U.S. Secretary of Education a question and receive a response posted on the site. The feature is a spin-off from the "Ask the White House" section, http://www.whitehouse.gov/ask/, which when launched in April 2003, was the first online interactive forum of its kind in politics. This section allows interaction with administration officials and has featured over 200 online discussions since its debut. Users can suggest the next administration official they would like to appear and also read transcripts of previous sessions.

edge initiative is the government's adaptability in venturing into this realm quickly to reach new audiences. FirstGov provides a list of all available government podcasts at http://www.firstgov.gov/Topics/Reference_Shelf/Libraries/Podcasts.shtml.

Canada's continued strong online presence is marked by consistency across sites and stages in terms of both the extent of information and services provided as well as the design and navigational standardization. These characteristics are reflected on its national site, http://canada.gc.ca, and also throughout its online presence, including most ministries as well as associated subsections and portals. Consequently, no matter where the user is on the various sites, the look and feel will largely be the same. While this is a tremendous undertaking in and of itself, it should be emphasized that it is also simultaneously implemented in two languages as all Canadian sites seemingly provide mirror English and French versions. In addition, all government sites surveyed link back to the gateway portal in an integrated fashion, a simple but commendable approach to e-government.

> Canada's continued strong online presence is marked by consistency across sites and stages in terms of both the extent of information and services provided as well as the design and navigational standardization.

Best Practice

Box 5. Canadian national site

The Canadian national site, http://canada.gc.ca, is an example of a best practice. Notably it is the highest quantitatively scoring national site in this year's web measure. Consequently, there are several interesting initiatives as well as best practices that are found either on the site itself or through one of its many associated portals. One such site is the Government On-Line (GOL) initiative, http://www.golged.gc.ca, which is the government agency tasked with implementing e-government. As its homepage states, "The goal of the Government On-Line initiative is to use information and communication technology to provide Canadians with enhanced access to improved citizen-centred, integrated services, anytime, anywhere and in the official language of their choice."

Best practices features explicitly on the national site include the "My Account" registration option, http://canada.gc.ca/MGA/intro_e.html, as well as the wireless access alternative, http://canada.gc.ca/mobile/wireless_e.html. Additionally, the "Contact Us" page, http://canada.gc.ca/comments/form_e.html, claims to respond within one Canadian business day as long as a return e-mail address is provided.

Another notable Canadian venture is the decision to utilize a private third-party commercial platform for certain government procurements. The procurement process as described in "Doing Business in the Government Procurement Marketplace" not only mentions the company but also provides a clear link to it under "Related Reading."[3] Logging on, the Merx.com website is self-described as the most complete source for public tenders and private construction available in Canada. The Canadian decision to outsource traditional government services to third-party providers may not be unique but it is certainly cutting-edge.

Best Practice

Box 6. One window for consultation in Canada

As in previous years, the Consulting With Canadians single-window, http://www. consultingcanadians.gc.ca, remains a best practice in the network presence realm as it provides a comprehensive list of formal consultations from selected government departments and agencies. Additionally, past consultations are archived and user-friendly navigational features such as a search engine and a consultations calendar have been implemented to ease the participatory process.

Europe

As in 2004, there are only minor changes in the rankings in Europe, where most countries further solidified their e-government efforts and maintained their relative positions in 2005. **Denmark** (0.9058) continues to lead, followed by **Sweden** (0.8983) and then the **United Kingdom** (0.8777). In the last two years, both Denmark and Sweden have furthered their e-government programmes, such that their provision of government service delivery was rated the best in Europe. **Finland** (0.8231) and **Norway** (0.8228) maintained their rankings; **Germany** (0.8050) gained one point while **Netherlands** (0.8021) lost one. A few others also shuffled one or two points.

In Europe Denmark continues to lead followed by Sweden and the United Kingdom.

Two things are notable in the performance of the countries of Europe. First, except in the case of Serbia and Montenegro, countries more or less maintained their relative global rankings, with only marginal changes in the case of a few. Second, 32 out of 42 countries, or around three fourths of the countries of Europe, fell within the top 50 countries of the world in 2005. All except eight of the countries of Europe have an e-government readiness higher than the world average.

The improvement in performance across the continent, especially in countries with economies-in-transition, is reflected in the higher regional index—at 0.6012 in 2005, compared to 0.5866 in 2004.

Many of the Eastern European countries fortified their e-services, providing greater access and inclusion to citizens. In numerous instances innovative approaches to e-inclusion were evident, especially in areas of e-health, e-learning, e-government applications, networking and other web services. Among others, **Hungary** (0.6536), **Latvia** (0.6050) and **Belarus** (0.5318) all improved their global rankings in 2005. Their improved performance is notable. The **Former Yugoslav Republic of Macedonia** added 28 points to its ranking, advancing from 97th position in 2004 to 69th in 2005.

Many of the Eastern European countries fortified their e-services providing greater access and inclusion to citizens.

Among others, Hungary, Latvia and Belarus all improved their global rankings in 2005.

Among the countries of the region that are global leaders, several offered examples of best practices. Denmark's online presence embodies a citizen-oriented approach with more interesting and amazing portals than can be listed. The strength of Denmark's online presence begins with its gateway portal, http://www.danmark.dk, which "shows the way to the correct agency or the information sought." While its development is a self-described "continuing process," it has already come a long way

Table 3.6.
E-government readiness rankings: Europe

	Country	Index 2005	Global rank in: 2005	Global rank in: 2004	Change
1	Denmark	0.9058	2	2	0
2	Sweden	0.8983	3	4	1
3	United Kingdom	0.8777	4	3	−1
4	Finland	0.8231	9	9	0
5	Norway	0.8228	10	10	0
6	Germany	0.8050	11	12	1
7	Netherlands	0.8021	12	11	−1
8	Iceland	0.7794	15	14	−1
9	Austria	0.7602	16	17	1
10	Switzerland	0.7548	17	15	−2
11	Belgium	0.7381	18	16	−2
12	Estonia	0.7347	19	20	1
13	Ireland	0.7251	20	19	−1
14	Malta	0.7012	21	21	0
15	France	0.6925	23	24	1
16	Italy	0.6794	25	26	1
17	Slovenia	0.6762	26	27	1
18	Hungary	0.6536	27	33	6
19	Luxembourg	0.6513	28	25	−3
20	Czech Republic	0.6396	29	28	−1
21	Portugal	0.6084	30	31	1
22	Latvia	0.6050	32	39	7
23	Greece	0.5921	35	36	1
24	Slovakia	0.5887	36	37	1
25	Poland	0.5872	38	29	−9
26	Spain	0.5847	39	34	−5
27	Lithuania	0.5786	40	43	3
28	Romania	0.5704	44	38	−6
29	Bulgaria	0.5605	45	41	−4
30	Croatia	0.5480	47	48	1
31	Ukraine	0.5456	48	45	−3
32	Russian Federation	0.5329	50	52	2
33	Belarus	0.5318	51	58	7
34	T.F.Y.R. Macedonia	0.4633	69	97	28
35	Bosnia and Herzegovina	0.4019	84	93	9
36	Albania	0.3732	102	110	8
37	Republic of Moldova	0.3459	109	106	−3
38	San Marino	0.3110	124	128	4
39	Monaco	0.2404	148	152	4
40	Serbia and Montenegro	0.1960	156	87	−69
41	Andorra	0.1836	159	167	8
42	Liechtenstein	0.1789	161	155	−6
	Average	0.6012			

in fulfilling its mission to create an overview of the public sector and what is has to offer. In fact, it is an e-government leader.

One minor interesting observation on the national gateway homepage is that the British flag icon for the English language version has been removed and replaced with a simple link, "Guest in Denmark," which reflects the approach of the portal. It is assumed that non-Danish speakers would not seek the same information. Consequently the Danish content on the portal is not translated; instead, the English version focuses on tourism and study and job opportunities for the visitor and provides the main links to such information, including one to "Denmark's official web site," http://www.denmark.dk. Meanwhile, the Danish version provides users with local content and, as noted, helps them locate the information and services they seek.

Best Practice

Box 7. Denmark: Promoting dialogue between government and citizen

Danish online presence in the form of the e-dialogue portal DanmarksDebatten, http://www.danmarksdebatten.dk, is a best practice. Because an important reference point for the Danish Government's IT and telecommunications policy is the individual citizen it seeks to further opportunities for active participation and contributory influence. As noted on the site itself, "DanmarksDebatten is a dialogue-oriented Internet-based tool to support these efforts via qualifying input from citizens and elected representatives," which empowers citizens by creating a central framework for such debates. The portal also distinguishes itself compared to similar sites in other countries because "Debates are linked and made accessible, whether they take part at national, county or municipal level." Such an innovative approach enables DanmarksDebatten to be "both a national debate portal and a local e-Dialogue tool."

One of the most useful sites in the Danish online presence is the "net-citizen" portal, http://www.netborger.dk, which is a shortcut guide to public self-services at all levels of government involving everything from school and family to work, pensions and taxes. It is also a model for how a public-private partnership can combine its services, to the benefit of citizens. A list of partners as well as more information can be found starting at http://www.netborger.dk/linkpartnere.asp.

Like other leading e-government countries, Denmark has established an office for cooperation and standardization for using IT in the public sector. The OIO— Offentlig Information Online (public information online) portal, http://www.oio.dk, offers information, knowledge and access to tools while primarily targeting public sector employees who deal with e-government and the implementation of IT in the public sector. Of related interest is "the public" search site, http://www.detoffentlige.dk, which claims to search all three million government web pages.

Sweden is a world leader in accessibility, accountability and transparency. Consequently, the national site, http://www.regeringen.se, not only provides lots of information but does so in an innovative way coupled with great accessibility features. Specifically, in addition to providing the more common advanced search feature, more cutting-edge highlights promoting accessibility include the ability to change the font size or select a "simple reading" version in which difficult words have been removed or replaced, as well as a word definition feature, which is always available to explain words. This is complemented with advanced newsletter subscriptions and live and archived web cast press conferences, as well as a detailed calendar of upcoming events for all ministries and ministers.

Not surprisingly then, the strength of Sweden's online presence derives mainly from its national site. Interestingly, as opposed to other top e-government countries, Sweden has integrated its ministries into the main government site. Compared to those countries that simply frame their ministries as a stand-alone part of the overall site, *Sweden actually seamlessly integrates the main site's features in a ministry-specific manner.* Notably, this enables each ministry to incorporate the centrally-developed advanced features while also providing consistency to the user. While the obvious drawback of such an approach is the limitation mandated by the overall framework, it works in Sweden's case because of its advanced starting point.

Sweden has a number of interesting stand alone sites. One is Sverige.se, http://www.sverige.se, which is the online gateway to Sweden's public sector. Previously known as SverigeDirekt, the re-branded Sverige.se was launched at the end of 2004. Hosted by the Swedish Agency for Public Management, the portal remains the starting point for all searches relating to public sector organizations at all levels of government.

One notable initiative is the Government Interoperability Board, http://www.e-namnden.se, which was established in January 2004. Similar to its U.K. counterpart, GovTalk, the mandate of the board is to establish common standards and issue guidelines, as well as to promote the availability of information exchange services and products. In addition, the 24/7 Agency, http://www.24-timmar smyndigheten.se, is the government's vision of the future public sector. As the site proclaims, "Extending the agencies' use of ICT strengthens the infrastructure, contributes to technological development and thus helps to boost Sweden's competitiveness [sic] as an ICT-nation." Consequently, its report, "The 24/7 Agency—Criteria for 24/7 Agencies in the Networked Public Administration," has proposed a "four-stage agency development towards fulfilling the aim of enhancing accessibility and providing service round the clock, seven days a week." Another simple but effective electronic ID information portal is http://www.e-legitimation.se, which briefly explains its purpose and where to receive an E-ID.

Overall, much like those of the United States, the United Kingdom's individual sites consolidate enormous amounts of information and are incredibly useful. The new-look entry portal, http://www.direct.gov.uk, illustrates this strength. Readily accessible, the national site enables users to browse its offerings by audience or topic, or jump right into the "Do it online" section. Equally impressive are the numerous portals, such as the Government Gateway, http://www.gateway.gov.uk, which is the central registration service for e-government services in the United Kingdom. Another cutting-edge collaborative initiate is the info4local project, http://www.info4local. gov.uk, which, as the header clearly notes, provides "information for local government

Sweden is a world leader in accessibility, accountability and transparency.

Sweden's approach actually seamlessly integrates the main site's features in a ministry-specific manner.

from central government." Specifically, six departments, with the Office of the Deputy Prime Minister in the lead, provide local authorities with quick and easy access to useful information from more than 65 government departments, agencies and public bodies.

Best Practice

Box 8. A focus on e-consultation in the United Kingdom

"[I]t is not simply about more open government" but also "listening to … the public" notes the United Kingdom's consultations portal, http://www.consultations.gov.uk, which is not only re-designed and easy to use but could serve as a model presence. The approach is simple but effective and contributes to the country's strong network presence. In fact, despite increased competition, the U.K. remains the leading e-participation country. Notably, in addition to providing a stand-alone portal, each department site surveyed provided a formal consultation facility directly linked from the homepage and also encouraged participation. The model implementation typically comes with detailed descriptions as well as instructions and information on what to expect from the consultations process. Accountability is provided by the Cabinet Office, http://www.cabinetoffice.gov.uk, which issues annual reports on compliance with the Code of Practice on Consultations.[4]

Another especially noteworthy U.K. initiative is the Government Interoperability Framework (e-GIF). At the centre of the project is GovTalk, http://www.govtalk.gov.uk, the purpose of which is to enable participants, both public and private, to work together to develop and agree on policies and standards for e-government through a consultation process. This public-private interoperability partnership has been very successful and is a definite best practice solution that has received wide attention.

Meanwhile, the Office of Government Commerce (OGC), http://www.ogc.gov.uk, has an important role in developing and promoting private sector involvement across the public sector. It is also tasked to work with the public sector as a catalyst to achieve efficiency in commercial activities and improve success in delivery. One such project is the e-procurement site, OGCbuying.solutions, http://www.ogc buyingsolutions.gov.uk, which is an Executive Agency within (OGC) that develops web-based solutions for transactional purchasing. In fact, it was recently announced that the U.K. government had signed a contract for the delivery of an e-procurement hub entitled "Zanzibar," which would further streamline the process.[5]

The United Kingdom's innovative, collaborative, integrated and interoperability approach to e-government is not only successful but also sets standards. While the Department of Education and Skills, http://www.dfes.gov.uk, was deemed a model at the ministerial level, it is perhaps no surprise that all surveyed sites offered a strong online presence. The approach may be simple, but it is effective.

Slovenia's national site, http://www.vlada.si, provides a solid gateway to the country's overall presence. It is, however, the e-government portal, http://e-uprava.gov.si/e-uprava, that is the highlight allowing it to advance one point in the global

The United Kingdom's innovative, collaborative, integrated and interoperability approach to e-government is not only successful but also sets standards.

rankings in 2005. Besides login and personalization features, the site features audience approach information architecture for a well-organized and user-friendly environment. The portal also encourages inclusiveness as it is made accessible at several levels. Specifically, in addition to providing a text only version, it includes an adjustable font size feature and—notably—a wireless WAP access alternative. The e-government services site is obviously also useful in and of itself. It offers up-to-date news, including an e-mail sign-up option, as well as numerous online forms, some of which can be signed electronically. A poll is also included on this site, as well as on the linked site dedicated to Slovenia's place in the European Union, http://evropa.gov.si, which also runs a list-serve through which individuals can discuss issues related to the EU.

Hungary continues to improve its online presence and this year made it to the group of global leaders at the 25th position on web assessment, though it was 27th on the global e-government readiness ranking. *The key to its success lies in the steady progress made each year,* with sites added and re-modelled. Hungary has never lost its commitment to continuous improvements across its government sites. Instead, the country illustrates *the value of long-term planning and dedication,* having enhanced its presence, site-by-site, feature-by-feature. The Hungarian government portal, http://www.magyarorszag.hu, is a case in point. It has continually been refined, bringing it up to par with some of the best national sites in the world. In addition to covering virtually all "basic" information and services, the site also features complete transaction and payment capabilities and online submission of forms, as well as a discussion forum and the ability to provide feedback on policies and activities.

The Hungarian ministries have not yet implemented true transactional capabilities but do offer a strong network presence. Notably, all surveyed ministries provided an open-ended discussion forum. Among them, the Ministry of Education, http://www.om.hu, continued to be the most impressive. It is notable that participatory services are provided through the websites with the response time from government to citizen stipulated as one day.

Many other countries of Europe show considerable progress and diversification in their online content and information. Latvia added key usability and access features to most of the surveyed sites. The Ministry of Education, http://www.izm.gov.lv, for example, featured a search engine as well as a site map to help users locate information quickly. Among features that will enhance social inclusion are the discussion forum included on the Ministry of Welfare site, http://www.lm.gov.lv, and the detailed daily calendar of events on the Ministry of Finance site, http://www.fm.gov.lv.

Having had a mediocre online presence in 2003, Belarus improved significantly last year and has continued to achieve notable progress. This year, it expanded its government web presence by adding a new stand-alone Ministry of Health site, http://www.minzdrav.by. This site is up-to-date and features current news as well as archived law and policy documents, which are available for download. Other government improvements include the Ministry of Education site, http://www.minedu.unibel.by, which has clearly solidified its network presence by adding even more participatory features than were available last year. Specifically, the site now features an online poll, a discussion forum and registration and e-mail sign-up options, as well as a statement

Hungary illustrates the value of long-term planning and dedication.

Many other countries of Europe show considerable progress and diversification in their online content and information.

encouraging citizen participation. Overall, Belarus has clearly fortified its online presence and simultaneously established a strong network presence, which is reflected in the e-participation module.

Many countries
of Southern Europe
improved their ranks in
2005 due to additions
to their e-government
features and services.

Many countries of Southern Europe also improved their ranks in 2005 due to additions to their e-government features and services. The Croatian national site, http://www.vlada.hr, has covered the basics as it provides standard information on laws, government structure, projects and activities, as well as an impressive collection of links organized both alphabetically and according to subject. Its homepage also provides links to several interesting associated government sites and portals. One such link site, http://www.otvorena-vrata.hr, is dedicated to informing the public about government incentive programmes aimed at stimulating the economy and encouraging business. Another, http://www.hitro.hr, contains information and forms for registering a new business while the e-government site, http://www.e-hrvatska.hr, allows citizens to look up land-registry information. While the online services offered are not yet substantiated, the creation of government portals promises more to come, both in terms of content as well as specific e-government features.

The Former Yugoslav Republic of Macedonia has significantly improved its online presence. The key to its success is its overall dedication to expanding the presence while also providing consistency. It starts with the national site, http://www.vlada.mk, which is completely re-designed and which has greatly increased the amount of information available to citizens. Among many other things, it provides up-to-date access to archived and current initiatives, such as the strategy for reform of the judiciary system and the plan for attaining future membership in NATO, as well as detailed answers to the questionnaire for the European Commission's opinion survey on European Union membership. It also links to Macedonia's Secretariat for European Integration, http://www.sei.gov.mk, and provides access to the online version of the country's Official Gazette at http://www.slvesnik.com.mk, where all laws, acts and regulations are published.

Improvement is also seen across the government as several previously inaccessible ministries are now available, such as the Ministry of Health, http://www.zdravstvo.gov.mk, and the Ministry of Education and Science, http://www.mon.gov.mk. The Ministry of Labour and Social Policy, http://www.mtsp.gov.mk, meanwhile, was also accessible during the survey period, though at the time of this writing it once again failed to open up. Clearly, the Macedonian sites are still largely informational but the overall enhancement and improved consistency signal a firmer commitment to investing in open and efficient access to information.

The website of the national government of Bosnia and Herzegovina is combined with the site for the Federation entity under the same URL, http://www.fbihvlada.gov.ba. Consequently, if one is not careful, it is easy to mistake the government entity section for the national site, although to a citizen of the country the distinction would be clear. Notably the site does not provide a link to the other of the two entities, the Republic of Srpska, http://www.vladars.net, which likewise does not provide a link to the national government site. Sorting through this, however, there is some valuable information to be found, including budget information, reports on economic policies and archived laws, as well as links to government agencies and local offices of international organizations. In addition, a useful collection of defined government-related terms is made available, allowing citizens to become better acquainted with their system of government and language. This is important for understanding the documents found on the sites.

The ascendancy of the countries of Europe in e-government reflects a major effort to propel the European Union's advance into the information society. It is notable that with a view to promoting social inclusion, many countries have fortified their participatory services.

However, the relative e-government maturity among countries remains varied. Many countries of Eastern Europe continued to be constrained by the lack of both finance and infrastructure as they attempted to reform their economies. As can be seen from the table above, most of the bottom 10 countries belong to Eastern Europe. E-readiness in countries such as Bosnia and Herzegovina (84th), Albania (102nd), the Republic of Moldova (109th) and Serbia and Montenegro (156th) needs to be strengthened.

South and Eastern Asia

The **Republic of Korea,** with an e-government readiness index of 0.8727, is 5th in the world ranking and the regional leader in South and Eastern Asia. It is closely followed by **Singapore** (0.8503) and **Japan** (0.7801) (Table 3.7). While the Republic of Korea maintained its global ranking in 2005, Singapore and Japan further advanced by one and four points, respectively. However, despite these minor differences in rankings, online services of all three countries are very close to those of the United States, which is the world leader. The Republic of Korea provides 96 per cent of the online services provided by the United States while Singapore and Japan provide 93 per cent and 86 per cent, respectively. *Part of the reason for the high e-readiness in the Asian economies is past investment in, and development of, infrastructure.* The Republic of Korea, Singapore and Japan have high levels of fixed line, mobile phone and Internet penetration.

Among other notable gainers in the region were the **Philippines** (+6), **Thailand** (+4), **China** (+10) and **Viet Nam** (+7). Overall the performance of the region was good in 2005. Three of the region's countries are among the top 25 world leaders while seven out of its 15 countries had e-government readiness higher than the world mean.

A strong commitment to promoting access and use of ICTs is a key ingredient of successful e-government development. Both the Republic of Korea and Singapore signify such commitment. The Republic of Korea remains one of the world leaders in e-government. Its central services portal, http://www.egov.go.kr, continues to offer citizens the opportunity to complete a vast array of government related transactions through several payment options, including digital currency. It also provides a "service cart" similar to the shopping cart feature on e-commerce sites, allowing the user to select, apply for and pay for several services in one transaction. The site also gives users the ability to register in order to personalize services. The Republic of Korea is also home to one of the most impressive e-procurement implementations through its

The Republic of Korea is the regional leader in South and Eastern Asia and is closely followed by Singapore and Japan.

Part of the reason for the high e-readiness in the Asian economies is past investment in, and development of, infrastructure.

Overall the performance of the region was good in 2005. Three of the region's countries are among the top 25 world leaders while seven out of its 15 countries had e-government readiness higher than the world mean.

A strong commitment to promoting access and use of ICTs is a key ingredient of successful e-government development. Both the Republic of Korea and Singapore signify such commitment.

Table 3.7.
E-government readiness rankings: South and Eastern Asia

	Country	Index 2005	Global rank in: 2005	Global rank in: 2004	Change
1	Republic of Korea	0.8727	5	5	0
2	Singapore	0.8503	7	8	1
3	Japan	0.7801	14	18	4
4	Philippines	0.5721	41	47	6
5	Malaysia	0.5706	43	42	–1
6	Thailand	0.5518	46	50	4
7	China	0.5078	57	67	10
8	Brunei Darussalam	0.4475	73	63	–10
9	Mongolia	0.3962	93	75	–18
10	Indonesia	0.3819	96	85	–11
11	Viet Nam	0.3640	105	112	7
12	Cambodia	0.2989	128	129	1
13	Myanmar	0.2959	129	123	–6
14	Timor-Leste	0.2512	144	174	30
15	Lao, P.D.R	0.2421	147	144	–3
	Average	0.4922			

continued development of the Government e-Procurement System (GePS), a single window for public procurement that allows for full integration—from initial purchase request and bid information to actual payment. While the system is centralized it provides multiple access points within its integrated system depending on the audience. (See http://www.g2b.go.kr.)[6]

Singapore is also a world leader in e-government. Its strong online presence is multi-faceted and stems from commitment, as well as continuing progress across all areas. Besides maintaining excellent, informative and up-to-date sites designed to make information easily accessible, *the country's innovative approach to e-government is exhibited in its numerous first-rate portals.* Notable examples include the Government Consultation Portal, http://www.feedback.gov.sg, which encourages feedback from citizens regarding policy, as well as the forum for suggesting ways to cut government waste, http://www.cutwaste.gov.sg.

There are also a variety of new interesting services and portals that have come online recently, such as Sprinter (Singapore Press Releases on the Internet), http://www.sprinter.gov.sg.

Another noteworthy initiative with its own online presence is the ZIP (Zero-In-Process) portal, http://www.zip.gov.sg, which is meant to decrease the number of cross-agency grey areas that can often frustrate citizens. The Secretariat asks citizens to write in with their problem; then decides which agency should be given clear authority over the issue or makes other arrangements for resolving the concern.

Singapore's strong online presence is multi-faceted and stems from commitment, as well as continuing progress across all areas.

In this way, it serves as an impartial and cohesive resource through which citizens can bring up cases of "getting the run-around" by any government agency (or combination of agencies) so that systemic oversights can be addressed to provide better service to Singaporean residents. This constitutes a best practice in improving public sector efficiency.

Given the multitude of impressive offerings perhaps the most noteworthy part of Singapore's overall online presence is the integration process. The national site, http://www.gov.sg, provides user-friendly access to all aspects of its e-government presence. Equally notable is the claim that all of Singapore's government sites link back to the national site in an integrated manner, making for yet another best practice and reinforcing the paradigm that integrated portals and one-stop-shop sites are an effective way forward in e-government.

Japan has progressively enhanced and expanded its online presence. This year, the government's dedication paid dividends as Japan markedly advanced in both e-government readiness and web measure rankings. *The achievement is clearly attributed to incremental development but also consistency.* The key to the overall leap is that all of

Japan has progressively enhanced and expanded its online presence.

Best Practice

Box 9. Singapore's eCitizen portal

The eCitizen portal, http://www.ecitizen.gov.sg, is a success story in Singapore. It is an internet portal created to provide Singaporeans with a single, organized access point to all government services.

Notably, it also allows for personalization through the new My.eCitizen project, http://my.ecitizen.gov.sg, which enables the user to receive e-mail and SMS alerts for such things as parliament notices, library book reminders and passport renewal notifications. Additionally, the eCitizen site, as well as the national site homepage, provides a gateway to the eNETS payment site, http://202.79.222.113/eNETS/Agencies.jsp, where payments owed to just about any government agency can be made. Currently eNETS enters users into weekly and monthly prize drawings in an effort to encourage residents to make payments electronically and decrease government transaction costs.

Singapore's governmental online presence is a best practice, especially in terms of the large number of transactions residents can carry out completely online simultaneously, earning the country top marks in the transactional stage. The eCitizen portal enables users to search for and access a diversity of information from government agencies and conduct a wide range of transactions online with these agencies. The eCitizen portal has the ambition to herald a new era for the Singapore Public Service by transforming the way in which the public interacts with government agencies. Under the e-Government Action Plan, all public services that are suitable for electronic delivery or can tap electronic channels to improve service delivery will be designated for transformation. This is in line with Singapore's vision for service excellence among all government agencies.

Japan's achievement is clearly attributed to incremental development but also consistency.

Japan's sites have been enhanced and consequently increased their numerical score. Especially prominent on an empirical level is Japan's move into the e-participation realm, incorporating features to encourage policy feedback at all surveyed sites; however, the country still lacks a formal online consultation mechanism. For example, the government portal, http://www.e-gov.go.jp, offers documents for consultation but requests feedback offline as opposed to online. While the generic web comment form provided on the site could be used, it is not the integrated and targeted effort that is associated with, and typifies, formal online consultation in the world's more sophisticated e-government websites.

The Japanese government portal, http://www.e-gov.go.jp, continues to develop and impress. Notably, Japan is one of only eight countries in the world that features a wireless access alternative. While it has yet to develop its full online transactional and payment facilities, it is notable that every ministerial site provides access to an associated e-procurement portal. The Japanese e-procurement examples include the Ministry of Health, Labour and Welfare, http://www.ebid.mhlw.go.jp and the Ministry of Education, Culture, Sports, Science and Technology, http://portal.bid.mext.go.jp, as well as the Ministry of Finance, http://portal.bid.mof.go.jp. This approach is in contrast to, for example, Ireland's centralized eTender portal, http://www.etenders.gov.ie, which integrates all public sector procurement opportunities in one place as opposed to having separate sites.

Best Practice

Box 10. Japan's M-Government

Japan's national site, http://www.e-gov.go.jp, is one of only eight worldwide that provides a wireless access alternative. The "m-government," or "keitai" section in Japanese, offers a collection of eight government entities that in turn provide content accessible via a mobile phone or other wireless device capable of browsing. Citizens using the service can, for example, surf the Ministry of Land, Infrastructure and Transport content to view information on road closures, traffic warnings, weather and road surface temperatures, as well as access phone numbers used to report problems. Similarly, the Maritime Safety Agency offers navigation warnings and local contact phone numbers accessible via a variety of wireless services.

Notable m-government content is also provided by the Ministry of Foreign Affairs, which offers passport and visa application instructions along with contact information for local offices as well as information on foreign embassies and consulates in Japan. Meanwhile, in an effort to help track down criminals, the National Police Agency provides pictures of wanted suspects along with information on their age, physical description and the crime they are suspected of committing.

Not to be outdone, the Office of the Prime Minister has also gone mobile and offers a wide variety of information. Especially noteworthy is a frequently-asked-questions section on policy that includes government answers and the ability to instantly send a question, comment or complaint via an e-mail option. Now that is cutting edge.

The Philippines has also developed a solid presence across all stages of e-government. In general it has covered most of the basic functions and features while simultaneously developing transactional facilities and venturing into the networked presence stage, though it still lacks a formal online consultations mechanism. The country needs to fortify sites at the ministerial level, which, though good, are far from matching the quality of its national site. The Philippines has also occasionally experienced other problems. For example, the Department of Finance site, http://www.dof.gov.ph, arguably its best one at the ministerial level, was unavailable during the entire window of the survey last year. A brand new, re-designed site is now online. It still has some parts under construction, though it is still very valuable. Its maintenance problems thus resolved, the site now sets the standard for the other departments in the country and consequently contributed to the Philippines' overall rise in ranking this year. Like the national site, the Department of Finance site offers everything from E-Services and E-Bidding to basic participatory features. Also, via a link, users can access the Revenue Integrity Protection Service site, http://www.rips.gov.ph, where they can find out how to file a corruption complaint either online, by phone or via SMS, and then come back later to track its status.

> The Philippines also developed a solid presence across all stages of e-government.

Good Practice

Box 11. The Philippines' integrated portal

The Philippines' online presence offers an integrated all-services national site, http://www.gov.ph, which is on a par with the best in the world and could be considered a good practice. Among the many notable features, the dedicated E-Services section illustrates that one can simply—but effectively—integrate information across departments, providing a single place for users to find what is available. More advanced tools include a multi-topic discussion forum, as well as a recent feature that enables citizens to comment directly on news items posted on the site as each piece provides a "Send your feedback about this article" button. In addition, it is one of the few national sites that offer a wireless access alternative. Impressively, it does so in three dedicated ways, namely via Short Message Service (SMS), Wireless Application Protocol (WAP) and through a Pocket PC section. Perhaps especially noteworthy, however, is the "Issuances for Comments" section on the national site homepage. It invites the user to take part in the policy-making process by providing feedback.

Thailand has continually solidified its online presence. The national site, http://www.thaigov.go.th, is a case in point as it has progressively covered the basic online government elements while simultaneously expanding into higher levels of e-government by incorporating advanced portals.

The most impressive single window in the Thai online presence is the eCitizen portal, http://www.ecitizen.go.th. In addition to offering personalization through registration, as well as targeting by audience, the site offers extensive sections on "eServices Online" and "eForms." While e-filing of taxes may be the prominent success story, the overall information, services and links offered here are all staples of Thailand's growing e-government achievements.[7]

Among the other government sites, the Ministry of Labour's http://www. mol.go.th was quite impressive and reflected the incremental approach embodied by the national site. More specifically, the Ministry of Labour also progressively covers the fundamental steps while making an initial foray into the upper stages of e-government by encouraging participation and providing several participatory features such as an open-ended discussion forum.

Commitment to e-government is a key ingredient in designing successful initiatives for service delivery. Illustrating the progress made in China, as well as the fast pace of e-government development in general, the country completely re-designed and revised its national site, http://www.gov.cn, between the survey period and the time of this writing. In fact, China exemplifies the success associated with dedicated continued development of government sites as the country has improved its online presence incrementally in each of the three years. It now finds itself among the top 50 in the web measurement. The national site that was surveyed before the recent enhancements is a case in point. Though it was mostly informational and static, it also featured more advanced features such as online submission of forms, as well as a discussion forum. Similarly, the Ministry of Education site, http://www.moe.edu.cn, has realized incremental but steady improvements and this year also featured a rudimentary English language version in addition to the standard Chinese one. Perhaps most impressive among the ministries' sites, however, was the one of the Ministry of Health, http://www.moh.gov.cn, which despite having certain features under construction ventured beyond the basics and entered the network presence realm, indicating the government's commitment to providing access and inclusion to citizens. Specifically, the site not only contained an online poll but also encouraged participation by providing the opportunity for citizens to provide feedback on government documents and policies via e-mail. Overall, however, China has yet to solidify its network presence and still remains underdeveloped in online transactional presence.

Despite incremental overall improvement, Viet Nam still has some ground to cover in solidifying its online presence. Notably, a small number of government sites remain inaccessible and the country lacks a true national site. Meanwhile the National Assembly site, http://www.na.gov.vn, is currently functioning as the gateway substitute. While the site is quite impressive (among other things it encourages citizens to become involved by submitting their opinions on how corruption could be curbed), the fact is that it remains an alternative, which should be superseded by a true national portal in order to consolidate the government's online presence.

Overall Vietnamese progress was instead captured at the ministerial level. Specifically, the Ministry of Health site, http://www.moh.gov.vn, became not only accessible but also rather impressive. It featured good information and useful links as well as its annual strategic plan, though it remained static and had no true services per se. Similarly, the Ministry of Finance site, http://www.mof.gov.vn, remained static in nature but provided useful information regarding the budget and exchange rate trends, as well as an extensive frequently-asked-questions (FAQ) section.

Although many exemplary cases of best practice exist in the region, there are also countries that need to further reinforce e-government programmes and initiatives. Among others, Brunei Darussalam, Mongolia, Indonesia, Viet Nam, Cambodia and Myanmar show progress but are way behind the top five in the region with e-government indices at 20–25% that of the regional leader. Countries such as Timor-Leste and the People's Democratic Republic of Korea belong to the least e-ready countries of the world. Their services are at stages I and II with limited forays into the more mature stages. Whereas some progress has been made, these countries will need to revisit their e-government development programmes in light of their goals, development plans and resource availability.

South and Central America

The relative performance of the region in 2005 was rather mixed with only five out of 20 countries able to advance their e-government readiness rankings. **Chile** (0.6963) maintained its position as the regional leader in 2005, followed by **Mexico** (0.6061), **Brazil** (0.5981) and **Argentina** (0.5971) (Table 3.8). Chile, which was 22nd in 2005, was also the only South or Central American country to make it to the global top 25.

Chile maintained its position as the regional leader in 2005, followed by Mexico, Brazil and Argentina

Table 3.8.
E-government readiness rankings: South and Central America

		Index 2005	Rank in: 2005	2004	Change
1	Chile	0.6963	22	22	0
2	Mexico	0.6061	31	30	−1
3	Brazil	0.5981	33	35	2
4	Argentina	0.5971	34	32	−2
5	Uruguay	0.5387	49	40	−9
6	Colombia	0.5221	54	44	−10
7	Venezuela	0.5161	55	56	1
8	Peru	0.5089	56	53	−3
9	Panama	0.4822	64	54	−10
10	Costa Rica	0.4612	70	73	3
11	El Salvador	0.4225	78	79	1
12	Bolivia	0.4017	85	88	3
13	Guyana	0.3985	89	71	−18
14	Ecuador	0.3966	92	82	−10
15	Belize	0.3815	97	76	−21
16	Guatemala	0.3777	100	111	11
17	Paraguay	0.3620	107	109	2
18	Suriname	0.3449	110	105	−5
19	Nicaragua	0.3383	113	121	8
20	Honduras	0.3348	115	113	−2
	Average	0.4643			

Notwithstanding the relative performance, the regional e-government readiness mean was 0.4643, which was above the world average, reflecting the consolidation and improvements in e-government programmes of several countries in the region such as **Venezuela** (0.5161; +1), **Costa Rica** (0.4612; +3) and **Bolivia** (0.4017; +3). A few countries in the region changed their global rankings. Uruguay (0.5387), Colombia (0.5221), Guyana (0.3985), Ecuador (0.3966) and Belize (0.3815) lost several points in the global rankings in 2005.

In Latin America the development of e-government has been rapidly brought about, in part, by the deregulation of the telecommunication industry. Privatization and regulatory reform have allowed many countries of the region to expand access considerably and further government e-services in recent years. In these times of technology transition a few countries acted upon their vision and capacity to promote access through reinforcement of e-government programmes. Among these are Chile, Mexico and Brazil, which have continued to expand their e-government offerings online at a steady pace.

Chile's national homepage, www.gobiernodechile.cl, is specifically directed at its citizens with easy access links on the front page. The website provides information on what the government is doing and its front page has links to all online transactions and services, regional government websites and sites for consumer safety and civil/criminal defence. This inclusion on the front page of links to the government's most important information and services for the citizen is an effective approach for Chile.

Best Practice

Box 12. Employment services in Chile

Chile has made a special effort in employing e-government for promoting employment. One such endeavour is the *InfoEmpleo,* www.infoempleo.cl, where Chile facilitates an online national employment database to help citizen-employees find jobs and private employers fill employment slots. This is the only such government-sponsored online employment network found in Latin America. The front page divides services into two main sections: (1) for employers to post job openings; and (2) for workers to find jobs for which they qualify. Employers can also scan the postings of potential employees. The government service is free and easy to use, and registration is required. Additionally, the front page lists those jobs that are most sought after and provides links to private employment websites and other useful resources.

Digitizing e-government is a complex and continuous process, with different countries at different stages. Innovative approaches to e-government development depend upon a country's commitment, level of development and resource availability. One approach is found in **Mexico**, where *@Campus* is an online learning programme for public servants intended to help consolidate civil service reform.[8] The project provides civil servants with an Internet-based education portal offering courses and information on how to receive certification.

Approaches to e-government programme offerings differ from country to country. The "how" of what countries choose to display on their websites is a function of the "what" they want to focus on and "why" they want to focus on the issue selected.

Whereas some countries closely follow the model of an integrated and multi-faceted approach to a portal others may spin off separate portals from one national site. Mexico's triple combination of online services and transactions provides citizens with easy-to-use methods to interact with government to address needs, comment on policy and find pertinent information. It provides a multi-faceted approach to online services and transactions. This *is an approach rich with potential for promoting access and inclusion for all groups of the population.*

Approaches to e-government programme offerings differ from country to country.

Mexico's triple combination of online services and transactions is an approach rich with potential for promoting access and inclusion for all groups of populations.

Best Practice

Box 13. Mexico's approach for promoting access and inclusion

Mexico has adopted a three-pronged approach to promote access and inclusion to its different population groups. First, Tramitanet, www.tramitanet.gob.mx, is a one-stop-shopping citizen portal with services for both citizens and businesses. Second, e-Mexico, www.e-mexico.gob.mx, is an extensive e-government site with online information and services categorized into ten "communities." Users are asked to click on the image that corresponds with their community—for example, *women, immigrants, senior citizens, business owners* or *students*—and the relevant online services and information are presented. The website also lists the most commonly requested services for each community. Last, Foros, www.foros.gob.mx, provides a networking presence for citizen discussion groups on national law and policy. Discussions and postings are divided by topics, as well as by specific legislation, and all registered citizens can post messages to be read by other citizens and the government. The website appears to be used extensively as, this year, over 100,000 messages had been posted by the time of its assessment.

Brazil improved its ranking in 2005 by reinforcing its infrastructure and services. Brazil's one-stop-shopping site, www.e.gov.br, is perhaps the most effective in Latin America. This website provides the most pertinent information and services, including 13 images with subtitles that represent the most desired citizen services, ranging from tax payment and health services to legislation information and utilities. The site's image logos make it particularly user-friendly. In addition, the Brazilian government provides an e-procurement website for government contracts for goods and services. *Comprasnet,* www.comprasnet.gov.br, contains information on relevant legislation and current news on the economic development of the country. More importantly, it provides an online bidding site for government contracts, as well as

Brazil's one-stop-shopping site is perhaps the most effective in Latin America.

links to services for new and emerging businesses in Brazil. To enable use of these online services, the website installs specific software on the user's computer and allows for online registration of potential government contractors.

Argentina offers a *comprehensive one-stop-shopping approach* with numerous links to various information sources and online services, www.gobiernoelectronico.ar. It groups the information into several clear categories. For instance, icons at the top of the web page list the services and information provided by the three branches of government while the local government divisions are listed in the left column of the web page. General transactions and services options are listed by category in the centre of the web page and additional links to national newspapers, weather outlets, tourism centres and so forth are listed in the right column. Current news, legislation and policy options are also listed, in a separate box at the bottom of the page. The Argentine approach to one-stop-shopping attempts to list all resources and is effective because it is clearly organized and user-friendly.

Western Asia

Countries of Western Asia have performed very well in 2005. In the last three years the region as a whole has advanced its e-government readiness to 0.4384, which is higher than the 2005 world average. While **Israel** (0.6903; 24th) remained among the top 25 world leaders and the regional leader, many other countries in the region substantially advanced their global rankings. Notable among the performers are **Cyprus** (0.5872; +12), **the United Arab Emirates** (0.5718; +18), **Qatar** (0.4895; +18), **Kuwait** (0.4431; +25), **Saudi Arabia** (0.4105; +10), **Georgia** (0.4034; +11), **Oman** (0.3405; +15) and the **Syrian Arab Republic** (0.2871; +5), all of which improved their global rankings in 2005 (Table 3.9).

Cyprus' performance in 2005 has been remarkable. It added 12 points to its ranking. Its overall web presence was enhanced with the addition of a new Cyprus Ministry of Health site, http://www.moh.gov.cy, that is a useful resource for obtaining health-related information and services. It features printable forms for requesting a medical card or health benefit entitlement prior to travel to certain countries, a listing of prices and fees for medical services, detailed information on the process of harmonization of health legislation with EU standards, as well as a tender announcements section.

The United Arab Emirates (UAE) posted one of the most impressive yearly gains among all the countries of the world in 2005. It advanced its ranking from 60 in 2004 to 42 in 2005. As with many other top gainers, it did so due to a revamped national site that integrates information and services into a single gateway where its offerings can be easily located. The UAE national site was not only completely re-done but also re-branded, from http://www.uae.gov.ae to the new http://www.government.ae. Furthermore, in a bid to provide access and inclusion to all, the UAE government expanded its Ministry of Education site, http://www.moe.gov.ae, to include participatory features. This was perhaps especially noteworthy because, in addition to having been re-branded, this is one of the few government sites in the Middle East that offers an open-ended discussion forum.

Table 3.9.

E-government readiness rankings: Western Asia

		Index 2005	Rank in: 2005	2004	Change
1	Israel	0.6903	24	23	−1
2	Cyprus	0.5872	37	49	12
3	United Arab Emirates	0.5718	42	60	18
4	Bahrain	0.5282	53	46	−7
5	Turkey	0.4960	60	57	−3
6	Qatar	0.4895	62	80	18
7	Jordan	0.4639	68	68	0
8	Lebanon	0.4560	71	74	3
9	Kuwait	0.4431	75	100	25
10	Saudi Arabia	0.4105	80	90	10
11	Georgia	0.4034	83	94	11
12	Azerbaijan	0.3773	101	89	−12
13	Armenia	0.3625	106	83	−23
14	Oman	0.3405	112	127	15
15	Iraq	0.3334	118	103	−15
16	Syrian Arab Republic	0.2871	132	137	5
17	Yemen	0.2125	154	154	0
	Average	0.4384			

Regional Best Practice

Box 14. The United Arab Emirates' Gateway to e-services

An interesting feature of the UAE gateway, http://www.government.ae, is that the government entry site is organized by end-user, providing information, services and transactions under separate sections for residents, business, visitors and government. Impressive features on the site itself include up-to-date information, as well as registration and e-Tenders, which incorporate online bidding for public tenders. In addition, the government gateway provides clear access to two excellent portals: the e-Dirham portal, http://www.e-dirham.gov.ae for transactions; and the e-Forms portal, http://www.uaesmartforms.com for online forms, advancing its interactive presence.

Continued improvement to its central services portal, http://www.e.gov.qa, has enabled Qatar to leapfrog into the top half in the web assessment. While some aspects of the country's overall online presence can be further enhanced, *the e-government portal can be considered a regional best practice and is on a par with integrated services portals elsewhere in the world. The e-government pilot project illustrates the success associated with a clear long-term vision that integrates not only front-end services but also coordinates back-end strategy.* Aimed at building a central foundation for a flexible e-service platform the portal's inter-departmental approach integrates public services

Qatar's e-government portal can be considered a regional best practice and the project illustrates the success associated with a clear long-term vision that integrates not only front-end services but also coordinates back-end strategy.

The e-government pilot project illustrates the success associated with a clear long-term vision that integrates not only front-end services but also coordinates back-end strategy.

for both companies and citizens onto a single window and facilitates a convenient and user-friendly approach.

Regional Best Practice

Box 15. Qatar e-government portal

As its "Government services made easier" slogan reflects, the site offers many useful services, ranging from student registration and the payment of fines for traffic violations to applying online for visas and permits. In August 2005, the site claimed 115,000 visitors—a growth of 66 per cent compared to July 2005—as well as 13,311 transactions during the month of August alone. Given the dedication of the project as well as the usefulness of the site, this is hardly surprising. The portal, which comes in a default Arabic version but with mirror English pages, is well worth a visit, both for its services and for inspiration. More information about the project can be found at http://www.e.gov.qa/eGovPortal/aboutus.jsp.

An important part of e-government service delivery is site maintenance and availability.

Kuwait made steady improvements over previous years in 2005. In large part the jump was due to the fact that the Ministry of Social Affairs and Labour site, http://www.mosal.gov.kw, was accessible. While this site is good in and of itself, its complete unavailability last year clearly hurt the country's overall presence, which it has now regained. This underscores the point that even though it is commendable to develop and implement a site, it also needs to be continuously maintained. *Sites with irregular availability are of limited value to the citizens and could even discourage usage. An important part of e-government service delivery is site maintenance and availability.*

The overall reason for Kuwait's achievement in 2005 is clearly due to the fact that all of its sites were accessible during the survey window. Another important development in creating an integrated and user-friendly online presence is the implementation of an official national government gateway. Though not fully implemented in Kuwait, it is the natural next step. Currently, its National Assembly site, http://www.alommah.gov.kw, which also experienced irregular availability during the review, is considered as a substitute national site. Most notable in the country's online presence is the Ministry of Finance site, http://www.mof.gov.kw, which not only consistently opened up but also offered more useful and extensive information than those of the other ministries.

Unlike many of its regional neighbours, Saudi Arabia has yet to develop and implement a true national portal. The deficit translates onto the ministerial level, which remains inconsistent but with flashes of positive signs. The Ministry of Education site, http://www.moe.gov.sa, for example, only opened up sporadically during the survey period but when available offered useful information, such as educational statistics. Meanwhile, the Ministry of Foreign Affairs site, http://www.mofa.gov.sa, functions as a gateway and provides an impressive collection of links, as well as an extensive archive of speeches by officials and a summary of the Kingdom's foreign policy. In addition, several of Saudi Arabia's ministerial sites contained basic network presence features, including online polls and e-mail sign-up options, which illustrates the interest in advancing the overall presence. Also impressive was the country's General Directorate of Passports site, http://www.gdp.gov.sa, which offers online forms for passports, permits and visas that can be filled in, as well as detailed instructions related to the various procedures for foreign nationals.

Another case of gradual progress is found in Georgia, where the parliament site, http://www.parliament.ge, remains the country's starting point. It features both current and archived information and includes a search feature as well as a site map to aid users in finding the information provided. On average, Georgia's status remains similar to that of last year. However, it has expanded its online presence slightly by providing brief sections for all its ministries. While the ministry information is currently limited to contact information it is a first step in making it easier for citizens to contact officials with questions or concerns. The only ministry with a stand-alone website is the Ministry of Finance, http://www.mof.ge, which also provides useful information but has thus far not taken the next step towards two-way communication. Overall, Georgia has solidified its online presence by providing the most basic information but has yet to venture towards any form of interactivity.

Notwithstanding the fact that many of the region's countries did well in 2005, only three countries of Western Asia are among the top 50. The bottom six countries fall among the 100–160 rankings of the world. These disparities in e-readiness reflect inequality in income and ICT availability within the region. More effort toward e-government is required to alleviate such disparities.

In the case of Iraq, which lost 15 points in the 2005 global ranking, it should be noted that in 2005 the UN E-government Survey continued to assess the available Coalition Provisional Authority (CPA) site because no other site was available (see box below).

Box 16. The special case of Iraq

Because of its special circumstances, Iraq's online presence in 2004 was measured via the Coalition Provisional Authority (CPA) website, http://www.cpa-iraq.org/, which remains available for historical purposes until 30 June 2006.[9] While it was explicitly acknowledged in last year's report that the site could change or become unavailable altogether, it did meet all the technical requirements as to what constituted a national government site at the time of the survey.

Simultaneously, however, Iraq petitioned the U.S.-based Internet Corporation for Assigned Names and Numbers (ICANN) for control of the .iq domain.[10] On 28 July 2005, ICANN voted to approve the proposed re-delegation of the .iq domain to the National Communications and Media Commission (NCMC) of Iraq.[11] While the country has now officially regained control over the domain, no website associated with the extension had been assigned up until the time of this writing. Consequently, the Iraqi Transitional Government website, http://www.iraqigovernment.org, was surveyed again in 2005 as the country's national site.

Like its counterpart last year, the site surveyed may be temporary, in development or possibly moving, but it was recognized as the official government site at the time of this year's web measure survey. It is quite informative, providing news and archived information as well as the constitution and overviews of the country's vital sectors. While parts of the site are under construction, it is being kept up-to-date and offers a fairly extensive English version in addition to the Arabic one. It is well worth a visit.

Caribbean

Around half of the countries of the Caribbean region are ranked in the 60th to 120th range, which places them at about average in the global rankings (Table 3.10). In 2005, a few countries among the top ones improved their positions marginally. Half of the countries of the region were above the world average. **Jamaica** (0.5064) continued to be the regional leader in the Caribbean, followed by **Barbados** (0.4920), **Trinidad and Tobago** (0.4768) and the **Bahamas** (0.4676). Barbados has done well in 2005, advancing by four points in the global rankings. **Antigua and Barbuda** (0.4010) and **Grenada** (0.3879) also did well, gaining thirteen and seven points, respectively. E-government readiness in the region as a whole improved marginally even though it remained around the level of the world average.

Table 3.10.
E-government readiness rankings: Caribbean

		Index 2005	Rank in: 2005	2004	Change
1	Jamaica	0.5064	59	59	0
2	Barbados	0.4920	61	65	4
3	Trinidad and Tobago	0.4768	66	61	−5
4	Bahamas	0.4676	67	62	−5
5	Saint Kitts and Nevis	0.4492	72	72	0
6	Saint Lucia	0.4467	74	64	−10
7	Dominican Republic	0.4076	82	77	−5
8	Antigua and Barbuda	0.4010	86	99	13
9	Saint Vincent and the Grenadines	0.4001	88	119	31
10	Grenada	0.3879	95	102	7
11	Cuba	0.3700	103	104	1
12	Dominica	0.3334	119	98	−21
	Average	0.4282			

Over the last few years the Government of Jamaica has made the integration of information technology into the Jamaican economy a high priority and a strategic imperative. It aims to promote Jamaica as a Caribbean hub for IT activities and investment.[12] In particular it aims to enhance access by transformations in connectivity, building human resource development, and the enactment of an enabling legislative and policy framework.

The Jamaica national gateway site, http://www.jis.gov.jm, *offers well-organized, in-depth information on almost all facets of the government.* Additionally, the site offers users the ability to listen to web broadcasts of speeches by officials, as well as 30 minutes of news and features on government policies and events. Through the various associated government sites, Jamaica residents can also access numerous forms, which can then be filled out and submitted online to the respective agency. Other notable advanced features include online transaction facilities, such as for payment of taxes and traffic fines, through the Jamaica Tax Administration site at http://www.jamaicatax-online.gov.jm/.

The Government of Barbados Information Network (GOBINET) portal, http://www.barbados.gov.bb, continues to provide a solid national site presence for the country. The relatively simple site is an excellent gateway to Barbados' overall presence, hence the information network label, and is quantitatively on a par with countries ranked twice as high. Impressively, the consolidation effort noted in last year's report has continued and the site now boasts an expanded "Downloadable Government Forms" section with more than 25 forms from six different ministries/agencies. In fact, the national site remains a good example of what can be accomplished through dedication, planning and targeted development despite limited resources. Moreover, Barbados continues to offer a full online transaction facility through its post office site, http://bps.gov.bb, which is remarkable given its overall position.

One limitation of the national gateway development is evident however, as several ministries remain offline altogether while those online typically offer limited value. For example, the Ministry of Labour and Social Security website, http://labour.gov.bb, mimics the overall targeted approach in that it is limited in scope and only provides the "Barbados Labour Market Information System" (BLMIS), which while useful in and of itself, clearly leaves the Ministry site with things to be wished for, such as general Ministry news and information. Even so, the BLMIS system provides a variety of useful career-specific bits of information, such as a jobs database and industry profiles with salary ranges, as well as interview and resume writing tips. Clearly, given the constraints in place, Barbados has been forced to selectively implement only parts of its desired presence; however, it has seemingly started in the right places.

During the survey period this year, the national government of Trinidad and Tobago had an impressive, re-designed site available at http://www.gov.tt. It features *easy navigation through an extensive collection of government sites* via a pull-down menu, and a section dedicated to forms. The homepage highlights links to the "Fast Forward" site, http://fastforward.tt, which focuses on initiatives to advance technology in the country, as well as the "Vision 2020" site, http://vision2020.info.tt, that focuses on the country's development goals, to be achieved by the year 2020. While the new national government site still has some sections with relatively little content, the smart design and sections already included promise more to come and show the country's willingness to invest in and improve its e-government capabilities.

The national government of Trinidad and Tobago features easy navigation through an extensive collection of government sites.

Antigua and Barbuda has committed itself to utilizing ICT for development. The devotion is demonstrated on its recently overhauled national site, http://www.ab.gov.ag, which not only provides a brief section on e-government but also clearly highlights the government's draft policy on Information and Communication Technologies (ICTs) at the top of the homepage. The policy, according to the introduction, "is a blueprint for the economic transformation of Antigua and Barbuda to a knowledge-based society. In its implementation, this policy will provide the requisite legal and regulatory framework as well as financial and social incentives, which will ensure that the people of Antigua and Barbuda are active participants in the Global Village and reap the full rewards of globalization."[13]

At an empirical level, the Antigua and Barbuda national site, http://www. ab.gov.ag, has indeed made progress compared to only a year ago. While previously the site consisted only of minimal text-based information, the newly re-designed government portal offers not just extensive information and basic services such as forms but has also ventured into the higher stages and provides a multi-topic, open-ended discussion forum where feedback is encouraged, especially on the draft ICT policy.

For the second straight year, Grenada's national gateway, http://www.gov.gd, remained under construction. Nevertheless, the site is kept current and offers the most basic information. Particularly noteworthy is that while it listed its ministries last year none of them were actually online; however, this year, three have been afforded their own online presence through a type of framed site. Out of the three, one is included in the web measure, namely the Ministry of Finance, http://finance.gov.gd. (The other two are the Ministries of Agriculture and Tourism.) Though the new ministry site is in its infancy and is limited in its offerings, it does, like the national site, provide a first step in the right direction.

The importance of consistency in the maintenance of e-government websites cannot be overstated. There is a need for countries to recognize that utilization of ICTs to provide online services, even at the rudimentary level, must go hand-in-hand with a commitment to maintain the site. *Effective e-government requires a vision, a plan and a strategy, which must be developed in conjunction with resource availability and the level of human and physical infrastructure on the ground.* In the last three years there have been several instances of e-government offerings that seemed to be making gradual progress going offline all of a sudden—sometimes for extended periods of time. An example is the national Saint Vincent and the Grenadines site, www.gov.vc, which at the time of the site survey in 2005 had made some progress. Even though the country ranked 119th in 2004, this progress allowed it to advance to the 88th position in 2005. At the time of this writing, however, the national site of Saint Vincent and the Grenadines was not online, which does not augur well in terms of the e-services it offers.

> Effective e-government requires a vision, a plan and a strategy, which must be developed in conjunction with resource availability and the level of human and physical infrastructure on the ground.

South and Central Asia

Many of the countries belonging to South and Central Asia continued to progress well in their e-government programmes. **Kazakhstan** (0.4813) bypassed Kyrgyzstan to arrive at the top, adding four points to its global ranking. It was followed by **Kyrgyzstan** (0.4417), **Maldives** (0.4321) and **Uzbekistan** (0.4114) (Table 3.11). Consolidation of their past investments led to around half of the countries increasing their relative rankings in the global e-government readiness index in 2005. Most notable among these were the countries of South Asia such as the **Islamic Republic of Iran** (0.3813), **Nepal** (0.3012) and **Bhutan** (0.2941).

The region as a whole, though, remained below the world average in e-readiness with some of the countries among the least e-ready countries in the world. Part of the reason is that though Asia is one of the largest regional Internet markets, with estimated potential users close to a billion, high access costs, poor infrastructure and the slow pace of deregulation have affected the growth of ICTs in general and the

> In South and Central Asia Kazakhstan was followed by Kyrgyzstan, Maldives and Uzbekistan.

Table 3.11.
E-government readiness rankings: South and Central Asia

		Index 2005	Rank in: 2005	2004	Change
1	Kazakhstan	0.4813	65	69	4
2	Kyrgyzstan	0.4417	76	66	−10
3	Maldives	0.4321	77	78	1
4	Uzbekistan	0.4114	79	81	2
5	India	0.4001	87	86	−1
6	Sri Lanka	0.3950	94	96	2
7	Iran (Islamic Republic of)	0.3813	98	115	17
8	Tajikistan	0.3346	117	—	—
9	Nepal	0.3021	126	132	6
10	Bhutan	0.2941	130	165	35
11	Pakistan	0.2836	136	122	−14
12	Bangladesh	0.1762	162	159	−3
13	Afghanistan	0.1490	168	171	3
	Average	0.3448			

Internet in particular. Along with Africa, South and Central Asia is the least e-ready region of the world, with a serious deficit in telecommunications infrastructure, which at present is 20 per cent of the world average and five per cent of the level of the United States and Canada taken together. Since the region is home to more than 1.5 billion people, lack of access to telecommunication has limited the potential for achieving the social and economic benefits of ICTs for this region. Limited e-government development is also the result of a lack of financial resources, more basic needs being the emergent priorities for most of the countries of the region. Newer technologies remain the domain of the elite in most of them. Large populations, especially in rural areas of countries like India, Pakistan and Afghanistan, remain without electricity and telephone service. Where access is available, lack of literacy and technical skills pose limiting constraints on the demand for e-services.

Despite these serious problems it is notable that all countries have an online presence at some level. A few are more developed than others. Moreover, armed with e-strategies, many countries of the region have made efforts to promote citizen participation on their e-government websites. Even though some are at the basic stages of e-government maturity, a few such as Kazakhstan and the Islamic Republic of Iran have taken steps to establish some participatory presence. Recently India added a policies portal for viewing government public policies—a definite step towards broader inclusion.

Kazakhstan has progressively improved in each of the three annual surveys. Thus, it is no surprise that it has markedly enhanced its overall position and solidified its online presence. Notably, its true national site, http://www.government.kz, is consistently accessible and provides extensive information and useful links. Moreover, the

Armed with e-strategies, many countries of the region have made efforts to promote citizen participation on their e-government websites.

President's site, http://www.president.kz, was completely re-designed between the time of this year's survey and this writing—a sign of the overall dedication to and progress in ICT. While the old version was quite average, the new-look site is clearly an improvement and provides a neat and useful framework for information. Also notable is the fact that the national site, as well as the President's site come in both Kazakh and Russian, as well as in a fairly extensive English version. The latter is also typical of the other government sites. This illustrates a commitment to preserving local and traditional identities while incorporating a global viewpoint.

The continued dedication and solidification of the overall online presence in Kazakhstan is also reflected at the ministerial level. Although the sites remain mostly informational and static, some of them, such as the sites of the Ministry of Education and Science, http://edu.gov.kz, and the Ministry of Labour and Social Protection, http://www.enbek.kz, not only cover most of the basics but have also made an initial foray into networked presence. Moreover, the Ministry of Finance site, http://mfn.minfin.kz, was self-described as undergoing re-construction during part of the survey period and appeared to be making promising progress as well. The overall maturity reached by Kazakhstan bodes well for the future as a stepping-stone into the higher stages of e-government.

Even though Kyrgyzstan slipped 10 points in 2005, it remained number two in the region. Kyrgyzstan's e-government initiative at http://www.gov.kg is proceeding according to well-set-out priorities and development plans. In 2005 its overall online presence was fortified with the expansion of information and services, as well as the promotion of participatory features across most ministries. The effort expended to bring these initiatives online still pays dividends as the sites and their offerings remain intact. Notably, the government access point, http://www.gov.kg, still provides a very user-friendly approach with links to a wide variety of sites, including ministries, as well as other government and non-government sites. Additionally, the site features a registration option as well as a multi-topic discussion forum. Notwithstanding this array of features, its ICT portal, which gives information on its e-government programmes, http://www.ict.gov.kg, did not open up during the review period and could not be verified this year (though it became accessible after the survey window had closed). This resulted in a decline of 10 points in Kyrgyzstan's ranking. While the country spent considerable effort in solidifying its online presence, its initiatives seem to have lost steam because little to no progress has been visibly achieved over the past year. This underscores the point that any e-government initiative needs to involve continuous development towards an ever-higher aspiration rather than being a one-time fix.

The Islamic Republic of Iran made impressive gains in the web measure compared to last year. This jump is attributed to the improvement in ministerial presence. While it was unavailable during the survey period last year, the Ministry of Education site, http://www.medu.ir, is now accessible. Like other Iranian sites, it is mostly static but provides plenty of useful information. However it is notable that despite being at stage II in most services the country encourages citizen feedback by providing both "Question & Answer" and "Opinions & Suggestions" e-mail forms and in this aspect is taking steps to promote participation and inclusion. The focus

Kyrgyzstan's e-government initiative is proceeding according to well-set-out priorities and development plans.

The Islamic Republic of Iran made impressive gains in the web measure compared to last year.

on participation was also visible on the new Ministry of Labour and Social Affairs site, http://www.irimlsa.ir, which despite having parts under construction, was impressive at the basic stages while also featuring an online poll. Likewise, the Ministry of Finance site, http://www.mefa.gov.ir, came online with its own URL, though at least half of the links on the site were not working at the time of the survey.

Meanwhile the Iranian President's site, http://www.president.ir, remains informational and up-to-date, though it provides little else and some parts are still under construction. Notable, however, is the "E-mail to President" feature, which is a sophisticated e-mail comment form, complete with attachment and formatting features, as well as the ability to provide a mailing address if the e-mail needs follow-up. Overall, the Iranian online presence is ever expanding, has covered the basic ground and is set to take the next step.

Though India slipped one point in the relative ranking in 2005 it nevertheless reinforced its offerings. A notable feature in promoting online participation is that India has added a Portal on Government Policies, http://policies.gov.in/, where agencies and departments are able to publish their policies for the public to view. Along with the downloadable policy document itself, contact information for the individual responsible for each policy is listed so that potentially affected parties can make comments, offer suggestions or provide other input related to the subject of the policy, usually by calling or e-mailing the responsible individual, or by using the online comment form provided. The site further promises that "queries and suggestions regarding any Policy shall be directly forwarded to the concerned Department." Another noteworthy site is provided by the Department of Administrative Reforms & Public Grievances within India's Ministry of Personnel, Public Grievances & Pensions. The Online Public Grievance Lodging and Monitoring site, http://www.darpg-grievance.nic.in/, enables users to lodge a complaint about an issue that was not resolved through the regular administrative procedure of the agency in question and to track the status of grievances so lodged. In addition to serving the purpose of allowing the Department to facilitate resolution of citizen grievances, with various agencies as third party mediators, the website also allows the government to track the number of grievances lodged against various agencies and departments in order to highlight problem areas that require improvement or reform. Through these two online mechanisms, India is increasing its citizens' access and soliciting their views to help shape how government fulfils its mandates in a more efficient manner.

Nepal has progressively improved its online presence in each of the three years of the survey. As an example, its national site, http://www.nepalhmg.gov.np, was re-designed between the close of this year's survey window and the time of this writing. It is interesting that while English was the default website language, the Nepali version of the site was under construction. With the introduction of the re-designed site, it now appears as though Nepali is the default website language with heavy, if not mirror, content provided in English. Similarly, the Ministry of Women, Children and Social Welfare site, http://www.mowcsw.gov.np, was also completely revamped after the survey collection had ended and is now afforded its own stand-alone web presence. Progress was evident too at the redesigned and enhanced Ministry of Labour and Transport Management site, http://www.moltm.gov.np.

Nepal has progressively improved its online presence in each of the three years.

Overall, Nepal has covered the basic stages of e-government well with its current commitment and now lacks only the advanced stage presence.

More countries are investing in and implementing an official national government gateway site as part of their strategy to provide citizens with better, faster and more convenient access to information and public services. Specifically, last year's survey found that 85 per cent of the Member States maintained a functioning official national government site, while this year's update found that this number had increased to 87 per cent.

Bhutan is one of the countries that, in the past, only had a limited official web presence, through alternative sites. However, this year it did much to improve its e-government standing by developing a national government portal to serve its citizens. Among many other things not previously available, the new entry portal, http://www.bhutan.gov.bt, features information on how to obtain a driver's license or register a vehicle, printable forms for requesting telephone service, making a customs declaration, reporting income or requesting a passport, as well as a comprehensive list of government department and agency sites.

Other countries in the region are also fortifying their e-government offerings to provide better access and inclusion. Sri Lanka hopes to achieve major progress in deploying ICTs for economic and social development by 2007. The Bangladesh Bureau of Manpower, Employment and Training (BMET) and the Ministry of Expatriate Welfare have developed a rich, interactive website that offers various services for job seekers and employers.[14] BMET has established a Data Bank of Prospective Overseas Job Seekers, which is web-based and offers overseas employers the facility to search for prospective overseas job seekers from Bangladesh through the Internet. The Pakistan Ministry of Information Technology, IT&T Division, has implemented a project aimed at providing basic infrastructure at the Federal Public Service Commission (FPSC), automating the seven major FPSC systems and providing an online recruitment system. These facilities will lay the foundations for government e-services in employment.[15] Tajikistan appeared for the first time, with its Ministry of Foreign Affairs site, http://www.mid.tj.

Overall the governments of the region are making efforts towards sustained and paced across-the-board e-government development. However, in the case of some countries the progress has been slow to moderate, resulting in relative declines when assessed against other countries of the world.

Oceania

Australia (0.8679) and **New Zealand** (0.7987) remain the regional leaders and among the top 25 world leaders in e-government readiness (Table 3.12). These two countries are also much farther advanced than the rest of the countries in Oceania and pull up the average e-readiness for the region, which at 0.2888, remains far below the world average.

Apart from Australia and New Zealand, which maintained their relative rankings, the region has not done well in 2005. Many of its countries have lost their relative positions due to greater efforts in other countries of the world. **Fiji** (0.4081)

Table 3.12.

E-government readiness rankings: Oceania

		Index 2005	Rank in: 2005	2004	Change
1	Australia	0.8679	6	6	0
2	New Zealand	0.7987	13	13	0
3	Fiji	0.4081	81	84	3
4	Samoa	0.3977	91	92	1
5	Tonga	0.3680	104	95	−9
6	Solomon Islands	0.2669	140	134	−6
7	Papua New Guinea	0.2539	142	142	0
8	Vanuatu	0.1664	165	164	−1
9	Palau	0.0564	175	177	2
10	Micronesia	0.0532	176	175	−1
11	Marshall Islands	0.0440	177	176	−1
12	Tuvalu	0.0370	178	—	—
13	Nauru	0.0357	179	178	−1
	Average	0.2888			

and **Samoa** (0.3977) were the only countries to add marginally to their rankings. In 2005, Tuvalu came online through the government's official tourism website, http://www.timelesstuvalu.com. Although not constituting a true national government site, this emerging presence constitutes a step in the right direction by providing some information and utilizing the Web as an outlet.

The New Zealand national site, http://www.govt.nz, has been re-designed over the past year. A highlight of the site is that it promises to help "Find out all that you need to know about everything that Government has to offer." Notably, it has retained its somewhat different approach, compared to others, as it is a "classic" portal, which only collects information and provides links to services themselves. For example, the recently prominently featured news section on the front page of the national site does not have links to a news section on the portal. Rather, it re-directs the user directly to the news items at the government/ministry site in question. Although the national site is limited in providing its own information, it should be noted that the re-design has increased national site content and that the general "classic" approach is definitely not a disadvantage. In fact, the collection, organization and standardization of information and services across government entities into a single portal is impressive and presented in a very user-friendly format.

Meanwhile, the New Zealand ministry sites are progressively improving and, perhaps as a case in point, two ministries had completely re-designed the sites they exhibited last year. Especially impressive is the fact that almost every site surveyed encouraged participation and/or promoted consultations. Among notable portals, the Ministry of Social Development, http://www.msd.govt.nz, offered an impressive one-stop site, http://www.studylink.govt.nz, that puts student loan services online. Other sites of interest include the New Zealand Government Jobs Online portal,

> **Best Practice**
>
> ## Box 17. Promoting participation and access in New Zealand
>
> While the national portal literally covers everything regarding government from A to Z, its most innovative feature is its targeting by audience structure, labelled "Things to Know When," http://www.govt.nz/ttkw, which is yet another way of intuitively guiding the user to the correct information and services without he or she having to know which government entity is responsible. The most impressive section, however, might be the "Participate in Government" feature, http://www.govt.nz/participate/, which is clearly highlighted on the homepage along with the tagline "Get involved with government and have your say." Even though the sub-section reflects the site's overall approach by only providing links along with brief descriptions, the collection as a whole is very impressive. The at-a-glance overview format makes it easy to find the many useful features, ranging from three links on "Have your say on a government consultation document" to one link provided by the Ministry of Justice, entitled "Start a citizens referendum." Overall, New Zealand is a leader in e-participation and its dedicated, easy-to-use and informative section on the national site clearly contributes to the progress.

http://www.jobs.govt.nz, as well as—of course—the e-government portal, http://www.e-government.govt.nz. In fact, the latter could serve as a model for others looking to develop a stand-alone portal on e-government as it is neatly organized, up-to-date, rich in content, and provides a great overview of e-government in general, as well as clarifying the specifics.

The foundation of strong online presence typically begins with a solid national site. Adopting this approach, Australia benefited from consolidating two somewhat overlapping portal sites, (http://www.fed.gov.au and http://australia.gov.au), into one. Re-designed and easy-to-use the national site slogan, "Your connection with government," lives up to its promise as it provides access to the large amount of information and many services that the government has to offer. In fact, the portal links to over 700 Australian federal government websites and searches over five million government web pages. Among the many impressive sites is the Centrelink agency, http://www.centrelink.gov.au, within the Department of Human Services, which delivers outstanding community services online.

Previously noted as a case study in excellence, the Workplace portal, http://www.workplace.gov.au, this year announced details of the Australian Government's move towards one, simpler national workplace relations system known as "WorkChoices," http://www.workchoices.gov.au, which will be an interesting initiative to follow.

Among the ministries, the Department of Education, Science and Training site, http://www.dest.gov.au, is a best practice in and of itself. Among other things, it offers formal consultation. The department also links to the enormously useful Education Portal, http://www.education.gov.au, which is yet another first-rate

The foundation of strong online presence typically begins with a solid national site.

> ### Best Practice
>
> ## Box 18. Australia's goldmine of information
>
> Similar to that of other leading e-government countries, Australia's online presence consists of numerous best practices portal sites. At the basic level, the Australian Government Online Directory (GOLD), http://www.gold.gov.au, is incredibly useful for finding government information. Meanwhile, in the higher echelons of e-government implementation, the AusTender site, https://www.tenders.gov.au, for government tenders is equally impressive in its own right as it enables efficiency at the larger transactional level. Similarly, though not related, it would be hard to discuss Australian transactional best practices without also referencing the Commonwealth Government Initiative on e-commerce best practices site, http://www.ecommerce. treasury.gov.au. Finally, a more recent addition to the online presence is the innovative country-wide pilot project, "Ask Now", http://www.asknow.gov.au, which is a virtual reference desk with live operators.

site. Progress is also seen at the Department of Health and Ageing site, http://www.health.gov.au, which has begun a pilot consultations programme. In fact, while formal consultation facilitation has previously been Australia's deficit, its inclusion on several ministry sites now indicates a strengthening of participatory initiatives.

Fiji maintains a true national site, http://www.fiji.gov.fj, which is clearly the strength of its overall online presence. Well-organized and up-to-date, the self-described "online portal" features a vast array of press releases, speeches and general information, such as the 88-page report entitled "Fiji Today," which summarizes policies, facts and statistical data. Another area of progress is in the Ministry of Labour, Industrial Relations & Productivity, http://www.labour.gov.fj, which since the previous survey has been afforded its own website in addition to the framed section under the national site. While Fiji made incremental improvements and strengthened its global ranking by three points, the country's overall online presence remains at a basic level compared to global standards. The country has yet to take initial steps in the more advanced stages. Some ministries do not have their own presence but remain framed within the national site while almost all ministries surveyed were outdated in terms of the content provided. Overall, therefore, improvement has clearly been made while the need for continued development remains.

Africa

As in 2004, a few countries deemed regional leaders in Africa generally improved or maintained their global positions. **Mauritius** (0.5317), at 52nd position in the global ranking, had the highest e-government readiness in the region, followed by **South Africa** (0.5075), and **Seychelles** (0.4884), which did well, advancing seven positions in the global ranking from 70th in 2004 to 63rd in 2005 (Table 3.13). Other notable advances were realized by **Egypt** (0.3793), which posted one of the greatest advances

Mauritius had the highest e-government readiness in the region, followed by South Africa and Seychelles.

Table 3.13.

E-government readiness rankings: Africa

		Index 2005	Global rank in: 2005	2004	Change
1	Mauritius	0.5317	52	51	−1
2	South Africa	0.5075	58	55	−3
3	Seychelles	0.4884	63	70	7
4	Botswana	0.3978	90	91	1
5	Egypt	0.3793	99	136	37
6	Swaziland	0.3593	108	101	−7
7	Namibia	0.3411	111	116	5
8	Lesotho	0.3373	114	117	3
9	Cape Verde	0.3346	116	107	−9
10	Zimbabwe	0.3316	120	130	10
11	Tunisia	0.3310	121	120	−1
12	Kenya	0.3298	122	126	4
13	Algeria	0.3242	123	118	−5
14	Uganda	0.3081	125	114	−11
15	United Republic of Tanzania	0.3020	127	131	4
16	Gabon	0.2928	131	124	−7
17	Ghana	0.2866	133	143	10
18	Congo	0.2855	134	125	−9
19	São Tomé and Principe	0.2837	135	133	−2
20	Malawi	0.2794	137	135	−2
21	Morocco	0.2774	138	138	0
22	Nigeria	0.2758	139	141	2
23	Madagascar	0.2641	141	148	7
24	Rwanda	0.2530	143	140	−3
25	Cameroon	0.2500	145	139	−6
26	Mozambique	0.2448	146	150	4
27	Djibouti	0.2381	149	153	4
28	Sudan	0.2370	150	147	−3
29	Benin	0.2309	151	149	−2
30	Togo	0.2274	152	146	−6
31	Senegal	0.2238	153	145	−8
32	Comoros	0.1974	155	157	2
33	Eritrea	0.1849	157	—	—
34	Angola	0.1840	158	151	−7
35	Côte d'Ivoire	0.1820	160	160	0
36	Gambia	0.1736	163	162	−1
37	Mauritania	0.1723	164	163	−1
38	Burundi	0.1643	166	166	0
39	Sierra Leone	0.1639	167	161	−6
40	Chad	0.1433	169	169	0
41	Guinea	0.1396	170	168	−2
42	Ethiopia	0.1360	171	170	−1
43	Burkina Faso	0.1329	172	158	−14
44	Mali	0.0925	173	172	−1
45	Niger	0.0661	174	173	−1
	Average	0.2642			

of all countries of the world in 2005. Among others, **Namibia** (0.3411) gained five points while **Zimbabwe** (0.3316) and **Ghana** (0.2866) posted gains of 10 points each.

Eighteen out of 43 countries of Africa either maintained their ranking or improved it; the rest lost out in the relative global rankings. Among others, Swaziland (–7), Cape Verde (–9), Uganda (–11), and Gabon (–7) did not maintain their rankings. In 2005, Eritrea came online with a Ministry of Information site, http://www.shabait.com, even though its offerings remained limited. The Democratic Republic of the Congo site disappeared as no government sites were available at the time of the survey. Further, the purported Zambian national site, http://www.statehouse.gov.zm, continued to be coming online "soon" for the third straight year.

Seychelles is gradually consolidating its e-government efforts. Since the last survey period in 2004, the country has made two additional sites available to inform and serve its citizens, easily found and accessible through the national government site. Whereas previously its online presence was in the form of framed sections on the national government web site, the Ministry of Health, http://www.moh.gov.sc, and the Ministry of Education, http://www.education.gov.sc, now maintain separate websites with their own URL. Another addition is the section on the Ministry of Economic Planning and Employment, which is now hosted on the main government website.

> Seychelles is gradually consolidating its e-government efforts.

Egypt has performed very well in 2005, advancing 37 points in its global ranking from 136th in 2004 to 99th in 2005. Egypt launched a new e-government central services portal, http://www.egypt.gov.eg, in 2004, which was further consolidated in 2005. This was a major first step towards coordinating and integrating government information and services. The website offers a wide array of e-services and can be considered a regional best practice in itself. However the country's e-readiness suffers because most Egyptian ministry sites still do not link to the portal, pointing to the need for them to be well integrated with, or promoted at, other Egyptian government sites. The e-government portal itself, however, provides a "Resources" section on its homepage with links to other Egyptian sites of interest, some of which link back to the portal, such as the Investment portal, http://www.investment.gov.eg, as well as the very useful Information portal, http://www.idsc.gov.eg/.

> Egypt launched a new e-government central services portal; a major first step towards coordinating and integrating government information and services.

Regional Best Practice

Box 19. Egypt's e-government central services portal

The e-government central services portal, http://www.egypt.gov.eg, offers a wide array of services. The E-Government programme's slogan that "The Government Now Delivers" is certainly true as the portal offers content in both Arabic and English with information related to more than 700 services, such as paying bills, fines and taxes, as well as reporting missing items or filing tourism complaints.

Among the countries of Africa, Namibia advanced five points in the global rankings in 2005. Namibia's current online presence continues to predominantly come in the form of its national government site, http://www.grnnet.gov.na.

Although the site features the most basic information and is being kept up-to-date, it made no progress and is in fact virtually identical to last year's. Positive signs are instead noted at the ministry level where the country has advanced from having only brief framed sections under one site to now enabling most ministries to have their own stand-alone URLs. While these sites are mostly in their infancy, with parts under construction or not yet updated, it is an important first step. Most notable is the Ministry of Finance site, http://www.mof.gov.na, which provides access to downloadable current budget documents, information on the ministry departments and statements regarding its Millennium Challenges.

Zimbabwe advanced 10 points on its global ranking by widening the scope of its sectoral websites. While Zimbabwe's national site, http://www.gta.gov.zw, made some incremental improvements, the country enhanced its e-readiness in several areas, notably by providing several stand-alone ministry sites, previously unavailable. The new Ministry of Education site, http://www.moesc.gov.zw, for example, features fairly substantial sections on programmes, services and publications, as well as news and other basic general information. While several areas of the site were still under construction at the time of review, its mere presence is a definitive first step towards offering Zimbabweans an online source for official information about the educational system.

> Zimbabwe's national site made some incremental improvements and the country enhanced its e-readiness in several areas.

The Madagascar national site, http://www.madagascar.gov.mg, was re-designed last year and large parts remain unavailable. In fact, there is a clear announcement at the top of the homepage that exclaims, "site under construction." Real progress, which allowed it to add seven points in the global ranking, from 148th in 2004 to 141st in 2005, is instead found at the ministerial level, where two sites that were inaccessible last year came online this year. Although both contributed to the overall online expansion, the Ministry of Finance and Budget site, http://www.mefb.gov.mg, offered less than that of the Ministry of Health, http://www.sante.gov.mg. At the enhanced presence level, the health site offers an extensive amount of information, archived as well as up-to-date. It also provides a detailed and complete directory of health-related resources and a discussion forum.

Despite progress in e-government readiness, access remains a serious issue in Africa with wide disparities between Africa and other regions of the world. Of the 12 countries not online, half are in Africa. The region as a whole had a mean e-government readiness at two thirds of the world average and 30 per cent of Northern America. Many countries, already among the least e-ready, again trailed behind the rest of the world. The majority of the countries of the region were among the bottom 40 per cent in terms of e-government readiness services with rankings below the world median. Information and services provided by these countries remained limited, for the most part at the emerging or enhanced stages. This lack of access for the millions of inhabitants of the region contributes to their exclusion from the benefits of the information society.

> The region, as a whole, had a mean e-government readiness at two thirds of the world average and 30 per cent of Northern America. Many countries, already among the least e-ready, again trailed behind the rest of the world.

In summary, patterns of e-government readiness across the world in 2005 reveal the following:

Most developing country governments around the world are promoting awareness about policies and programmes, approaches and strategies to the citizen on their websites. They are making an effort to engage multiple stakeholders in participatory decision-making—in some cases through the use of innovative means aimed at greater access and inclusion.

A strong commitment to promoting access and use of ICTs is a key ingredient of successful e-government development. Innovative approaches to e-government development depend upon a vision, long-term planning and dedication.

Approaches to e-government programme offerings differ from country to country. The "how" of what countries choose to display on their websites is a function of the "what" they want to focus on and the "why" they want to focus on the issue selected. Whereas some countries closely follow the model of an integrated and multi-faceted approach to a portal others may spin off separate portals from one national site.

Effective organization and integration of a large amount of information and a number of services in an easy to use and convenient manner is critical to the success of portals. Innovative, collaborative and integrated portals mindful of interoperability issues supported e-government efforts of many countries. It was notable that several noteworthy portals were also multi-faceted.

An important part of e-government service delivery is site maintenance and availability. Consistency in maintaining sites came across as an important issue. Sites with irregular availability will be of limited value and could even discourage usage. Consistency across all sites in terms of design and navigational standardization led to high e-government readiness.

E-government appears to be strongly related to income per capita. Resource availability appears to be a critical factor inhibiting e-government initiatives in many countries. Part of the reason for the high e-readiness in most of the developed economies is past investment in, and development of, infrastructure.

A serious access-divide exists across the world between the developed and the developing countries. Of particular concern are the countries belonging to the regions of South and Central Asia and Africa, which together house one third of humanity. The 32 least e-ready countries show little relative progress compared to the developed countries, which are already far advanced in their provision of services, outreach and access to citizens. Access and use of ICTs for development is at a rudimentary level in these countries, where millions of people are outside the inclusive net of the ICTs. Lack of telecommunication infrastructure and education are the key factors limiting both access and inclusion of societies in the developing world.

A few of the best practice approaches seen in 2005 are presented below:

Some best practice approaches in the world

Country	Best Practice model for:	Location
United States' FirstGov	A true universal portal with excellent integration of information	http://www.firstgov.gov
U.S. Department of Education	Government–Educationists consultation	http://www.ed.gov

Approaches to e-government programme offerings differ from country to country.

Effective organization and integration of a large amount of information and services in an easy to use and convenient manner is critical to the success of portals.

Resource availability appears to be a critical factor inhibiting e-government initiatives in many countries.

A serious access-divide exists across the world between the developed and the developing countries.

Some best practice approaches in the world (*continued*)

Country	Best Practice model for:	Location
Canada	Consistency of design, effective integration of information & services	http://canada.gc.ca
Canada	One window for consultation	http://www.consulting canadians.gc.ca
Denmark	Dialogue between government and citizen	http://www.danmarks debatten.dk
United Kingdom	Integrated portal	http://www.direct.gov.uk
United Kingdom	Focus on e-consultation	http://www.consultations. gov.uk
Singapore	E-consultation	http://www.ecitizen.gov.sg
Japan	Japan m-government	http://www.e-gov.go.jp
Philippines	Offers an integrated all-services national site	http://www.gov.ph
Chile's *InfoEmpleo*	Employment portal	www.infoempleo.cl
Mexico	Promoting access and inclusion	Tramitanet www.tramitanet.gob.mx eMexico www.e-mexico.gob.mx Foros www.foros.gob.mx
United Arab Emirates	Gateway to e-services	http://www.government.ae
United Arab Emirates	E-Dirham portal	http://www.e-dirham.gov.ae
Qatar	E-government portal	http://www.e.gov.qa/ eGovPortal/aboutus.jsp
Egypt	E-government central services portal	http://www.egypt.gov.eg
Australia	Government Online Directory (GOLD)	http://www.gold.gov.au
Australia AusTender site	E-tenders	https://www.tenders.gov.au
New Zealand	Promoting participation	http://www.govt.nz/ttkw http://www.govt.nz/ participate/

Notes

1   In regional presentations, the Survey follows the "Composition of macro geographical (continental) regions, geographical sub-regions, and selected economic and other groupings" of the UNDESA Statistics Division, http://unstats.un.org/unsd/methods/m49/,49regin.htm.

2   See recent article in *Government Technology,* http://www.govtech.net/news/news.php?id=96736.

3   For the overview, see http://www.cbsc.org/servlet/ContentServer?pagename=CBSC_FE/ display&c=GuideFactSheet&cid=1081945277357&lang=en.

4   See http://www.cabinetoffice.gov.uk/regulation/consultation/index.asp.

5   For more about the OGC and Zanzibar, see http://europa.eu.int/idabc/en/document/4986/194.

6   For more information about the entire project, see http://www.pps.go.kr/neweng/html/geps/ i_geps_010.html.

7   For the e-filing success story, see, for example, an article in *Public Sector Technology & Management,* http://www.pstm.net/article/index.php?articleid=662.

8   http://www.itu.int/osg/spu/wsis-themes/ict_stories/Themes/e-Government.html.

9   The URL indicated last year, http://www.cpa.gov, was a mirror/re-direct with the URL mentioned here. Also, last year's site indicated it would expire on 30 June 2005; however, the deadline has apparently been extended for another year.

10   For a recent summary of previous events see http://www.foreignpolicy.com/story/cms.php?story_id=3207.

11   See http://www.icann.org/minutes/minutes-28jul05.htm. Further, the root record is available at http://www.iana.org/root-whois/iq.htm.

12   http://www.iicd.org/articles/IICDnews.import2144.

13   http://www.ab.gov.ag/gov_v2/government/parliament/laws/itc_draft_policy.pdf.

14   International Telecommunication Union, http://www.itu.int/wsis/stocktaking/.

15   Ibid.

Chapter IV
Web measure assessment

While the e-government readiness of a country in this Report is assessed by the effort a government makes for the provision of e-services, the extent of connectivity it has provided and the human skills available to access these services, it is important to take a closer look at the online public sector offerings in and of themselves. The web measure index assesses the websites of the governments to determine if they are employing e-government to the fullest. The web measure rankings are different from the e-government readiness rankings given in the previous chapter, which are based on a composite index comprising web measure, infrastructure and human capital assessment.

Table 4.1 shows the top 25 countries ranked by the web measure index with the United States, which scored the highest, as the comparator. Three things are

The web measure index assesses the websites of the governments to determine if they are employing e-government to the fullest.

Table 4.1.
Web measure index 2005: top 25 countries

	Country	Index	Rank
1	United States	1.0000	1
2	United Kingdom	0.9962	2
3	Singapore	0.9962	2
4	Republic of Korea	0.9769	3
5	Denmark	0.9731	4
6	Chile	0.9115	5
7	Australia	0.9038	6
8	Canada	0.8923	7
9	Sweden	0.8654	8
10	Germany	0.8423	9
11	Finland	0.8269	10
12	Mexico	0.8192	11
13	Japan	0.8154	12
14	New Zealand	0.8038	13
15	Norway	0.7962	14
16	Malta	0.7923	15
17	Brazil	0.7500	16
18	Austria	0.7423	17
19	Philippines	0.7423	17
20	Netherlands	0.7346	18
21	Israel	0.7308	19
22	Belgium	0.7115	20
23	Ireland	0.7115	20
24	Hungary	0.7038	21
25	Estonia	0.6962	22

Except for two, all
of the top 25 countries
are the same, which
made it to the
list of the top 25
e-government
readiness index.

notable. First, except for two of them, all of the top 25 countries are the same ones that made it onto the list of the top 25 countries on the E-government readiness index presented in Chapter III. Most of these are industrialized countries with high-income economies. The United States is the global leader, followed by the United Kingdom (0.9962) and Singapore (0.9962). It is notable that, due to consistent efforts at new and innovative e-government initiatives, Singapore climbed to the 2nd position, with the United Kingdom, in 2005. The performance of Japan (0.8154) was notable as well, inasmuch as it advanced its ranking from 25th in 2004 to 12th in 2005.

Second, the top 25 countries with the most e-services are also the same countries that made it to the top in 2004. In 2005, consistent progress among this group has brought them closer together, implying that the majority now provide most of the services and features in health, education, welfare, employment and finance assessed in this survey. For example, the United Kingdom and Singapore, which together occupy the 2nd position, provide almost the same services as the United States, which is the global leader. A measure of the small spread among these leaders is that Estonia, which is the 25th country in the group, provides 70 per cent of what the United States does as measured here.

Third, although the majority of countries in the top 25 group are from industrialized economies they include six developing countries as well. Chile (0.9115), Mexico (0.81912), Malta (0.7923), Brazil (0.7500), Philippines (0.7423) and Estonia (0.6962) stand out as examples of good e-government for development in 2005. Planning and investment in e-government initiatives have placed these countries in the vanguard. Of these, Chile is the only country from Latin America that is among the top 25 global leaders in e-government. Mexico (0.8192) in recent years invested a lot in online e-services. As a result it climbed to 11th in web assessment compared to its ranking (31st) in e-government readiness. Mexico's web measure score in 2005 was around 82 per cent of that of the United States, the top scoring country in the five sectors assessed here. However it did not make it to the top e-ready countries because access to infrastructure remains a constraining factor. The same was the case for the Philippines and Brazil, both of which do not figure in the top 25 e-ready countries but are included in the top 25 countries when assessed by websites. Brazil was 33rd and the Philippines 41st in the e-government readiness rankings presented in Chapter III. Both of these countries have put a lot of effort into improving e-government services in the past few years. Brazil provides around three-fourths of all the services that the United States does on its websites. The Philippines, ranked the same as Austria, also provides around 75 per cent of the services of the U.S. Notwithstanding the expansion in e-government programmes, access to all in these developing countries remains limited, with greater efforts needed to expand the outreach of basic telecommunication infrastructure to all people. A few of the greatest advances are given in Figure 4.1.

Although the majority
of countries in
the top 25 group are
from industrialized
economies they
include six developing
countries as well.

Table 4.2 represents the next 25 countries and their web measure index. Among these, the scores of Thailand (0.6654, 23rd), Argentina (0.6577, 24th) and Romania (0.6423, 25th) are close to those of the top 25 group. The regional leader in Africa—Mauritius (0.6288, 26th)—provided around 63 per cent of the services of the U.S. It is notable that efforts toward citizen-oriented services by these developing

Figure 4.1.
Greatest advances in top 25 countries

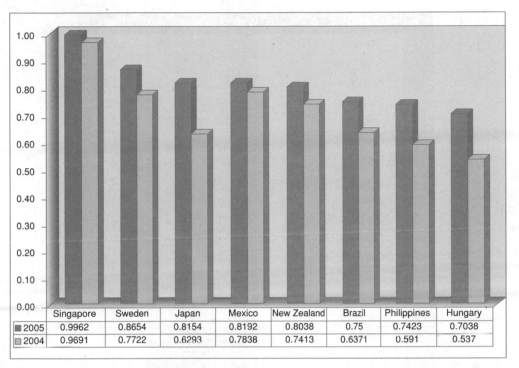

	Singapore	Sweden	Japan	Mexico	New Zealand	Brazil	Philippines	Hungary
■ 2005	0.9962	0.8654	0.8154	0.8192	0.8038	0.75	0.7423	0.7038
■ 2004	0.9691	0.7722	0.6293	0.7838	0.7413	0.6371	0.591	0.537

countries have been at a level higher than those in some of the high-income countries such as France (0.6115, 29th), Iceland (0.6077, 30th) and Switzerland (0.6038, 31st). A few of the high performing developing countries from among this group are presented in Figure 4.2.

Figure 4.2.
Greatest advances in e-government services delivery, selected countries

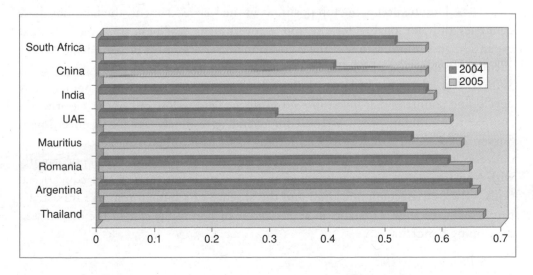

Table 4.2.

Web assessment: next 25 countries 2005

	Country	Web measure index	Rank
1	Thailand	0.6654	23
2	Argentina	0.6577	24
3	Romania	0.6423	25
4	Mauritius	0.6288	26
5	Italy	0.6269	27
6	Colombia	0.6154	28
7	France	0.6115	29
8	United Arab Emirates	0.6115	29
9	Iceland	0.6077	30
10	Switzerland	0.6038	31
11	Slovenia	0.5923	32
12	Czech Republic	0.5885	33
13	India	0.5827	33
14	Ukraine	0.5808	34
15	Malaysia	0.5769	34
16	Venezuela	0.5769	34
17	China	0.5692	35
18	South Africa	0.5692	35
19	Peru	0.5577	36
20	Slovakia	0.5385	37
21	Lithuania	0.5231	38
22	Turkey	0.5231	38
23	Bulgaria	0.5192	39
24	Greece	0.5115	40
25	Poland	0.5115	40

Expansion and consolidation of the e-government services must be complemented by adequate human and technological infrastructure expansion to provide access to all.

Despite occupying top positions in the web assessment, the fact that these countries did not qualify for the top e-government readiness slots suggests that expansion and consolidation of the e-government services must be complemented by adequate human and technological infrastructure expansion to provide access to all. With a weak platform of human skills and inadequate infrastructure support, many developing countries that invest in e-government tend to lose out in the set of world comparative rankings when assessed for overall e-readiness. As the E-government Survey 2004 stated "whereas it is important to focus on improving access to service delivery, e-government programmes must be placed in—and run concurrently with—an integrated framework aimed at improving infrastructure and educational skills." Lack of telecommunication and the absence of a human resource infrastructure remain the limiting factors in access and inclusion in the case of the majority of developing countries.

Government provision of e-services

As e-government services have continued to expand around the world, website assessment in 2005 indicates that the majority of the UN Member States have embraced electronic service delivery. Of the 191 Member States, 179 were online in some form or another in 2005. There were three new additions to online government this year, from Tuvalu, Eritrea and Tajikistan. On the other hand, two countries (i.e. Democratic Republic of the Congo and Turkmenistan) joined the 12 countries which did not provide any services online this year.

The website assessment in 2005 indicates that of the 191 Member States, 179 were online in some form or another.

> ## No online presence
>
> Central African Republic, Democratic People's Republic of Korea, Democratic Republic of the Congo, Equatorial Guinea, Guinea-Bissau, Haiti, Kiribati, Liberia, Libyan Arab Jamahiriya, Somalia, Turkmenistan and Zambia

Not only did more countries come online, they further expanded and consolidated their e-services. Table 4.3 below indicates steady progress in the provision of key (Stage II-Enhanced presence) features in the last three years. E-government policy statements on the national portals gave way to stand-alone websites as an increasing number of countries opted to establish separate e-government portals, which provide a one-stop-shop window for easy access to all public services. Around half of the countries had some form of integrated portals or one-stop-shop windows compared to 35 per cent last year. Thirty-nine per cent of the countries put out their e-government policy statements on their websites compared to 42 per cent last year.

Not only did more countries come online, they expanded and consolidated their e-services further.

Around half of the countries had some form of integrated portals or one-stop-shop windows compared to 35 per cent last year.

Figure 4.3.
Governments online 2005

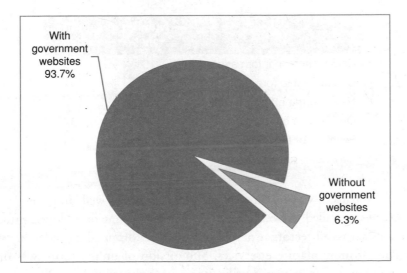

With government websites 93.7%

Without government websites 6.3%

Table 4.3.

Stage II characteristics of country websites

	Per cent of countries		
	2005	2004	2003
One-stop-shops (single windows)	47	35	26
Sources of archived information (laws, policy documents, etc.)	95	92	90
E-government portal	31	29	—
E-government policy statement	39	42	—
Databases (e.g., web access to downloadable statistics)	88	85	79
Wireless/WAP/PDA access	4.5	—	—

More and more countries' national sites are also their all-services portals (i.e., the National Site itself contains forms, transactions or participation features). In some cases governments have a separate portal for citizen services as a one-stop window that is integrated within, and thus a part of, a "national" portal site. At other times it is a stand-alone website, not integrated or even linked to a national site. Generally, specific "e-government" portals focused only on the country's e-government policies, plans and regulations rather than actually providing any e-services. Some large economies have fashioned "stand alone" portals by theme. For example the United States' site, www.forms.gov, contains all the federal government forms for all departments. The Department of the Treasury then provides a link to this portal, integrating the services offered there.

First level participatory features such as contact information or e-mail were increasingly the norm, with the overwhelming majority of countries providing some means for the public to contact the government officials. Furthermore, in the last few years almost all countries have started providing laws and policy documents.

Table 4.4.

Selected interactive and transactional services

	Number of countries	
	2005	2004
Contact person information	164	159
Downloadable forms	125	104
E-mail to the official	168	167
Online payment by credit card	44	32
Payment of fees online	46	38
Play video/audio capability	106	83

The pattern was repeated in sectoral services as well. In general, a majority of countries provided the basic services such as current or archived information and databases across all sectors reviewed but the level dropped considerably with the requirements of more mature e-services. Submission of online forms was one category showing lower than expected utilization with only around 23 per cent in health

First level participatory features such as contact information or e-mail were increasingly the norm, with the overwhelming majority of countries providing some means to the public to contact the government officials.

and 28 per cent in education. In the labour sector, around two thirds of all countries offered the facility of downloading forms for employment.

Figure 4.4.
Some enhanced presence services

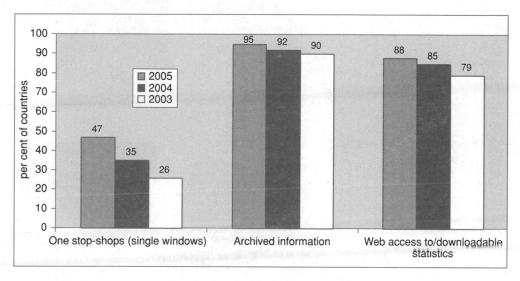

Figure 4.5.
Countries having e-government portal and policy statement

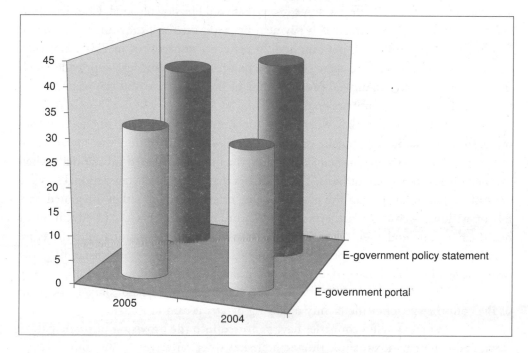

In a bid to make the government more effective and reduce costs, governments are choosing to provide an increasing number of public services online. While this was the domain of the developed countries a few years ago, more and more developing countries are putting basic interactive services in Stage III online. As seen in Table 4.4,

In a bid to make the government more effective and reduce costs, governments are choosing to provide an increasing number of public services online.

Figure 4.6.

Number of countries providing selected interactive and transactional services 2005

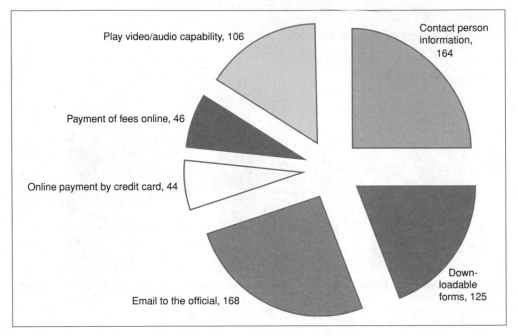

More and more developing countries are putting basic interactive services in Stage III online.

in the last year alone there was a 20 per cent increase in downloadable forms online with 125 countries out of 179 offering some forms that could be downloaded. Countries providing more mature services, such as payment by credit card and the online payment of fees, increased by around 38 per cent and 20 per cent, respectively, in 2005. Notwithstanding this progress, in the aggregate only a quarter of all countries yet provided such transactional services. Figure 4.6 presents some of the interactive and transactional feature availability in the countries graphically.

It was notable that whereas 44 (or around 25 per cent) of the countries offered online payment by credit card/debit card when this option was measured as being available on any one of their six websites, the number declined substantially when assessed on a sector by sector basis. This indicates that, in general, transactional services are still in their infancy, with the majority being offered through either integrated portals or national websites. Furthermore, the nature of citizen services in education or health may not lend themselves easily to transactional interactions and therefore may not be a priority area for the governments. These factors notwithstanding, the overall level of transactional services on sectoral sites is relatively low. For example, even in the case of the finance websites, where fees and taxes can be paid, only 17 per cent of the countries yet offer the facility of paying by credit card (Table 4.5).

Around 18 countries provided feedback on policies.

Whereas many countries have ventured into the provision of participatory services on their national sites, the sectoral sites offer far fewer of the more mature Stage V services, with only around 10–15 per cent of the countries allowing for online polling and half that number providing a facility for actual online consultation. A mere 10 per cent, or around 18 countries, provided feedback on policies. Figures 4.7 and 4.8 present key features of citizen participation graphically.

Table 4.5.
Provision of services by sector

	Per cent of countries				
	Health	Education	Welfare	Labour	Finance
Stage II					
Archived information (laws, policy documents, etc.)	83	90	82	83	93
Current information (e.g., reports, newsletters, press)	76	80	76	77	85
Databases (web access to/ downloadable statistics)	71	72	74	71	90
One-stop-shops/"single window" available?	29	35	40	41	28
Stage III					
Download/print forms	48	58	59	63	59
Submission of online forms	23	28	31	39	29
Audio, video capability	15	20	16	19	16
Electronic signature	7	8	14	14	16
Stage IV					
Any online transaction services	15	15	21	22	26
Credit, debit, or other card payment	8	6	11	10	17
Stage V					
Online poll/survey	10	15	14	16	12
Formal online consultation facility	7	7	7	7	6
Allow feedback on policies	10	10	10	10	8
Encourage citizen participation	9	16	14	17	13

Figure 4.7.
Online poll and consultation services

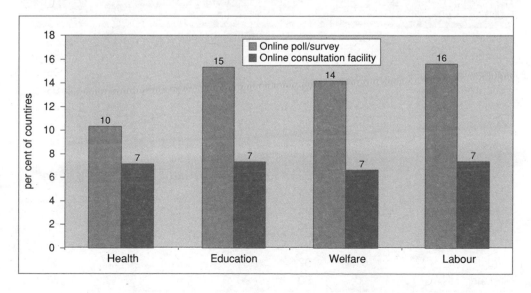

Figure 4.8.

Government encouraging feedback on policies and citizen participation

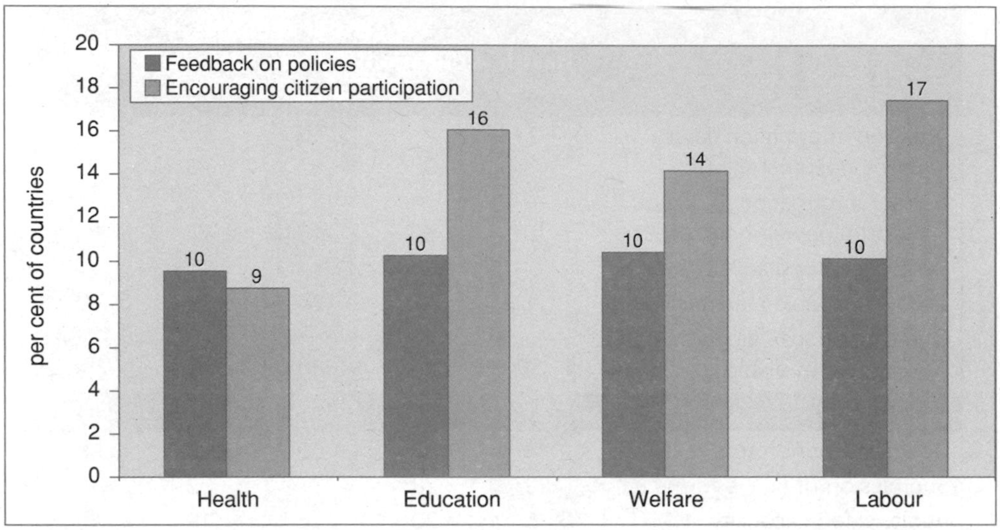

Stages of service delivery by country

Table 4.6 provides a breakdown of the number of top, mid-range and lowest scoring countries in 2005 by the five stages. There is gradual progress in utilization of e-government for the provision of services to the citizen. Utilization is defined as services provided as a percentage of the maximum services in a category. In 2005,

Table 4.6.

Scores by stages, selected countries 2005

	Per cent utilization					
	I	II	III	IV	V	
	Emerging	Enhanced	Interactive	Transactional	Networked	TOTAL
			67–100% utilization			
United States	100	99	100	100	76	95
United Kingdom	100	99	99	100	76	95
Singapore	100	94	99	100	83	95
Republic of Korea	100	98	96	90	80	93
Chile	100	93	93	85	65	86
Australia	100	95	93	80	61	86
Canada	100	99	90	61	69	85
Germany	100	95	100	54	41	80
Mexico	100	93	86	46	61	78
Japan	100	94	92	37	56	77
New Zealand	100	92	86	46	56	76
Brazil	100	90	77	63	33	71
Philippines	100	91	82	44	35	70
Israel	100	92	81	54	22	69
Ireland	100	90	80	61	13	68

Table 4.6. (*continued*)

	I	II	III	IV	V	
	Per cent utilization					
	Emerging	Enhanced	Interactive	Transactional	Networked	TOTAL
34–66% utilization						
Estonia	100	87	85	27	28	66
Thailand	88	89	76	20	31	63
Argentina	100	83	74	39	24	62
Romania	100	82	79	20	26	61
Mauritius	100	80	83	27	9	60
Italy	100	94	64	15	24	59
Colombia	100	84	70	15	26	58
United Arab Emirates	75	62	79	59	17	58
Czech Republic	100	85	65	5	26	56
India	100	77	72	17	17	55
Ukraine	100	87	55	0	39	55
South Africa	100	79	62	17	22	54
China	100	75	71	5	24	54
Greece	88	86	44	10	19	49
Jamaica	100	56	64	17	17	46
Russian Federation	100	76	39	0	20	43
Kazakhstan	100	74	36	0	28	43
Egypt	88	53	60	22	7	42
Jordan	88	62	58	0	6	41
Pakistan	100	62	51	0	11	41
Spain	100	66	42	0	4	37
Bhutan	100	51	49	0	13	36
Botswana	75	49	52	0	6	35
Kyrgyzstan	100	56	36	0	15	35
1–33% utilization						
Lebanon	100	46	43	0	9	32
Iran (Islamic Republic of)	0	60	23	0	11	28
Indonesia	100	49	15	0	24	28
Mozambique	75	34	38	0	9	26
Costa Rica	75	45	24	0	2	24
Kuwait	0	40	26	0	15	24
Nigeria	100	24	26	5	9	21
Madagascar	88	26	15	0	9	18
Cuba	50	25	11	0	7	14
Tonga	63	22	10	0	2	12
Yemen	75	17	5	0	0	9
Mali	13	9	8	0	0	6
Tajikistan	0	11	7	0	0	6
Togo	25	7	0	0	0	3
Tuvalu	0	1	7	0	0	3
Ethiopia	0	2	2	0	0	1
São Tomé and Principe	0	0	2	0	2	1
Niger	0	3	0	0	0	1
Chad	13	0	1	0	0	1

Note: For the complete set of countries by groups see Annex 1, Table 9.

seven more countries advanced their services to join the first group, which had 67–100 per cent utilization; five countries joined the 2nd group (34–66 per cent); while 10 more graduated from the 0–33 per cent to the next higher group.

Despite this advancement, progress appears to have been confined to the top echelons. Analysis of scores by stage reveals that the majority of countries are not using the full potential of e-government online. As Figure 4.9 indicates, of the countries of the world that were online, only 24 provided 67–100 per cent of "what they could have provided" as measured by this survey; a little more than 50 provided 34–66 per cent, while the majority (104 countries) provided a mere 1–33 per cent of the services. Details on all Member States appear in Annex 1, Table 9.

As in the past, the experience of individual countries in progressing from one stage to the next was not strictly additive, nor was there much evidence of a linear progression in e-government stages. Countries provided online features in line with the political, economic and social systems they had in place. A case in point is Ukraine, where no transactional services are provided but networked and participatory services are available on almost all sites.

The top countries provide mature e-services across all five stages with very little spread among them in Stages I to III but tapering off thereafter. The United States and the United Kingdom provide 100 per cent of the services across Stages I to IV as measured here, and Singapore follows very closely. With the advancement in e-government service delivery in the last three years, the gap between the top 16 was reduced further, especially in Stages I–III.

Whereas the majority of developing countries remained within the first three stages, a few were featured in the next two stages as well. Figure 4.9 presents the differences among a few developing countries across the five stages.

> Analysis of scores by stage reveals that the majority of countries are not using the full potential of e-government online.
>
> The experience of individual countries in progressing from one stage to the next was not strictly additive, nor was there much evidence of a linear progression in e-government stages. Countries provided online features in line with the political, economic and social systems they had in place.

Figure 4.9.

E-government service delivery

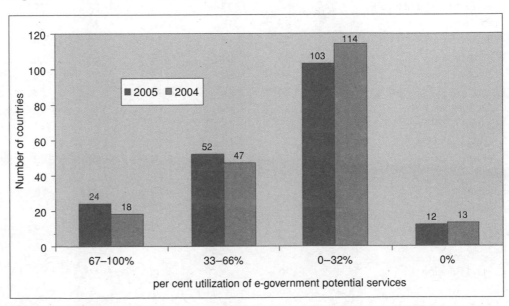

per cent utilization of e-government potential services

Table 4.7.

Progress in e-government, selected countries

	Per cent of utilization in all five stages		
	2003	2004	2005
Malta	49	70	75
Hungary	27	51	67
Slovenia	38	49	56
Czech Republic	30	52	56
Malaysia	42	46	55
Ukraine	30	53	55
Saudi Arabia	16	29	36
Lebanon	22	23	32
Qatar	12	8	31
Iran (Islamic Republic of)	13	15	28

Tracking the progress of developing countries over the last three years indicates that many of the developing countries have consistently consolidated their e-government offerings. Table 4.7 presents total services offered as a per cent of utilization from 2003 to 2005. As can be seen, the e-government services in Malta advanced from 49 per cent in 2003 to 75 per cent in 2005; in Hungary they tripled, from 27 per cent in 2003 to 67 per cent in 2005. Among others, there was notable progress in the cases of Ukraine, Slovenia and the Czech Republic, where the percentage of service utilization went from being around one third in 2003 to more than half in 2005. See Figure 4.10.

What is provided on websites is a function of the willingness and the capacity of the countries to engage in e-government and as such reflects the priorities of the

Tracking the progress of developing countries over the last three years indicates that many of the developing countries have consistently consolidated their e-government offerings.

Figure 4.10.

Stages of e-government, 2005, selected countries

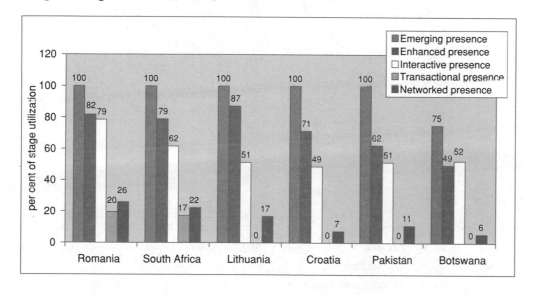

government. As in 2004, a few countries did not score on Stage I but in subsequent stages. This indicates no integrated portal, no links to ministries or other national sites and limited static information on the national page. Examples of these countries are Kuwait and Tajikistan, among others. Although Kuwait scores nothing in Stage I, it is worth noting that it has a 40 per cent and 26 per cent utilization on enhanced and interactive stages, which is higher than the scores of many other countries. Some others, such as Egypt, Jamaica and Greece, have taken a more step-by-step approach so that their e-government development programmes resemble a linear pattern.

Another measure of the progress in 2005 is that the number of countries offering some of the transactional features of Stage IV involving payment rose from 38 in 2004 to 46 in 2005. Table 4.8 presents the countries offering online payment in descending order of the number of transactions available. Among the top five countries, the United States, the United Kingdom and Singapore provided 100 per cent of these services as measured in this Survey, with the Republic of Korea close behind.

Figure 4.11 presents the progress in various transactional services for the top 10 countries. As can be seen, the most spectacular jump was in the performance

Table 4.8.

Countries offering facility of online payment for any public service

1	United States	24	New Zealand
2	United Kingdom	25	Norway
3	Singapore	26	Philippines
4	Chile	27	United Arab Emirates
5	Denmark	28	Barbados
6	Republic of Korea	29	Egypt
7	Australia	30	France
8	Brazil	31	Guatemala
9	Canada	32	Hungary
10	Finland	33	India
11	Israel	34	Italy
12	Sweden	35	Jamaica
13	Argentina	36	Japan
14	Austria	37	Malaysia
15	Belgium	38	Nigeria
16	Estonia	39	Panama
17	Germany	40	Portugal
18	Greece	41	Qatar
19	Ireland	42	Romania
20	Malta	43	Slovenia
21	Mauritius	44	South Africa
22	Mexico	45	Thailand
23	Netherlands	46	Uruguay
	26% of total countries		

Figure 4.11.
Transactional services: top 10 countries

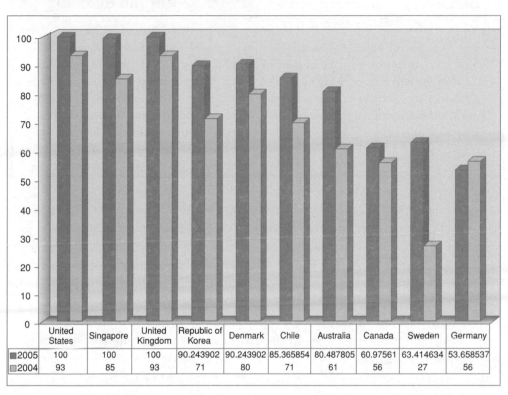

	United States	Singapore	United Kingdom	Republic of Korea	Denmark	Chile	Australia	Canada	Sweden	Germany
■2005	100	100	100	90.243902	90.243902	85.365854	80.487805	60.97561	63.414634	53.658537
■2004	93	85	93	71	80	71	61	56	27	56

of Sweden, where transactional services on the government websites jumped from a mere 27 to 63 per cent in one year. No less spectacular was the performance of Australia, Singapore and the Republic of Korea.

      Lack of development of domestic financial systems is an impediment to online transactional services in many developing countries. Moreover, online transactions require a platform of adequate regulatory and legal systems to allow for electronic payments by credit card, debit card or some other e-payment system. In many countries such systems are yet to be put fully in place. Most developing countries provided substantial services in Stages I to III, and then a few in Stage V but almost nothing in the transactional Stage IV, due to lack of development of financial markets. For example, Jordan, Kyrgyzstan and Pakistan all had substantial Stage I–III services but zero transactional services in 2005. E-transactions and e-payments also need a secure environment and are dependant on sophisticated levels of technology that for many countries may be costly and difficult to implement and operate. In all, only 56 countries, or 31 per cent of the total number surveyed, offered any online transactional services.

      Political will or "willingness of the countries" is an important factor in terms of the type of services provided online. Some countries invest more in employing e-government to engage the citizen in a dialogue. In such cases their websites are endowed with features and services aimed at encouraging partnership with the citizen for public policy making. Singapore is notable inasmuch as it has become the global leader in the provision of Stage V participatory-networked services, with the Republic of Korea close behind.

Lack of development of domestic financial systems is an impediment to online transactional services in many developing countries.

Political will or "willingness of the countries" is an important factor in terms of the type of services provided online.

> **Box 20. E-consultation further fortified in the Republic of Korea**
>
> The Republic of Korea encourages participation and provides an advanced feedback mechanism on policies and activities on all its surveyed sites. The Government of the Republic of Korea national site, http://www.egov.go.kr, further fortified e-participatory services to offer a formal e-consultation facility where users can submit their views and opinions on specific government policies and proposals. As the site itself proclaims, "Through the online exchange of information between the government and the people, public opinion can be reflected in government policy."

Participatory services scores indicate that most countries are still behind their potential in the provision of avenues for feedback and participation to the citizen, even among the more mature e-ready countries.

However, in general, participatory services scores indicate that most countries are still behind their potential in the provision of avenues for feedback and participation to the citizen, even among the more mature e-ready countries. For example, whereas the United States, the United Kingdom and the Republic of Korea follow Singapore closely and are almost at full potential as measured by this survey, Australia provides 61 per cent, New Zealand, 56 per cent, and Germany, 41 per cent of Stage V services. In the last three years a few developing countries also put in a relatively greater effort into developing networked-participatory features compared to their level of overall service delivery. For example, Indonesia falls within the 0–33 per cent utilization bracket, providing around 50 per cent of enhanced (Stage II) and 15 per cent of interactive (Stage III) services and zero transactional services. However, it does provide 24 per cent of the participatory and networked services in Stage V, which is higher than many other countries with more mature e-services. Similarly, Ukraine's overall utilization is at half its potential and it does not provide any interactive services

> **Box 21. Ukraine bypasses transactional stage to networked presence**
>
> While e-government implementation is often incremental, piece-by-piece and stage-by-stage, Ukraine's online presence proves that this need not be the case as the country has completely bypassed the transactional stage in favour of a networked presence, which is the foundation for e-participation. The Ukrainian national site, http://www.kmu.gov.ua, for example, provides no clear indication of any transaction features. However, it encourages participation and provides an advanced type of open-ended discussion forum whereby the government can (and does) provide answers and other users can make remarks on posted comments.
>
> Ukraine's success in networked presence stems from the fact that almost all of its national government sites integrate discussion forums and polls to gauge public opinion as well as an e-mail sign-up option for users to stay up-to-date on government information, all of which enables its citizens to actively discuss issues and concerns. Most notable in this year's survey was the Ministry of Social Welfare and Labour site, http://www.mlsp.gov.ua, which improved its networked presence with the addition of both an online poll and an open-ended discussion forum.

on its national government websites. However its participatory services to citizens in Stage V are higher than those of Brazil, the Philippines, Israel, Ireland and Estonia, all countries at a higher e-government readiness than Ukraine.

The least e-ready countries

Table 4.9 presents the pattern of e-services in the bottom 32 countries in 2005 with less than 10 per cent average utilization across all five stages. Whereas in the last years

Table 4.9.

Countries with the lowest aggregate utilization 2005: range 0–10%

| | Per cent utilization | | | | | |
	Emerging presence	Enhanced presence	Interactive presence	Transactional presence	Networked presence	TOTAL
Micronesia	75	11	14	0	0	10
Solomon Islands	0	13	18	0	0	9
Cameroon	38	13	11	0	4	9
Gambia	38	13	11	0	4	9
Sierra Leone	75	11	7	0	6	9
Yemen	75	17	5	0	0	9
Gabon	0	17	11	0	0	9
Marshall Islands	0	10	17	0	0	9
Grenada	38	16	7	0	0	8
Lao P.D.R.	0	8	16	0	0	7
Bangladesh	88	11	1	0	2	7
Mauritania	63	10	2	0	4	7
Dominica	0	10	8	0	4	7
Syrian Arab Republic	0	13	4	0	6	6
Mali	13	9	8	0	0	6
Tajikistan	0	11	7	0	0	6
Eritrea	0	8	7	0	4	5
Nauru	0	9	8	0	0	5
Comoros	25	8	6	0	0	5
Côte d'Ivoire	50	9	1	0	2	5
Iraq	25	10	2	0	2	5
Republic of Moldova	0	10	6	0	0	5
Suriname	0	8	7	0	0	5
Vanuatu	25	7	6	0	0	5
Burundi	13	7	4	0	0	4
Guinea	25	2	7	0	0	4
Togo	25	7	0	0	0	3
Tuvalu	0	1	7	0	0	3
Ethiopia	0	2	2	0	0	1
São Tomé and Principe	0	0	2	0	2	1
Niger	0	3	0	0	0	1
Chad	13	0	1	0	0	1

there were around 40 countries in this group, eight advanced to higher utilization groups. Among the remaining countries, most had an e-presence reflecting a static national website with few links to ministerial sites and some downloadable features. The majority had a limited range of Stage III features, essentially phone, fax and e-mail contact information. None of these 32 countries provided any transactional services and only very few had the basic one or two features in the networked presence.

In summary, broad trends of e-government development around the world in 2005 confirm that political ideology, economic and social systems, level of development, resource availability, human and technological infrastructure, institutional framework and cultural patterns all have a bearing on the level of e-government service delivery. Where countries have substantially improved their performance in the last few years, e-government programmes have been built on the foundations of already existing access opportunities, pervasive infrastructure and a high level of human resources development. Notwithstanding the steady progress, mature interactive, transactional and networked online services remain limited mainly to the developed countries. The majority of countries are not yet exploiting the full potential of ICTs and e-government for promoting access.

Chapter V
E-participation as the means to access and inclusion

The responsibility for successful governance rests equally with the government, the private sector and the citizenry. The concept of e-participation espouses the critical element by which inclusion is achieved. The e-participation index assesses "how relevant and useful the e-participation features of government websites around the world are; and how well they are deployed by the governments for promoting participatory decision-making." Though a qualitative assessment, it is a useful tool in making a broad appraisal of the quality and relevancy of participatory services provided through e-government readiness initiatives.

Table 5.1 presents the e-participation rankings for the top 25 countries. As in the case of the other indices presented in this Report, the rankings closely mirror the e-government readiness and the web measure assessment, reinforcing the theory that the developed economies of the world have the resources and the wherewithal to invest in e-participation endeavours more effectively. These countries are in the vanguard of providing access and opportunity to the citizen through development of participatory initiatives via ICT.

The e-participation index assesses "how relevant and useful the e-participation features of government websites around the world are; and how well they are deployed by the governments for promoting participatory decision-making."

Figure 5.1.
E-participation index 2005: top 25 countries

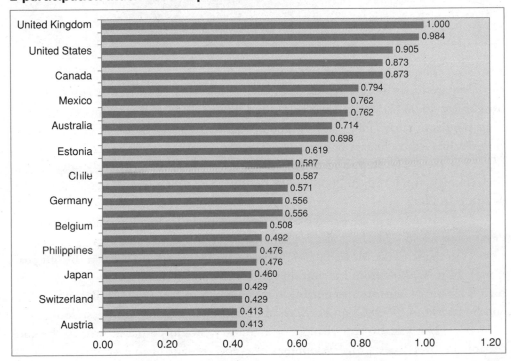

Table 5.1.

E-participation index 2005: top 25 countries

	Country	Index 2005	2005	Rank in: 2004	2003	Change 2004–2005
1	United Kingdom	1.0000	1	1	1	0
2	Singapore	0.9841	2	4	13	+2
3	United States	0.9048	3	2	2	–1
4	Canada	0.8730	4 (tie)	3	3	–1
5	Republic of Korea	0.8730	4 (tie)	6	12	+2
6	New Zealand	0.7937	5	6	5	+1
7	Denmark	0.7619	6 (tie)	7	14	+1
8	Mexico	0.7619	6 (tie)	6	9	0
9	Australia	0.7143	7	8	8	+1
10	Netherlands	0.6984	8	5	7	–3
11	Estonia	0.6190	9	9	4	0
12	Chile	0.5873	10 (tie)	11	3	+1
13	Colombia	0.5873	10 (tie)	10	28	0
14	Sweden	0.5714	11	13	10	+2
15	Finland	0.5556	12 (tie)	13	14	+1
16	Germany	0.5556	12 (tie)	12	11	0
17	Belgium	0.5079	13	11	21	–2
18	Brazil	0.4921	14	23	16	+9
19	Malta	0.4762	15 (tie)	14	18	–1
20	Philippines	0.4762	15 (tie)	17	6	+2
21	Japan	0.4603	16	21	15	+5
22	Switzerland	0.4286	17 (tie)	20	13	+3
23	Venezuela	0.4286	17 (tie)	21	28	+4
24	Austria	0.4127	18 (tie)	15	29	–3
25	France	0.4127	18 (tie)	14	7	–4

The United Kingdom, as in previous years, scores the highest and forms the comparator for the relative performance of all other countries. It is followed by **Singapore** (0.9841) and then the **United States** (0.9048). The performance of Singapore is notable (Table 5.1). In 2005 consistent consolidation of its e-participation services led to Singapore bypassing all other countries to rank second among the top 25 leaders. The **Republic of Korea** (0.8730) has also consistently advanced in the rankings, from 12th in 2003 to 6th in 2004, and along with Canada, to the 4th position in 2005.

The United Kingdom is followed by Singapore and the United States.

Around a quarter of the countries figuring in the top 25 group are from the developing world. They have also made an effort toward developing their participatory services in the last year. **Mexico** (0.7619), tied with **Denmark** (0.7619) at the 6th position, held its ranking from last year due to further improvements in providing participation services. Gains are also notable in the case of **Sweden** (0.5714), **Brazil** (0.4921) and **Switzerland** (0.4286), all of which improved their rankings from last year.

Around a quarter of the countries figured in the top 25 group are from the developing world.

The year-by-year changes of a country should be placed within the context of the overall level of development of e-government in that country. It should also be kept in mind that the e-participation index is a relative measure (i.e., each country is measured against the performance of the other countries). As such, a lower ranking may not reflect deterioration in the e-participation services of the country but show that other countries did better.

However, the focus of the e-government action plan, the policy and strategy of e-participation development, and the overall direction of where the country is headed in terms of its ICT development are key indicators of its e-readiness. Moreover, the quality and relevance of e-participation endeavours appear to be a function of the income level of a country. Table 5.2 provides countries that had e-participation scores above and below the mean for all countries. As can be seen, of the 40 high-income countries two thirds had scores above the mean. The situation was reversed in the case of all other groups, with the proportion of countries below the average rising as income levels declined. Whereas around 60 per cent of the upper middle income countries and 72 per cent of those at the lower middle income level were below average, this ratio rose to cover almost the entire low income group, which scored below average.

> The focus of the e-government action plan, the policy and strategy of e-participation development, and the overall direction of where the country is headed in terms of its ICT development are key indicators of its e-readiness.

Table 5.2.
E-participation by income group 2005

Income Class	Number of countries		% of countries	
	Above Mean	Below Mean	Above Mean	Below Mean
High Income (n = 40)	25	15	63	38
Upper Middle Income (n = 38)	15	23	39	61
Lower Middle Income (n = 54)	15	39	28	72
Low Income (n = 59)	5	54	8	92
Total Countries	60	131	31	69
Mean = 9.62				

Note: Two countries, Nauru and Tuvalu, are not members of, and therefore not included in, the World Bank dataset. In the absence of GNI data GDP is used. Nauru has an estimated GDP per capita of US$5000 while Tuvalu's is US$100.
Income Source: http://www.worldbank.org/data/countryclass/countryclass.html
Income group: Economies are divided according to 2004 GNI per capita, calculated using the World Bank Atlas method. The groups are: low income, US$825 or less; lower middle income, US$826–US$3,255; upper middle income, US$3,256–US$10,065; and high income, US$10,066 or more.

It should be noted that the measurement of willingness, quality and relevancy of e-participation rests primarily on the content available on the websites. Second, e-participation development is still in its early stages for most of the countries of the world. In the interest of reality the survey assesses the relevance and quality of basic e-participation tools. The survey questionnaire assumes existence of e-participation at a rather rudimentary level. Constructing a questionnaire with all the features of mature deliberative participation would render the results for the majority of the countries as zero or very close to zero. As such, the comparative ranking of countries should be considered a work in progress and used purely for illustrative purposes.

Table 5.3.
E-participation profile of UN Member States 2005

	67–100%	34–66%	1–33%	No score
2005				
No. of countries	3	18	129	41
% of countries	2	9	68	21
2004				
No. of countries	2	15	133	28
% of countries	1	8	75	16
No. of countries online in 2005 = 179				

Top ⅓ = 67–100%
Middle = 34–66%
Lowest ⅓ = 1–33%
No score = Countries scored a zero on e-participation

The e-participation scores comprise an assessment of e-information, e-consultation and e-decision making. Table 5.3 and Figure 5.2 indicate that the quality and relevance of e-participation remain limited in their utilization. Only three countries have e-participation scores in the top utilization bracket, indicating high quality and relevance of the services. Another 18 countries, or nine per cent, have scores within the 34–66 per cent range, while more than half of what all countries in the 0–33 per cent range provide is of mediocre quality. The remaining 21 per cent offer no e-participation services at all.

A closer look at how these scores are distributed across the three categories of e-information, e-consultation and e-decision-making in Table 5.4 indicates that no

Figure 5.2.
E-participation utilization levels 2005

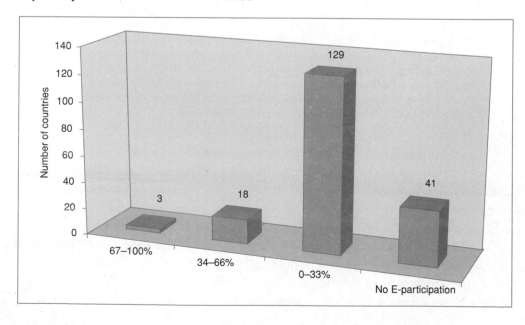

Table 5.4.
Quality and relevance of e-participation initiatives, selected countries

	E-information	E-consultation	E-decision-making	Total
67–100 percent				
United Kingdom	85	75	67	75
Singapore	90	75	58	74
United States	80	70	54	68
34–66 per cent				
Canada	80	65	54	65
Republic of Korea	85	60	58	65
Mexico	70	60	42	57
Australia	75	45	50	54
Estonia	75	43	29	46
Chile	75	30	42	44
Colombia	65	40	33	44
Sweden	80	30	33	43
Belgium	60	33	29	38
Brazil	75	28	21	37
Malta	60	20	42	36
Philippines	60	33	21	36
10–33 per cent				
Venezuela	50	28	25	32
Norway	65	13	29	30
Hungary	50	25	17	29
Ukraine	50	18	25	27
Poland	45	20	21	26
Mozambique	35	30	8	25
Indonesia	35	18	17	21
Turkey	40	15	17	21
Guatemala	30	18	17	20
Honduras	40	18	8	20
Panama	50	13	8	20
Mongolia	30	18	13	19
Kazakhstan	25	15	8	15
China	35	8	8	14
Slovakia	30	10	4	13
El Salvador	40	0	8	12
Greece	25	8	8	12
India	30	3	13	12
Kyrgyzstan	15	10	13	12
Russian Federation	25	0	17	11

country provides more than three fourths of the services for e-participation. As expected, quality and relevance of information tools is the highest, with percentage of utilization tapering off in e-consultation and e-decision-making categories. The United Kingdom retains its lead in overall e-participation as in the past, followed in the 2nd position by Singapore, which has done very well in 2005 on all indices, including e-participation. The United States is the 3rd country with top bracket utilization.

E-information assesses the relevance and quality of features on the websites that would inform citizens about the benefits of e-information, looking at items such as the links to policies, programmes, laws, mandates and other briefs on key public issues of interest. It also assesses the quality of tools that governments employ on the websites for dissemination of information. For example, among other things, it assesses the relevance of "the use of e-mail notification and web personalization for timely access;" "the use of public information on key issues;" "the relevance of the 'calendar of events/events listing';" "the listing for issue-specific topics open to citizen participation;" and "relevant citizen-to-citizen web forums and newsgroups."

The countries that score high have a meticulous approach to e-participation. For example, all of Singapore's websites provide the most relevant and highest quality of information about its policies, programmes and "how to" manuals. Information is complemented by frequent and relevant online listings of events on specific topics to further knowledge to the citizen. It is especially notable that Singapore scores the highest in e-information, at 90 per cent, and along with the United Kingdom, in e-consultation at 75 per cent. The United States, Canada and the Republic of Korea, all of which have invested considerably in making access to citizens a priority, follow them in this category.

Eighty-nine countries (or around 50 per cent) provided some information on the benefits of e-information, including in some instances the role of ICTs in providing information to the citizen. The majority of industrialized countries provided the relevant policies, programmes, laws, and other briefs on key public issues of interest. Denmark and Singapore were the best sites in e-participation, especially in terms of timely access and use of public participation on key issues through e-mail notification and web personalization. The Republic of Korea's websites had the most relevant citizen-to-citizen web forums, e-mail lists, newsgroups and chat rooms, while Sweden and the United States provided the most up-to-date events listings on issue-specific topics for citizen participation (Table 5.5).

Table 5.5.
Countries providing e-information

	Number of countries	Per cent
Government information to citizens about the benefits of e-information	89	50
Calendar of events/events listing for issue-specific topics open to citizen participation	74	41
Relevant citizen-to-citizen web forums, e-mail lists, newsgroups, chat rooms, etc.	71	40

It is notable that the e-participation utilization scores drop fast as the list of countries descends. Mexico, which is among the top countries in the 34–66 per cent group, though higher than Australia and the Netherlands, provides only a little more than half of all services.

Though not scoring the highest, many developing countries were employing e-government to involve greater participation of the citizen. A few of the countries that have taken steps towards online citizen participation are given below.

It is notable that the e-participation utilization scores drop fast as the list of countries goes down.

Selected developing countries providing benefits of e-information to citizens

Colombia, Malaysia, Malta, Mauritius, Slovenia, Argentina, China, Croatia, Egypt, Hungary, India, Lebanon, Myanmar, Pakistan, Panama, Philippines, Qatar, Romania, Sri Lanka, Thailand, Trinidad and Tobago, Turkey, Ukraine, United Arab Emirates and Venezuela

---

E-consultation constitutes the use of ICTs for promoting access and inclusion. As Table 5.6 shows, less than 20 per cent of all countries explained what e-consultation was, why it was important and where citizens should provide inputs to the government. Canada, Singapore, the United Kingdom and the United States scored the highest when it came to explaining e-consultation and informing citizens of ways to provide input. An even lesser number—13 per cent—provided the opportunity to citizens to comment publicly via a web forum on topics chosen by the government, even though 15 per cent provided an index or a directory of online consultations. Along with many of the developed

Less than 20 per cent of all countries explained what e-consultation was, why it was important and where citizens should provide inputs to the government.

Table 5.6.
Quality and relevance of e-consultation

	Number of countries	Per cent
Explaining e-consultation and informing citizens of ways to provide input	32	18
Online consultation mechanisms and tools (providing opportunities to citizens to comment publicly via a web forum on topics chosen by the government etc.)	23	13
Citizen usage and quality of discussion as judged by the content on discussion forums/lists, web casts/meetings and list-servs between citizen and government	42	23
Choice of topics for online discussion	47	26
Availability of an index/directory of online consultations/hearings/ proposed rules and links to documents	26	15
Encouraging citizens to participate in surveys/polling	53	30
Inviting citizen participation in agenda setting	18	10
Encouraging citizens to participate in discussing key issues	55	31

countries, Mexico, the Philippines, Chile, China, Colombia, Estonia, Romania and South Africa provided some facility for public comment.

As Table 5.6 indicates, 55 countries (or 31 per cent) encouraged citizens to participate in discussing key issues of importance. Forty-seven countries (or 26 per cent) also allowed the citizen some choice of topics for online discussion. Canada, Mexico, Netherlands and New Zealand are the best in this but some developing countries have made gains too. Among those with the best sites are Belarus, Brazil and Colombia. On the other hand, the Mexican sites provided high quality and relevant discussion forums or web casts, meetings or list-servs between citizens and the government, with Brazil and Estonia not far behind. Overall however, a lesser number of countries of the world provide relevant and quality facilities for e-consultation. It is notable that 53 countries, or 30 per cent, had statements encouraging citizens to participate in online polls. In this group, the Republic of Korea, Mexico, Belgium, Chile, Colombia, Estonia and Indonesia were in the forefront. Selected e-consultation services are presented in Figure 5.3.

> Fifty-five countries (or 31 per cent) encouraged citizens to participate in discussing key issues of importance.

> Fifty-three countries, or 30 per cent, had statements encouraging citizens to participate in online polls.

Figure 5.3.

E-consultation, selected services

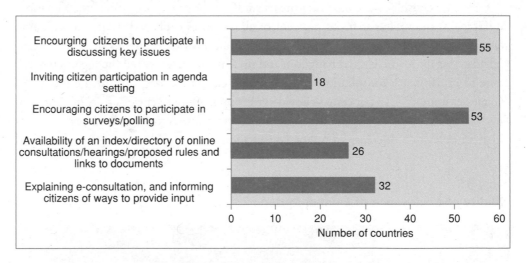

E-decision-making is the mature use of ICTs and e-government towards a partnership between the government and the citizen for participatory and deliberative decision-making on public policy. It involves use of ICTs to allow the government to actively solicit citizens' views and take citizen input into account in decision-making. It is a key tool for promoting inclusion.

Among the countries that allowed for e-decision-making the performance was mixed. Whereas 80 countries, or 47 per cent of the total, had some basic feature such as use of e-mail for feedback, quality services for citizen participation were relatively scarce. Only 28 countries gave the assurance that the government would take citizen input into account in decision-making. Expectedly, the top scorers among these were Singapore, the United Kingdom and the United States. A few of the countries that were in this group are listed below. Their performance in this respect is notable.

> Whereas 80 countries, or 47 per cent of the total, had some basic feature such as use of e-mail for feedback, quality services for citizen participation were relatively scarce. Only 28 countries gave the assurance that the government would take citizen input into account in decision-making.

Table 5.7.
E-decision-making

	Number of countries	Per cent
Allows citizens to petition online	14	8
Indicates the government will take citizen input into account in decision-making	28	16
Indicates government provides a "sent receipt" for citizen-sent communication, including copy of what was received, by whom, time/date received and response time estimate	15	8
Indicates government feedback on specific issues	16	9

Countries indicating the government will take citizen input in decision-making

Canada, Singapore, United Kingdom, United States of America, Australia, Denmark, Estonia, Finland, Malta, New Zealand, Republic of Korea, Austria, Belgium, Brazil, Colombia, Guatemala, Hungary, Mexico, Mongolia, Netherlands, Philippines, Poland, Saint Kitts and Nevis, South Africa, Switzerland, Ukraine, Venezuela and Viet Nam.

In a special focus on promoting access the *UN Global E-government Survey 2005* explored country approaches to participation by assessing whether websites provided a response time to citizen e-mails. It is notable that only 18 countries out of 179 clearly provided a response timeframe on any of their surveyed sites. These are given in Table 5.8. Moreover, there were considerable differences in the response times indicated (Box 22).

Only 18 countries out of 179 clearly provided a response timeframe on any of their surveyed sites.

Table 5.8.
Countries providing receipts to citizen

Australia	Dominican Republic	Republic of Korea
Bhutan	Hungary	Singapore
Canada	Italy	Sweden
Chile	Malta	Trinidad and Tobago
Colombia	Mexico	United Kingdom
Denmark	Norway	United States

In another bid at citizen participation, the government provided "feedback to the citizen on issues" in only 16 countries. These are listed in Table 5.9.

Table 5.9.
Countries providing feedback on issues

Australia	Chile	Mexico	Singapore
Belgium	Colombia	Netherlands	South Africa
Cambodia	Denmark	New Zealand	United Kingdom
Canada	Malta	Republic of Korea	United States

Box 22. An assessment of government attention to citizen feedback

For each country researchers are asked to assess whether their sites have a "response timeframe indicated by the government to forms/e-mails submitted by the citizen." Providing the general public with a clearly identifiable and specific timeframe for response to inquiries by citizens increases transparency and accountability at all levels. From a user perspective it offers a sign of commitment on behalf of the government entity and allows for more effective communications. Clearly, a second prompt won't be necessary before the stated deadline but—lacking a response—a reminder is obviously called for. Meanwhile, from the government standpoint it increases efficiency and creates additional responsibility while also generating better organization, enabling a "citizen-centric" approach.

Given the many positive benefits associated with providing a clear response timeframe, it is unfortunate that only 18 countries provided the feature on any of their surveyed sites. While there is no "best practice" timeframe per se—though sooner would arguably be better—it is interesting to observe the variations given.

The U.S. FirstGov feedback mechanism, http://answers.firstgov.gov/cgi-bin/ gsa_ict.cfg/php/enduser/ask.php, for example, states that "a member of our Citizen Response Team will respond to you within two business days." Not to be outdone, Canada's national site contact page, http://canada.gc.ca/comments/form_e.html, informs the user that its "service standard is to respond within one Canadian business day." Meanwhile, the Health Canada site, http://www.hc-sc.gc.ca/home-accueil/contact/general_e.html, apparently uses a different approach as it states, "Our service standard is to respond to English and French inquiries only, within 10 Canadian business days." Obtaining a promised reply from the U.K.'s HM Treasury, http://www.hm-treasury.gov.uk/contact/contact_index.cfm, is not quite as fast, as "All correspondence received is replied to, within 15 working days, and so you will receive a response." But then again, those e-mails are also sent to the Chancellor's Private Office, which may explain the comparative delay. For faster service, visit the U.K.'s national site helpdesk, http://www.direct.gov.uk/Hl1/Help/ContactUs/ ContactUsForm/fs/en, which promises to "reply to all reasonable requests within five working days." Reasonable or not, the U.S. Department of Labor page, http://www.dol.gov/dol/contact/contact-email.htm, meanwhile only provided a generic timeframe by noting that it would "respond to your e-mail inquiry as soon as possible." Such a general statement is neither especially helpful nor quantitatively scored. Finally, it should be noted that providing a response timeframe is not limited to large developed countries. Bhutan's new national portal, http:// www.bhutan.gov.bt/contactus.php, for example, promises to "respond within a day or two provided that you give us the return e-mail address."

In summary, the potential of e-participation remains yet to be fully exploited. For the majority of countries, especially developing countries, meaningful qualitative or relevant services to encourage deliberative participatory dialogue on public policy decision-making are still in their infancy.

Figure 5.4.

Key decision-making services provided by countries

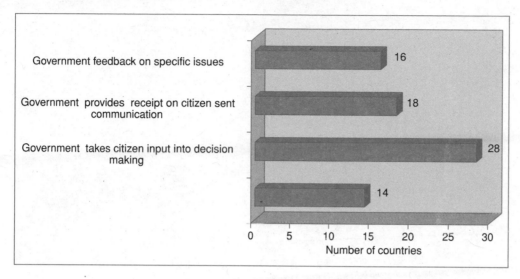

Part II

From E-Government to E-Inclusion

Chapter VI
The emerging socially inclusive government paradigm: from e-government to e-inclusion

The importance of governance in development is accepted worldwide.[1] The cognizance of close linkages between good governance and development stem, in part, from past failures of policy and programme approaches and the search for a more holistic path to equitable human development. The speed with which the new paradigms in development are changing is in large part due to the emerging realities at the nation-state level brought on by the increasing globalization of the world economy and the urgency of adapting to the information society.

Patterns of ICT diffusion worldwide indicate that the policy-programme approach of the past few years has fallen far short of providing opportunity for all. Though in part successful in some countries, it has left gaps which can only be filled through a systemic approach to development, focusing on both the emerging realities of the information society and the need to remodel the functioning of the institutions and mechanisms in place to implement the programmes and the processes through which the state, the private sector and the civil society interact.

There is a need to rethink the paradigms of development and redirect them towards citizen-oriented participatory and inclusive models of governance and development. To transform the role of government from that of a managerial authority to one of leadership in a multi-centred setting, the culture of governance needs to change its orientation—from bureaucratic to participatory; from authoritative to accountable; from monopolistic to competitive and innovative; from closed to open; from autocratic to democratic; and from exclusive to inclusive.

Such a holistic approach requires cognizance of the inter-linkages among the various players at the level of the state, the private sector and the civil society. In short, it requires a new model of governance.

Socially inclusive governance for the information society

The vision of good governance today requires a rethinking towards a Socially Inclusive Governance Model that broadens the parameters of access to "inclusion" for opportunity and empowerment of all and considers inclusion as broader than—and encompassing both—access and connectivity.

The underlying premise of the Socially Inclusive Governance Framework is that to build an Information Society for the future, ICT-led development is an imperative. As such, the concept of socially inclusive governance in this Report assumes a systemic integration of ICT into development programmes and processes as a given. Socially

Patterns of ICT diffusion worldwide indicate that the policy-programme approach of the past few years has fallen far short of providing opportunity for all.

There is a need to rethink the paradigms of development towards citizen-oriented participatory and inclusive models of governance and development.

The vision of good governance today requires a rethinking towards a Socially Inclusive Governance Model that broadens the parameters of access to "inclusion" for opportunity and empowerment of all where inclusion is considered as broader than—and encompassing both—access and connectivity.

The Socially Inclusive
Governance, then, is a
model for governance
in an Information
Society using ICT
to include all in
the benefits.

Inclusive Governance, then, is a model for governance in an Information Society using ICT to include all in its benefits.

Information technologies have begun to be thought of as the conduit for promoting inclusion. The concept of technology for social inclusion maintains that since technology is woven into the social system in place, attempts to bring technology to the marginalized should not be considered as only an issue of overcoming the digital divide but also as a process of social inclusion.[2] In recent years there has been a growing recognition of the social inclusion, ICTs and development nexus. Some are beginning to apply social policy concepts to ICTs for development.

In some countries around the world digital divide issues have begun to be addressed within the confines of social inclusion. There is a growing realization that people's ability to use a computer in meaningful social practices is far more important than its mere availability.[3] The European Union (EU) is among those in the vanguard in adopting inclusion approaches in the use of ICTs. Building upon the *Lisbon Strategy*, the EU "Information Society for All 2010" initiative focuses on achieving an inclusive European Information Society that promotes growth and jobs in a manner that is consistent with sustainable development, and that prioritizes better public services and quality of life.[4] The EU e-inclusion approach towards promoting participation in the information society focuses on people who are disadvantaged due to limited resources or education, age, gender or ethnicity; people with disabilities; and those living in less favoured areas. Since 2001 all EU Member States have produced biennial National Action Plans for Social Inclusion. Although these are called plans for social inclusion, they are actually part of the EU strategy against social exclusion.[5] The Social Inclusion Initiative in South Australia is about finding ways to make sure everyone who lives has access to all that the society offers; it is about helping people to live fulfilling lives and to feel that they are a part of the community.[6]

The private sector is not behind in defining its own concepts. The Laidlaw Foundation of Canada is in the vanguard in exploring concepts and practices for social inclusion. In the last few years it has commissioned research into what social inclusion means and how it can be applied to various sectors. It defines social inclusion as "… the capacity and willingness of our society to keep all groups within reach of what we expect as a society—the social commitments and investments needed to ensure that all people are within reach of (close to) our common aspirations, common life and its common wealth …"[7] Among ICT industry firms, Hewlett Packard's (HP's) vision of e-inclusion is about contributing to the empowerment of people to access the social and economic opportunities of the digital age. HP is working with a range of local and global partners to develop and deliver sustainable information solutions targeted at the four billion people with very low incomes in the developing world. The purpose is to close the gap between the technology-empowered and the technology-excluded communities.

In these initial stages of concept development, social inclusion means different things to different people. Today much of the focus of social inclusion initiatives in the public sector revolves around bringing the marginalized groups living in hardship on the fringes of society into the mainstream. The issue is defined in terms of inclusion for those with persistent lack of income, disability and unemployment or the disadvantaged who lack the resources needed to participate fully in the society. Most concepts of social inclusion have revolved around the same theme. In Ireland,

"Combat Poverty," a non-governmental organization working on ways to prevent and eliminate poverty and social exclusion, defines social inclusion as "... to ensure that the marginalized and the poor have greater participation in decision making which affects their lives, allowing them to improve their living standards and their overall well-being ..."[8] Broader concepts of social inclusion have, at other times, implied exclusion of groups due to social, cultural or ethnic factors. But most of these concepts have focused on social inclusion by defining the "excluded."

These models have inherent difficulties for many developing countries, where life chances are not equal, not only for the disadvantaged and the elderly but in many cases *for the majority of their populations*. Such is the evidence from many countries: where ICT-related benefits are concentrated among small elite populations; where hundreds of millions living in poverty have no resources and no skills to utilize newer technologies to their benefit; where women, comprising 50 per cent of the population, are mostly outside the ambit of connectivity and opportunity; where large populations living in the rural areas cannot employ the Internet to obtain time-sensitive farming data; where the majority of youth attend schools with few or no computers; and where all these groups lack the awareness to demand access to ICTs and the opportunities that flow from them.

Box 23. Nine reasons why a focus on "e-inclusion" is necessary in the developing countries

1. Low literacy rate and lack of technical skills set limits to using ICTs as a medium.

2. Available content may not be accessible in the required language—75 per cent of the websites are still in English.

3. Existing software, including search engines, is targeted towards the needs of better-off people.

4. Information needs of rural and urban poor differ from the information accessible on most of the existing websites—relevant content is lacking.

5. There is limited connectivity in rural areas.

6. The poor and the marginalized suffer from barriers in mobility that prevent their reaching ICT centres.

7. Women and the poor, disabled and marginalized cannot afford sufficient time and incur income losses when they attend training classes.

8. Costs of hardware, software and connectivity are still considerable for poor people.

9. The majority lack awareness of how beneficial and powerful the Internet could be in their hands.

Adapted from Richard Gerster and Sonja Zimmermann. *Up-Scaling Pro-Poor ICT-Policies and Practices: A Review of Experience with Emphasis on Low Income Countries in Asia and Africa.* http://www.eldis.org/static/DOC18032.htm.
Accessed 8 October 2005.

Because recent patterns of ICT development are unlikely to promote equality, there is a need to revisit the conceptual framework governing ICT-led development for the developing countries if the vision of access for all is to become a reality.

The Socially Inclusive Governance Model

The *Socially Inclusive Governance Model* presents a holistic framework in which to think about the role of ICTs in providing access to the benefits of society. Assembling strands of recent state-of-the-art thinking it weaves together emerging concepts of inclusion, technology and development to present a model for thinking about access-for-all.[9]

The Socially Inclusive Governance Model is a call to developing countries to shed the emphasis on connectivity and access and replace it with a focus on inclusion of all groups in the population. It is a call to focus on programmes and policies aimed at the diversification of the ICT base so that those with low income, women, youth, the disadvantaged and those living in rural areas are systematically included in the impending benefits from newer technologies.

It is a "vision" for restructured thinking about developing an inclusive information society based on the appreciation of the capabilities of each and every person; the dignity that economic and social choice brings; and the freedom to partake of it all. If one takes the belief underlying the UN Human Rights Charter that "all human beings are born free and equal in dignity and rights"[10] as the basis of fair and equitable development for all then *equality of opportunity* becomes an important goal on which to focus. The moral equality of human beings gives rise to a fair claim to certain types of treatment at the hands of society and politics that must respect and promote the liberty of choice and the equal worth of people as choosers.[11]

Universal inclusion stems from a vision in which every person has a "right of inclusion" by virtue of his or her membership in a global community committed to principles of democracy, security and development.[12] In this vision of social inclusion, people have social rights to be defended and observed, freedom is the liberty to pursue a meaningful life, and states of social well-being are better advanced through improved states of social cohesion.[13] This vision of the world, then, has no room for inequality and exclusion.

The underlying concept of a Socially Inclusive Governance Framework draws upon Amartya Sen's approach of "capabilities as freedom" that focuses on the expansion of the "capabilities" of people to lead the lives they most value.[14] It applies Sen's concept to advance the case for an all-inclusive society aimed at reducing inequality in people's life chances. In this model inequality leads to deprivation and poverty, which is "un-freedom." A human-centred, pluralistic society is based on removing inequalities and deprivations of income, illiteracy, morbidity, persecution, security and lack of social choice. This requires a different set of allocational decisions and growth strategies than those of the traditional real-income framework.[15] It requires an open debate and policy making that "explicitly acknowledges the importance of collective action, public mores that are open to contestation and collective struggles, and focused efforts to stimulate and sustain organizations that transcend primordial and parochial interests—all necessary components in the quest for development as freedom."[16]

The concept of social inclusion in this report encompasses systemic interactions within a society that lead to different life chances for different people. Social

The Socially Inclusive Governance Model is a call to developing countries to shed the emphasis on connectivity and access and substituting it with a focus on inclusion of all groups in the population.

It is a "vision" for restructured thinking about developing an inclusive information society based on the appreciation of the capabilities of each and every person; the dignity that economic and social choice brings; and the freedom to partake of it all.

inclusion then becomes an effort to ensure that each person gets an equal chance to enhance his or her inherent economic and social capabilities. Social inclusion is about providing equal opportunity for life chances.

Capabilities are defined as the access and opportunity to do things a person values. They are a set of "well-being indicators," including income.[17] Public policy choices about what constitutes "well-being" indicators can be arrived at by consensus. In practical terms this implies two things:

1. access to information and informed decision-making; and

2. a system of citizen input into public policy decision making to ensure that policies and programmes represent choices reflecting what the citizens value.

A Socially Inclusive Government promotes "access for all" either directly or through legitimate intermediate institutions that represent its intentions. A flourishing civil society is the conduit through which people carry out economic and social participation in ways that can influence public policies, provide access to public resources and manage conflict. Socially inclusive government provides opportunities for participatory decision-making and inclusion of all segments of the society. While states and governments remain primary actors, they do not bear the whole burden of governance. *Social inclusion is as much about the government providing opportunities as willingness on part of the society to become involved in participation.* As such, socially inclusive government is a partnership among the government, the private sector and the civil society in pursuit of opportunity-for-all.

The cornerstone of the *Socially Inclusive Governance Model* is a focus on the reduction in inequality of opportunity. As such, the imperative for progress towards a socially inclusive government is access-to-all. Participation is possible only if political, economic, technological and social barriers are removed and access to opportunities is equitably distributed.

A Socially Inclusive Government promotes "access for all" either directly or through legitimate intermediate institutions that represent their intention.

Social inclusion is as much about the government providing opportunities as willingness on part of the society to become involved in participation.

The cornerstone of the Socially Inclusive Governance Model is a focus on the reduction in inequality of opportunity. As such, the imperative for progress towards a socially inclusive government is access-to-all.

Box 24. What is socially inclusive government

- **Vision of a pluralistic inclusive society;**
- **Appreciation of the inherent capabilities of each and every person;**
- **Cognizance of the role of ICTs in ameliorating inequality;**
- **Willingness and political commitment to undertake needed reforms and changes;**
- **Making ICTs the integrating cohesive underpinnings of the national development plans for social inclusion;**
- **Enabling environment promoting access, participation and inclusion for all;**
- **Employing inclusive approaches to setting objectives;**
- **Allowing for collective approaches to public policy based on consensus of public value.**

The information technology revolution has afforded a unique opportunity to realize this vision of the world. Advances in information technology have made possible the structural capacity of nations that provide access to information and services to everyone. This potential stems from the unique ability of ICTs to provide access to unlimited information to every person at any time, irrespective of distance and location, and to enable everyone to participate in proffering what he/she values, which should be produced by the society. Information technologies facilitate the dissemination of information and the opportunity for feedback as they promote access to government. They are the perfect conduit for citizen-government partnerships to promote public value, and therefore, inclusion.

Inclusion and participation through ICTs, or e-inclusion, then becomes the key tool at the disposal of a socially inclusive government.

From e-government to e-inclusion

Blending information technology with the need for good governance places e-government at the centre of the government's leadership role in promoting equitable human and social inclusion. In this context, the definition of e-government needs to be enhanced from simply "government-to-government networking" or "use of ICTs by governments to provide information and services to citizens" to one that encompasses the government's role as an equitable and socially inclusive force.

E-inclusion goes beyond e-government. It is defined as the use of modern information technologies to 1) address the issues of access-divide and inclusion; and 2) promote opportunities for economic and social empowerment of the citizen. Among the objectives of e-inclusion the following are of paramount importance and relevance here:

- Building inclusion for all;
- Efficient and transparent service delivery to citizens;
- Empowerment of the people through access to information;
- Efficient government management of information to the citizen;
- Promoting awareness about the information society;
- Building social and cultural consensus.

E-inclusion necessitates a shift in focus from technology per se to promoting equal access to ICT-centred economic, social and cultural opportunities to people. E-inclusion presents a holistic approach to prevent the risks of widening the access-divide, to ensure that disadvantaged people are not left behind, and to avoid new forms of exclusion due to income, educational, gender, language and content barriers. It means that each individual has the same chance to participate in—and derive benefits from—income, employment etc. in the society. In allows for a space where each individual has an equal chance for equal access. As depicted graphically in Figure 6.1, e-inclusion envisages that the average distance of each group or individual from the benefits of technology must be the same.

Inclusion and participation through ICTs, or e-inclusion, then becomes the key tool at the disposal of a socially inclusive government.

E-inclusion goes beyond e-government. It means employing modern ICTs to address the issues of access-divide and promote opportunities for economic and social empowerment of all citizens.

E-inclusion necessitates a shift in focus from technology per se to promoting equal access to ICT-centred economic, social and cultural opportunities to people.

Figure 6.1.
A model of e-inclusion

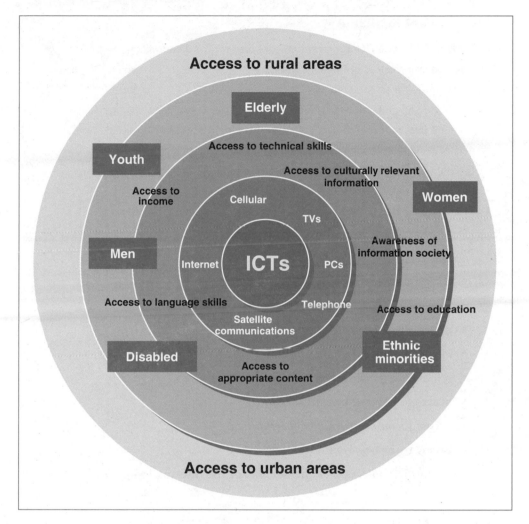

As Box 25 indicates, the evolved concept of e-inclusion allows the leadership role of the government to be multi-dimensional and multi-centred. The government still needs to be a facilitator of the right environment for the market economy; it retains the managerial authority to oversee the regulatory framework; it focuses on internal government networks to ensure transparency and efficiency; it partners with the public sector for the diffusion of ICT infrastructures; and it promotes participation of the citizen. But in addition it focuses on promoting access to the disadvantaged and marginalized groups; creating a level playing field for access to ICT tools; and supporting the use of ICTs for socio-economic development. In short, it needs to be socially inclusive.

In addition to promoting digital access, e-inclusion envisions supportive socio-economic, educational, gender, language, content, regulatory, awareness and policy-making activities. The socially inclusive governance agenda of e-inclusion adopted in the Report encompasses:

**Box 25. Guidelines for promoting accessibility
         and inclusion**

- Provide an enabling environment and policies for the development of ICTs;
- Develop IT infrastructure and networks;
- Employ ICTs for e-inclusion;
- Facilitate and promote widespread and varied uses of ICTs by society;
- Promote human resource capacities for the development of ICT skills;
- Aim to provide access to disadvantaged groups;
- Create a level playing field for cultural access to ICT tools and applications;
- Support uses of ICTs for socio-economic development;
- Promote cohesion and consensus on socially inclusive approaches.

- universal access to *physical infrastructure;*
- universal access to *education and ICT skills training;*
- appropriate access to *language tools;*
- access to culturally relevant and *appropriate content;*
- a focus *on gender access to ICTs;*
- access to population with *disability;*
- access to *income earning opportunities;*
- access to *information;*
- promoting *awareness* of the benefits of the information society.

Worldwide disparity in access and inclusion

But what is the current state of access and inclusion in the world today?

In a special focus on access and inclusion this chapter explores the various aspects of the lack of real access and inclusion that pose a challenge to the majority of countries in the world. Keeping in view the above-posed model of social inclusion, the following sections offer insights into the extent of the existing access-divide. The basic thesis tested here is whether existing disparities in income, infrastructure and education among and between countries and regions of the world have mapped onto disparities in ICTs, making access and inclusion for less developed countries and regions difficult.

Using the statistical databases of the *UN Global E-government Readiness Survey 2005,* supplemented by other data sources, the sections below present a better understanding of the comprehensive set of issues, which, together, are responsible for the lack of real access and inclusion. By presenting a snapshot of the current state of access-divide in today's world it is hoped that the Report will reiterate the importance of the need for restructured thinking towards a new model of ICT and social governance.

In addition to the access parameters presented in this section, *lack of affordability* and the *lack of an enabling regulatory environment* are of key importance in a holistic approach to access and inclusion. While acknowledging their importance, analysis of the two areas is outside the scope of this Report and left for a later opportunity.

Income access-divide

Accumulating evidence in recent years suggests that disparities in new information technologies mirror economic inequalities.[18] Table 6.1 maps these relationships between Gross National Income (GNI) and e-government programmes across countries. The pattern of diffusion of information technology across countries is closely related to levels of income: rich countries enjoy higher technological progress. Income per capita appears to be related to the maturity and sophistication of the web services offered by governments. The 40 high-income countries, with Gross National Income (GNI) per capita more than US$10,066, depicted below, provide 39 per cent

Table 6.1.
E-government development by income classification

Income group	I	II	III	IV	V	2005	2004	% Change
High Income								
(n = 40; average score)	7.1	66.9	56.4	14.1	16.8	161.2	147.1	9.58
% of total services provided	88	77	67	34	31	59	54	
Upper Middle Income								
(n = 38; average score)	5.9	44.3	38.7	3.8	8.1	100.8	87.5	15.20
% of total services provided	74	51	46	9	15	37	32	
Lower Middle Income								
(n = 54; average score)	5.3	36.3	28.7	1.7	5.6	77.6	69.2	12.11
% of total services provided	66	42	34	4	10	28	25	
Low Income								
(n = 59; average score)	4.0	17.1	14.1	0.2	1.9	37.4	31.4	19.08
% of total services provided	50	20	17	0	4	14	11	

Note: 1. The table includes all 191 Member States, including those with no web presence, in order to have a more accurate income group comparison; n = number of countries in the class.
2. Two countries, Nauru and Tuvalu, are not members of, and are therefore not included in, the World Bank dataset. In the absence of GNI data, GDP is used. Nauru has an estimated GDP per capita of US$5000 while Tuvalu's is US$1100.
Income Source: http://www.worldbank.org/data/countryclass/countryclass.html
Income group: Economies are divided according to 2004 GNI per capita, calculated using the World Bank Atlas method. The groups are: low income, $825 or less; lower middle income, $826–$3,255; upper middle income, $3,256–$10,065; and high income, $10,066 or more.
3. The number of countries in each income group in 2004 were: High income = 39; Upper Middle Income = 36; Lower Middle Income = 55; and Low Income = 61.

Figure 6.2.
Average scores of countries by income group: Stage II enhanced presence

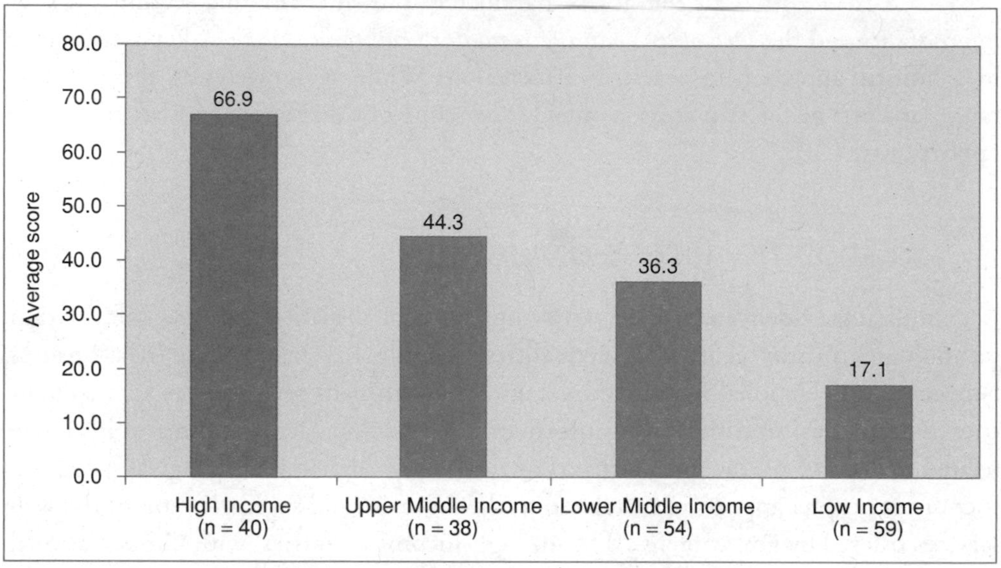

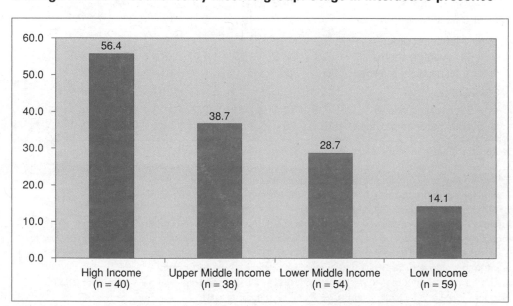

of the overall services across all five stages. Whereas the high income group provided one third of the networked services and the middle income group half of that amount, the networked services were very limited in the lower middle income and low income countries, providing only 10 per cent and four per cent of the potential services, respectively.

Around 60 per cent of the world's countries fall into two categories—low income with per capita of less than $825, and lower middle income with per capita

Figure 6.3.
Average scores of countries by income group: Stage III interactive presence

Figure 6.4.

Average scores of countries by income group: Stage IV transactional presence

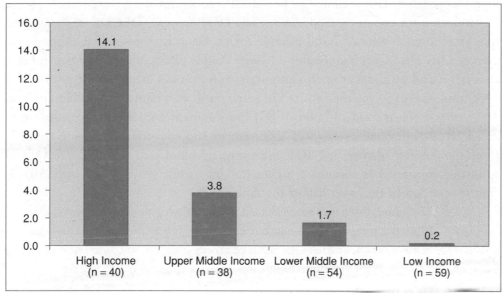

of \$826–\$3255. Together these 111 countries were far behind the others. As a whole they provided only 14–28 per cent of the e-government services. On an aggregate level, the low income countries accounted for a little more than 14 per cent of the potential services through the Web, zero transactional services and only four per cent of the participatory services.

Not only disparities in economic growth across regions are reflected in technology choices; data show that the pattern takes time to break. In 1999 a research

Figure 6.5.

Average scores of countries by income group: Stage V networked services

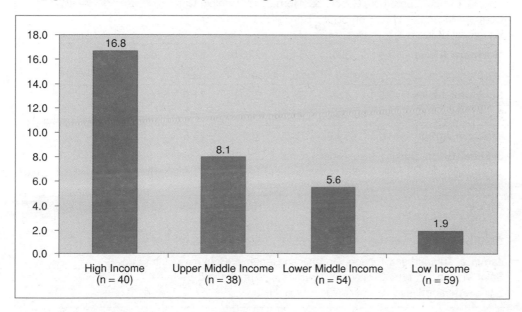

study constructed an Index of Technological Progress, which showed that the highly skewed distribution of technology found among the 110 countries of the world was highly correlated with income.[19] The top 10 economies were all members of the Organization for Economic Cooperation and Development (OECD); while the bottom 10 economies were all in sub-Saharan Africa. Data also showed that although the average OECD country had roughly 11 times the per capita income of a South Asian country, it had 40 times as many computers, 146 times as many mobile phones and 1036 times as many Internet hosts. The same result was found by another study in 2004, which constructed an index of ICT development encompassing connectivity, access, ICT policy and overall ICT diffusion in 165 countries. Exploring the relationship between income and ICT diffusion, it found that high-income OECD countries continued to dominate higher rankings while South Asian and African countries occupied the lower half of the rankings.[20]

The same disparities are reflected at the sub-regional level as well.

Table 6.2 presents an assessment of the government websites across the various sub-regions of the world. As the average scores indicate, there is wide disparity between the scores of the developed high income countries in Northern America and

Table 6.2.

Disparity in e-government outreach by regions of the world

Sub-region	No. of countries	2005		2004		% change	Notes
		Total score	Average score	Total score	Average score		
Eastern Africa	n=17	763.5	44.9	534.0	31.4	43	
Mauritius, Seychelles, Mozambique, United Republic of Tanzania, Kenya, Uganda, Madagascar, Djibouti, Malawi, Zimbabwe, Rwanda, Eritrea, Comoros, Burundi, Ethiopia, Somalia, Zambia							
Middle Africa	n=9	132	14.7	163.0	18.1	–19	Lowest scoring sub-region
Angola, Congo, Cameroon, Gabon, São Tomé and Principe, Chad, Central African Republic, Democratic Republic of the Congo, Equatorial Guinea							
Northern Africa	n=6	324	54.0	226.0	37.7	43	
Egypt, Algeria, Morocco, Sudan, Tunisia, Libyan Arab Jamahiriya							
Southern Africa	n=5	425	85.0	359.5	71.9	18	
South Africa, Botswana, Swaziland, Lesotho, Namibia							
Western Africa	n=16	459.5	28.7	407.5	25.5	13	
Senegal, Benin, Burkina Faso, Nigeria, Ghana, Cape Verde, Gambia, Sierra Leone, Mauritania, Mali, Côte d'Ivoire, Guinea, Togo, Niger, Guinea-Bissau. Liberia							
Africa	n=53	2104	39.7	1690.0	31.9	24	Lowest scoring region
Caribbean	n=13	725	55.8	598.0	46.0	21	
Jamaica, Trinidad and Tobago, Dominican Republic, Bahamas, Saint Lucia, Saint Vincent and the Grenadines, Barbados, Antigua and Barbuda, Cuba, Saint Kitts and Nevis, Grenada, Dominica, Haiti							

Table 6.2. *(continued)*

Sub-region	No. of countries	2005 Total score	2005 Average score	2004 Total score	2004 Average score	% change	Notes
Central America	n=8	819	102.4	757.0	94.7	8	
Mexico, Panama, Guatemala, El Salvador, Belize, Costa Rica, Nicaragua, Honduras							
Northern America	n=2	492	246.0	485.0	242.5	1	Highest scoring sub-region
United States, Canada							
South America	n=12	1419	118.3	1350.5	112.5	5	
Chile, Brazil, Argentina, Colombia, Venezuela, Peru, Uruguay, Bolivia, Ecuador, Guyana, Paraguay, Suriname							
Americas	n=35	3455	98.7	3191.0	91.2	8	
Eastern Asia	n=5	674	134.8	561.0	112.2	20	
Republic of Korea, Japan, China, Mongolia, Democratic People's Republic of Korea							
South and Central Asia	n=14	1071.5	76.5	860.0	61.4	25	
India, Kazakhstan, Pakistan, Nepal, Bhutan, Kyrgyzstan, Sri Lanka, Maldives, Iran (Islamic Republic of), Uzbekistan, Afghanistan, Bangladesh, Tajikistan, Turkmenistan							
South and Eastern Asia	n=11	1124	102.2	1013.0	92.1	11	
Singapore, Philippines, Thailand, Malaysia, Indonesia, Brunei Darussalam, Cambodia, Viet Nam, Myanmar, Timor-Leste, Lao People's Democratic Republic							
Western Asia	n=17	1396	82.1	1079.0	63.5	29	
Israel, United Arab Emirates, Turkey, Cyprus, Jordan, Bahrain, Saudi Arabia, Lebanon, Qatar, Kuwait, Georgia, Azerbaijan, Oman, Armenia, Yemen, Syrian Arab Republic, Iraq							
Asia	n=47	4265.5	90.8	3513.0	74.7	22	
Eastern Europe	n=10	1321	132.1	1213.0	121.3	9	
Hungary, Romania, Czech Republic, Ukraine, Slovakia, Bulgaria, Poland, Belarus, Russian Federation, Republic of Moldova							
Northern Europe	n=10	1945	194.5	1792.0	179.2	9	
United Kingdom, Denmark, Sweden, Finland, Norway, Ireland, Estonia, Iceland, Lithuania, Latvia							
Southern Europe	n=13	1455.5	112.0	1194.0	91.8	22	
Malta, Italy, Slovenia, Greece, Serbia and Montenegro, Croatia, Portugal, T.F.Y.R. Macedonia, Spain, San Marino, Bosnia and Herzegovina, Andorra, Albania							
Western Europe	n=9	1310	145.6	1288.0	143.1	2	
Germany, Austria, Netherlands, Belgium, France, Switzerland, Luxembourg, Monaco, Liechtenstein							
Europe	n=42	6031.5	143.6	5487.0	130.6	10	Highest scoring region
Oceania	n=14	817.5	58.4	728.0	52.0	12	

Note: UN classification sub-regions Central Asia and South Asia are combined here for consistency purposes. Sub regional classification is revised, as of August 23, 2005, taken from the UN Statistics Division, http://unstats.un.org/unsd/methods/m49/m49regin.htm. Accessed September 16, 2005.

Figure 6.6.

Average e-government scores in Africa

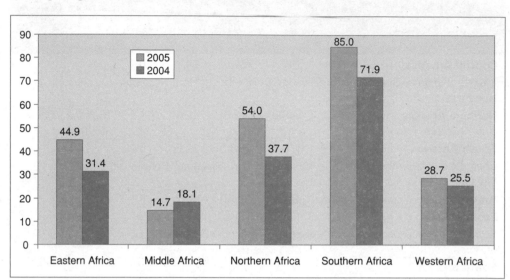

Europe and those in Africa and South Asia. Africa is the lowest scoring region. With an average score of 39.7, 53 countries of Africa have, collectively, a mere 16 per cent of the average access of two countries in Northern America. All sub-regions of Africa have low scores. "Middle Africa" (comprising Angola, Cameroon, Central African Republic, Chad, Congo, Democratic Republic of the Congo, Equatorial Guinea, Gabon, and São Tomé and Principe) has the lowest score of 14.1, or only about six per cent of the highest scoring sub-region of Northern America. This was also the only sub-region to have a lower score in 2005 compared to last year. As in 2004, the highest scoring sub-region in Africa—Southern Africa (home to Botswana, Lesotho, Namibia, South Africa and Swaziland)—was only 1.5 times higher than the Caribbean, the lowest scoring sub-region in the Americas, and only 10 per cent higher than South and Central Asia, the lowest scoring sub-region in Asia.

The region of South and Central Asia has done better in 2005 compared to last year. Bangladesh, Bhutan, India, the Islamic Republic of Iran, Kazakhstan, Kyrgyzstan, Maldives, Nepal, Pakistan, Sri Lanka, Tajikistan, Turkmenistan and Uzbekistan, as a whole, improved their average score by 25 per cent. As in 2004, however, the 1.5 billion people of this region had access to only about two thirds of the e-government services available to the least e-ready countries of Europe.

Telecommunication access-divide

Access to information technologies has become crucial to development. Technologies impact development by increasing the efficiency and competitiveness of the economy; enabling better service delivery to the citizens and creating new sources of income and opportunities.[21] Advancements in technology have opened up possibilities for improving living conditions. ICTs have created unprecedented opportunities for countries to leapfrog traditional modes of service delivery and make manifold improvements in process effectiveness and efficiency. Governments can now deliver better, more cost-effective services more speedily. Citizens, for their part, have been given chances to employ new forms of technology to absorb, deploy and utilize information and knowledge in their jobs, at home and in society. By bringing the activity *to the citizen* ICTs allow a unique opportunity for the development and empowerment of both individuals and societies.

> By bringing the activity to the citizen ICTs allow a unique opportunity for the development and empowerment of both individuals and societies.

The technological revolution has brought ICTs to much of the world and, on the whole, considerable progress has been made in recent years. Between 1991 and 2003 telephone lines doubled and the availability of personal computers grew five-fold. However as costs became affordable, the most revolutionizing progress was in the newer technologies such as mobile technology and the Internet. Compared to 12 years ago, 83 times as many people are now cellular telephone subscribers while the number of Internet users in the world has increased by a whopping 151 times! (See Figure 6.7.) Recently, developing regions have also speeded up their use of modern information technology. In the last few years there has been phenomenal growth in the use of the Internet in all regions of the world and especially in the developing regions. For example, from 2000 to 2005 Internet growth was the highest in the Middle East (312 per cent) and Africa (258 per cent).[22]

Notwithstanding progress made over the past decade, current technology data do not present a pretty picture of access for the average citizen of the world. As Table 6.3 shows, currently only around 20 per cent of the world's population has a telephone or a cell phone. Less than 15 per cent of the people are Internet users, while only one in 10 has a personal computer.

These disparities exist despite recent progress. Gini coefficients, which measure relative inequalities, compare cumulative shares of technology users and

Figure 6.7.
World growth in key ICTs 1991–2003

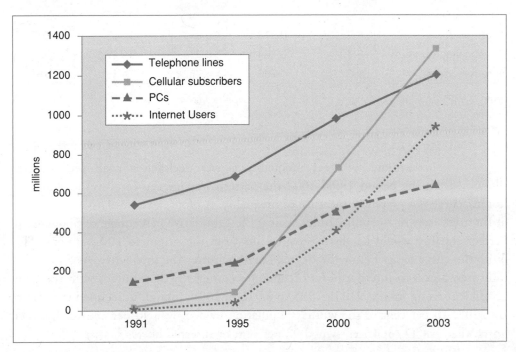

Table 6.3.
World Access to ICT

Millions	1991	1995	2002	2003	As % of world population in 2003
Telephone lines	546	689	983	1210	19
Cellular subscribers	16	91	740	1329	21
Personal computers	130	235	500	650	10
Internet users	4.4	40	399	938	15

Note: World population = 6420 million
Source: International Telecommunication Union, http://www.itu.int/ITU-D/ict/statistics/at_glance/KeyTelecom99.html, Accessed 25 August 2005. Internet usage and world population from Internet world stats. http://www.internetworldstats.com/stats.htm, Accessed 15 August 2005.

Existing distribution of ICTs is highly concentrated in a few countries of the world. This unequal distribution is particularly striking in the case of newer technologies, such as Internet hosts, than some of the traditional ones, such as telephone.

ICT hardware relative to the cumulative share of the world's population. Higher Gini coefficients imply higher inequality. Table 6.4 indicates that the existing distribution of ICTs is highly concentrated in a few countries. This unequal distribution is particularly striking in the case of newer technologies, such as Internet hosts, as compared to traditional ones such as the telephone. As can be seen in the table, the Gini coefficient for Internet hosts ranged from a high 0.910 in 1995 to 0.913 in 2002, indicating high inequality, compared to that for the telephone, which was 0.551 in 2002.

Table 6.4.
Worldwide inequality in the distribution of ICTs

	1995	1999	2000	2001	2002
Telephone mainlines	0.688	0.614	0.592	0.567	0.551
Mobile subscribers	0.822	0.735	0.703	0.655	0.609
Internet hosts	0.910	0.913	0.916	0.915	0.913
Personal computers	0.791	0.764	0.754	0.747	0.730
Internet users	0.871	0.786	0.757	0.735	0.761

Note: Numbers are Gini coefficients of relevant information technology.
Source: UNCTAD. *The Digital Divide: ICT Development Indices 2004*. P. 10.

Furthermore, whereas inequality slowly declined for all technologies shown during the period 1995–2002 the pattern was uneven for Internet hosts. A Lorenz curve is a graphical measure of inequality. It plots the cumulative percentage of Internet users in ascending order against the cumulative percentage of population. Perfect equality would be the 45-degree line from the origin to 100 per cent. The more the curve hangs below the degree line the greater the inequality. As Figure 6.8 indicates, access to Internet hosts became more unevenly distributed, with the Gini coefficient rising from 0.910 in 1995 to 0.916 in 2000, though it declined thereafter. By 2002, 10 per cent of the world's population owned over 90 per cent of Internet hosts; the OECD countries owned 93 per cent of Internet hosts.[23]

Figure 6.8.
Trends in the Lorenz curve for Internet Hosts, 1995–2002

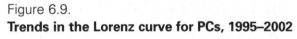

Source: UNCTAD. *ICT Development Indices 2004*. UNCTAD/ ITE/IPC/2005/4. P 13.

Further, these world aggregates hide wide disparities, which exist among different regions and countries of the world. Since many of the recent advances have been concentrated in the developed world, the disparities in traditional technologies have mapped onto the newer technologies, and especially the Internet, as evidenced by the fact that 81 per cent of some 1 billion Internet users in the world reside in only 20 countries.[24]

Figure 6.9.
Trends in the Lorenz curve for PCs, 1995–2002

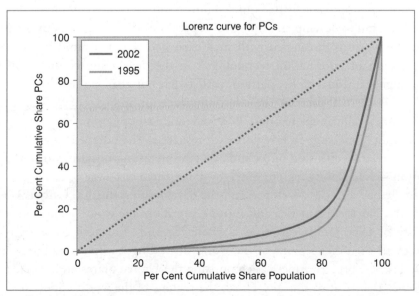

Source: UNCTAD. *ICT Development Indices 2004*. UNCTAD/ ITE/IPC/2005/4. P 14.

The inequality in technology is significant in the case of developing countries, where an inadequate telecommunication infrastructure and low Internet penetration have given rise to a huge telecommunication access-divide. Taken together low-income countries account for 40 per cent of the world's population and 11 per cent of the world's gross national income, yet comprise only two per cent of the world's Internet users.[25]

Two world regions in particular lag behind: South Asia and Africa. As Table 6.5 indicates, whereas Asia encompasses more than half of humanity only 8.9 per cent of its population uses the Internet. Of the entire population of Africa, only about two per cent uses the Internet compared to 68 per cent in North America, 37 per cent in Europe and around half in Oceania. (See Figure 6.7.) In fact, there are as many Internet users in Finland alone, with a population of five million, as there are in sub-Saharan Africa, with a population of 643 million.[26]

Two world regions in particular lag behind: South Asia and Africa.

Table 6.5.
Disparity in Internet usage

	As % of:		% of national
	World population	World users	population as Internet users
Africa	14.0	1.7	1.8
Asia	56.4	34.5	8.9
Europe	11.4	28.7	36.8
Middle East	4.1	2.3	8.3
North America	5.1	23.8	68.0
Latin America/Caribbean	8.5	7.3	12.5
Oceania	0.5	1.8	49.2

Source: Internet World Stats. http://www.internetworldstats.com/stats.htm Accessed 25 August 2005.

Despite rapid investments in and acquisition of information technologies in the developing countries in recent years the highly unequal global pattern of ICTs has not changed much.

The importance of ICTs in economic and social activity means that those countries that fail to develop technological capabilities risk being left out. At present, much of the world is threatened with such exclusion. Despite rapid investments in and acquisition of information technologies in the developing countries in recent years the highly unequal global pattern of ICTs has not changed much.

Figure 6.10 presents the telecommunication indices comprising Internet, TV, telephone, cellular telephones, PCs and online population for the regions.[27] Since the indices measure each region with respect to the other, they give an assessment of the relative diffusion of technology. An interesting insight into the telecommunication divide among regions emerges. First, there is a large telecommunication access-divide between the developed and the developing countries. Only two regions of the world, Northern America and Europe, are above the world average in terms of availability of telecommunication as a whole. Second, Northern America is far in advance of all the other regions of the world, including Europe. The telecommunication index of Northern America, comprising the United States and Canada, is 1.7 times higher than that of Europe. Third, the regions of the world appear to fall into

Figure 6.10.

Disparity in Internet use by region 2005

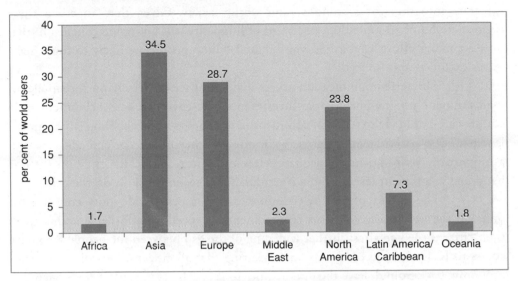

three categories. The first category is the two developed regions of Northern America and Europe, with high telecommunication services. Regions of South-Eastern Asia, the Caribbean, Western Asia, Oceania and South & Central America, together, comprise the second category, where ICT infrastructure level, though far below that of Northern America and Europe, will allow for some effective utilization of the ICTs. This group has telecommunication levels at 20–28 per cent those of Northern America. In the third category, comprising South and Central Asia and Africa, are the least e-ready regions. They have a gaping deficit in telecommunication infrastructure compared to the developed regions of the world. Both regions have a telecommunication infrastructure level that is five per cent that of Northern America! This kind

Figure 6.11.

Regional telecommunication indices 2005

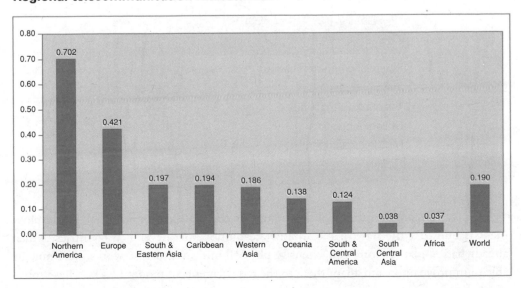

Large investments in e-government development by a country are not likely to result in commensurate benefits if the enabling environment is weak. For e-government initiatives to be effective they need to be embedded within a supporting environment of adequate telecommunication infrastructure on the one hand and a sufficient level of human resources and technical skills on the other.

The extent of this telecommunication access-divide puts considerable onus on the developing countries' governments to speed up affordable access to all their citizens so as to arrest further widening of the gap between the people who have access to ICTs and those who do not.

Inequalities in information and telecommunication technologies are mapped onto inequalities in e-government readiness.

of disparity is not going to be overtaken any time soon. Moreover, with newer technologies emerging at a rapid pace, it is also unlikely that these regions will be able to integrate into the world economy and world society. Given that, together, these regions are home to more than one third of humanity it is a forgone conclusion that unless a major effort is mounted more than 2 billion people are likely to find themselves excluded and isolated.

The telecommunication access-divide impacts adversely on the uptake of e-government programmes. Large investments in e-government development by a country are not likely to result in commensurate benefits if the enabling environment is weak. For e-government initiatives to be effective they need to be embedded within a supporting environment of adequate telecommunication infrastructure on the one hand and a sufficient level of human resources and technical skills on the other.

The extent of this telecommunication access-divide puts considerable onus on the developing countries' governments to speed up affordable access to all their citizens so as to arrest further widening of the gap between the people who have access to ICTs and those who do not. Ensuring that all citizens, regardless of socio-economic background, have the opportunity to access ICTs to exploit their talents to the fullest becomes a key challenge.

Further, inequalities in information and telecommunication technologies are mapped onto inequalities in e-government readiness. The correlation coefficients below indicate the relationship between the e-government websites and key technologies. A positive correlation exists when movements in one variable are associated with movements, in the same direction, in the other. As Table 6.6 indicates, the correlation coefficients for online population, Internet users and mobile telephone subscribers are high, indicating that generally a country's website development is positively linked to the levels of these key access indicators.

Table 6.6.

Correlation between web assessment and telecommunication indicators

Key access indicator	Correlation coefficient
Personal computers Index	0.6834
Internet users Index	0.7051
Telephone lines Index	0.6421
Online population	0.7460
Mobile subscribers	0.7267
TV sets	0.6408

Telecommunication infrastructure is the platform on which ICT development is built. At the start of the Internet revolution, the developed countries, which already had in place mature and extensive physical infrastructure networks, were quickly able to improve upon and adapt them to the requirements of modern ICTs. These coun-

Figure 6.12.

Interlinkages between telecommunication and e-government

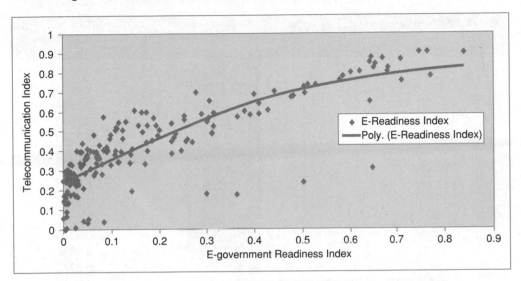

tries have since achieved high levels of e-readiness. Figure 6.12 shows the close relationship between greater e-government development and indicators of information and communication technologies. The bunching of countries in the left hand corner indicates a moderate level of telecommunication but not enough to provide access for all.

In a special focus on the least e-ready region in the world, Table 6.7 presents the relationship between telecommunication infrastructure and e-government readiness indices for 2005 for African countries. As stated before, all countries of Africa have a serious telecommunication deficit compared to the rest of the world. Whereas Mauritius and Seychelles are leaders in infrastructure availability and use, their infrastructural indices are only 25 per cent and 18 per cent, respectively, those of the United States and Canada taken together. Second, there is wide disparity within the region. Countries such as Mozambique, Uganda, Rwanda, Chad, Ethiopia, Malawi and Angola have levels of telecommunication that are a mere two-to-five per cent of the already low levels of Mauritius and Seychelles.

This grave lack of telecommunication infrastructure is the major impediment to e-readiness in the countries of the region. Of the 12 governments in the world that are still not online, more than half are in Africa. Most of those in the region that do have an online presence provide rudimentary services, evident in their low e-government readiness.

Inequalities in telecommunication access in Africa are the result of several factors. Poor electricity infrastructure is a key problem in many of the developing countries, especially in the rural or far-flung areas. Limited or erratic power distribution poses a barrier to the access and use of ICTs. In many instances this is compounded by the lack of an adequate road and rail network, needed to support a pervasive ICT infrastructure. Furthermore, many countries levy import taxes on computers and cell phones, treating them as luxury items and raising their costs beyond the reach of the majority of the populations.

Of the 12 governments in the world that are still not online, more than half are from Africa.

Table 6.7.

Telecommunication infrastructure and e-government in Africa 2005

	Country	Telecommunication Infrastructure Index	E-Readiness Index
1	Mauritius	0.1762	0.5317
2	South Africa	0.1234	0.5075
3	Seychelles	0.2343	0.4884
4	Botswana	0.0640	0.3978
5	Egypt	0.0717	0.3793
6	Swaziland	0.0456	0.3593
7	Namibia	0.0678	0.3411
8	Lesotho	0.0135	0.3373
9	Cape Verde	0.0808	0.3346
10	Zimbabwe	0.0395	0.3316
11	Tunisia	0.0993	0.3310
12	Kenya	0.0187	0.3298
13	Algeria	0.0365	0.3242
14	Uganda	0.0090	0.3081
15	United Republic of Tanzania	0.0110	0.3020
16	Gabon	0.0662	0.2928
17	Ghana	0.0214	0.2866
18	Congo	0.0119	0.2855
19	São Tomé and Principe	0.0797	0.2837
20	Malawi	0.0053	0.2794
21	Morocco	0.0637	0.2774
22	Nigeria	0.0143	0.2758
23	Madagascar	0.0075	0.2641
24	Rwanda	0.0035	0.2530
25	Cameroon	0.0139	0.2500
26	Mozambique	0.0057	0.2448
27	Djibouti	0.0211	0.2381
28	Sudan	0.0293	0.2370
29	Benin	0.0142	0.2309
30	Togo	0.0313	0.2274
31	Senegal	0.0275	0.2238
32	Comoros	0.0082	0.1974
33	Eritrea	0.0069	0.1849
34	Angola	0.0066	0.1840
35	Côte d'Ivoire	0.0223	0.1820
36	Gambia	0.0248	0.1736
37	Mauritania	0.0278	0.1723
38	Burundi	0.0043	0.1643
39	Sierra Leone	0.0056	0.1639
40	Chad	0.0023	0.1433
41	Guinea	0.0102	0.1396
42	Ethiopia	0.0027	0.1360
43	Burkina Faso	0.0060	0.1329
44	Mali	0.0060	0.0925
45	Niger	0.0069	0.0661
	Regional Average	0.0366	0.2642
	World Average	0.1898	0.4267

Figure 6.13.
Infrastructure indices for African countries

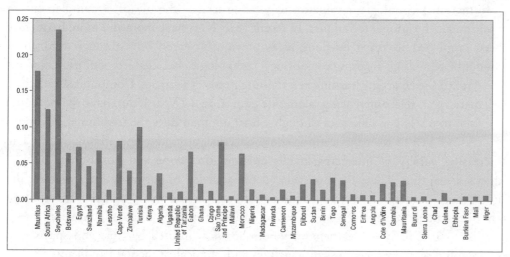

E-government readiness depends upon a combination of a country's economic, technological and human resource development. Weak access to ICT in Africa and other developing countries poses serious constraints on the empowerment of the people. Though many countries have undertaken privatization reforms and invested in telecommunication infrastructure, the long gestation periods of projects in this sector indicate that providing access to all will take time.

The following box presents a set of guidelines for consideration when devising pro-access ICT policies. They have been culled from various sources.

Formulating pro-access ICT policies: some thoughts to keep in mind[28]

- Governments should formulate effective strategies to facilitate a regulatory structure capable of managing a market economy, with competing firms involved in laying the telecommunications infrastructure. Regulatory bodies set up by the government can ensure fair competition among the competing firms to bring prices down and save scarce government funds in this regard.

- Wireless internet is a good mechanism for improving access and connectivity in remote areas. In areas of difficult terrain, connectivity can be achieved by providing wireless internet connectivity as low investment in equipment can be used to connect a very large area. Also, in some poor countries where copper and wire commodities are vulnerable to theft, wireless provides a tamper-proof solution.

- Governments can collaborate with other regional governments to bring down satellite technology rates. Collaboration between neighbouring states can bolster research and also reduce the costs of satellite technology.

- Internet kiosks can be set up and other telecommunication points opened in schools, local council halls and post offices to strengthen the telecommunications infrastructure.

Educational access-divide

Information technologies are increasingly being seen as the means of complementing traditional educational techniques. In recent years ICTs have more and more frequently been employed to reach far-flung areas previously served only through traditional modes of schooling. Incorporation of new technologies has enabled education systems to adapt to the emerging learning and training needs of societies. Computer simulation, telematics and teleconferencing, alongside educational TV or radio, have the potential to reach much larger audiences through e-learning than does the traditional classroom process, as well as to make learning more effective, attractive and stimulating.[29] The increasing variety of interactive media enlarges the scope and possibilities of self-directed learning. These tools provide an unparalleled opportunity for "reaching the unreached, particularly the 900 million illiterates in the world and the 130 million children unable to attend primary school, and for making lifelong education for all feasible, particularly for learners for whom access is limited by time and space, age, socio-cultural environment, work schedules and physical or mental handicaps."[30]

There is a positive link between high human capital and e-government readiness. With a higher level of education and skill the general populace is likely to have greater access to ICTs and be more likely to embrace modern ICTs quickly and efficiently. In turn, a populace skilled in the use of emerging technologies is more likely to adapt them towards greater gains of economic and social productivity. *A key benefit of ICTs is their ability to diffuse learning, information and knowledge more speedily, more widely and more deeply than ever before.*

However, at present there is wide variability worldwide in the literacy and education skills needed to operate these technologies. One of the three pillars of the e-government readiness index in the *UN Global E-government Survey* is the extent of human resource development in a country. As is shown in Figure 6.14, countries with a high education index are also countries with a higher level of e-government readiness. On the other hand, low levels of literacy and skill in a country are likely to impact adversely on its e-readiness as well. The average regional human capital indices for Africa and Oceania (as a whole) are around half those for North America and Europe. As can be seen, countries such as Burkina Faso and Chad will require a much greater effort to promote education if the benefits of ICTs are to be shared by all.

More than just literacy and primary education are required to master the technical skills needed to access and use ICTs. As more and more people around the world go online, traditional social science education is not sufficient for developing countries if they are to achieve effective integration within the digital world society. Whereas technical skills to access and use newer technologies can easily be imported online from the developed nations the ubiquitous nature of ICTs in education allows for the blending of local knowledge and cultures with modern science for adaptation to local use. In fact skills that allow for the use of ICTs within local indigenous processes are the conduit through which the benefits of ICTs will reach millions of hitherto disadvantaged populations.

In addition, one of the greatest opportunities the information technology revolution offers the world is to further develop the capabilities of the individual mind. This ability to expand capabilities is behind Amartya Sen's approach and

A key benefit of ICTs is their ability to diffuse learning, information and knowledge more speedily, more widely and more deeply than ever before.

Figure 6.14.

Education access-divide between countries

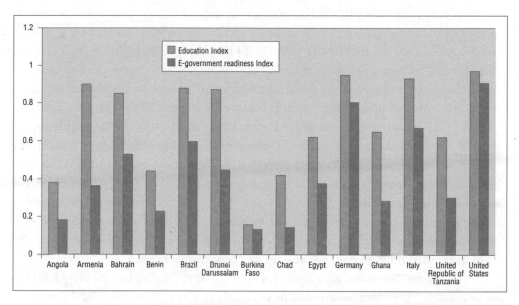

the building block of the Model of Socially Inclusive Governance. ICTs allow for the development of individual capabilities through the infinite medium of learning, doing and expanding knowledge. The opportunity ICTs offer is for learning individually and sharing collectively with millions around the world. This unique opportunity is the bedrock of innovation, progress and the future of development.

There is a need to invest in technical education, which allows for the building of skills as well as for promoting innovation in the use of ICTs.

Table 6.8 presents the interlinkages among knowledge, innovation, education and ICTs. The Knowledge Index (KI) is the average of the performance of a

Table 6.8.

Knowledge index, education and ICTs

Region/Group	KI	Innovation	Education	Information Infrastructure
G7	8.51	8.68	8.21	8.64
Western Europe	8.28	8.12	8.09	8.62
Europe and Central Asia	5.81	5.46	6.73	5.25
East Asia	5.25	5.31	4.96	5.48
Latin America	4.18	3.30	4.50	4.73
Middle East and North Africa	4.11	3.66	3.88	4.81
South Asia	1.98	2.51	2.10	1.34
Africa	1.69	1.70	1.51	1.87
World	4.91	4.86	4.91	4.96

KI (Knowledge Index) is the simple average of the performance of a region or country in three KI pillars: Education, Innovation and Information Communications & Technology.
Source: The World Bank. Knowledge Assessment Matrix (KAM) database.
http://info.worldbank.org/etools/kam2005/index.htm

One of the greatest opportunities the information technology revolution offers the world is to further develop the capabilities of the individual mind.

This unique opportunity is the bedrock of innovation, progress and the future of development.

There is a need to invest in technical education, which allows for the building of skills as well as for promoting innovation in the use of ICTs.

As expected, the knowledge index (KI) is the highest for the highly industrialized countries, comprising the G7 group (8.51), followed by Western Europe (8.28) and then Europe and Central Asia (5.81).

The extent of disparity between regions can be gauged by the fact that the G7 knowledge index is four times that of South Asia and Africa.

High per capita income countries have high human development index (HDI), higher public spending on education and more indigenous scientific and technical research. More schools are connected with the Internet in such economies.

region or country in education, innovation and ICT. Education includes indicators of literacy and enrolment, including secondary and tertiary enrolment, both of which are important in utilizing ICTs. The innovation index reflects "how well" the education system is being put to use. It includes indicators such as researchers in R&D, patent applications granted by the U.S. Patent and Trademark Office (USPTO), and scientific and technical journal articles, all of which combine to represent the level of innovation in an economy. Information infrastructure comprises telephone mainlines and mobile phones, plus computers and Internet users, per 10,000 population.

As expected, the knowledge index (KI) is the highest for the highly industrialized countries, comprising the G7 group (8.51), followed by Western Europe (8.28) and then Europe and Central Asia (5.81). The innovative use of ICTs in education and knowledge is dominated by the developed economies. Further, as in the case of the e-readiness index, South Asia and Africa bring in the rear. The extent of disparity between regions can be gauged by the fact that the G7 knowledge index is four times that of South Asia and Africa. Both of these regions are far below the world average at only 40 per cent and 34 per cent, respectively.

These disparities are further highlighted at the individual country level. As proxies, public spending as a per cent of GDP and the availability of Internet in schools both give an idea about the availability of financial resources and the extent of seriousness and commitment to education and knowledge. Table 6.9 presents key education and innovation indicators for selected developing and developed countries arranged in descending order of GDP per capita. The table shows the Human Development Index (HDI), which measures the level of literacy and education in a country; the scientific and technical research papers and patents granted by the U.S. Patent Office (USPTO) per million of population, which is a proxy measure of the relative innovation in a country; the public spending as a per cent of GDP; and the extent of Internet access in schools. A strikingly positive relationship appears with regard to income, education and innovation. High per capita income countries have high ranking on the HDI, higher public spending on education and more indigenous scientific and technical research. More schools are connected with the Internet in such economies. Most of the developed economies shown in the table score around six on "whether they have Internet in schools," indicating that it is "pervasive" (i.e., most children have frequent access). The converse is true as well. Lower per capita incomes are associated with lower human development, little original scientific and technical research and limited levels of Internet in schools.

Canada was the first country in the world to connect 100 per cent of its schools to the Internet, in 1999.[31] Since then many others, including Denmark, Iceland, Estonia and Japan have followed a similar path. A recent study of national e-strategies found that 88 per cent of the national ICT strategies had e-education as a focus area. The objective of the focus was e-literacy (i.e. basic computer and application skills such as using spreadsheets and surfing the Web) in the formal and informal education system across the primary, secondary, and tertiary institutions as well as adult/community training centres.[32] More importantly, the study found that income levels partly dictated the e-education priorities of countries.

It is true that lack of financial resources is always a constraint in the developing countries and a barrier to ICT diffusion in education, as in other sectors.

Table 6.9.
Indicators of education and innovation

		GDP per capita (Current PPP US$)	Human Development Index	Scientific and technical journal articles/ million pop	Patent applications granted by USPTO/ mill pop	Public spending as % of GDP	Internet access in schools
1	United States	37352	0.94	586.8	338.8	4.9	6.0
2	Denmark	31630	0.93	776.7	113.4	8.3	6.0
3	Netherlands	29412	0.94	660.6	96.8	4.8	5.7
4	Australia	29143	0.95	660.4	52.6	4.6	6.2
5	United Kingdom	27106	0.94	677.4	68.0	4.4	5.8
6	Singapore	24480	0.90	418.3	108.2	3.1	6.6
7	New Zealand	21177	0.93	623.3	41.2	6.6	5.7
8	United Arab Emirates	19429	0.82	41.9	—	1.9	—
9	Republic of Korea	17908	0.89	143.2	86.3	3.6	6.4
10	Czech Republic	16448	0.87	195.0	4.2	4.4	4.6
11	Hungary	14572	0.85	194.48	7.1	4.9	4.8
12	Estonia	13348	0.85	189.7	2.2	7.4	5.9
13	Saudi Arabia	12845	0.77	26.1	0.8	8.3	—
14	Latvia	9981	0.82	64.0	1.7	5.9	4.7
15	Mexico	9136	0.80	3.7	0.9	4.4	3.4
16	Iran (Islamic Republic of)	7145	0.73	5.5	0.0	5.0	—
17	Namibia	6375	0.61	7.6	0.0	8.1	3.8
18	China	4995	0.75	9.3	0.3	2.2	3.5
19	Philippines	4321	0.75	2.2	0.3	3.2	3.5
20	Egypt	3950	0.65	18.3	0.1	4.7	3.9
21	Cameroon	2069	0.50	4.2	—	3.2	1.6
22	Pakistan	1971	0.50	2.1	0.0	1.8	3.0
23	Bangladesh	1786	0.51	1.2	0.0	2.3	1.8
24	Yemen	889	0.48	0.6	0.0	10.0	—
25	Madagascar	808	0.47	—	0.0	2.5	1.5

Note: Figures are for the latest year available. GDP is for 2003; Human Development Index is for 2004; Internet access is based on the statistical score on a 1–7 scale of a large sample group in a particular country responding to the question of whether "Internet access in schools" in their country is (1 = very limited, 7 = pervasive—most children have frequent access).
Source: The World Bank. Knowledge Assessment Matrix (KAM) database.
http://info.worldbank.org/etools/kam2005/index.htm

However it is also true that in some countries the importance of the role of newer technologies in education and knowledge development is not fully recognized. On the other hand, the crucial nexus between ICTs and learning has become the platform of e-government strategies in the developed world. There, commitment to

The crucial nexus between ICTs and learning has become the platform of e-government strategies in the developed world.

Lack of education and technical skills widens the gap in economic and social opportunities, which stem from technology.

The education access-divide compounds all other access divides. Those with low levels of literacy and formal education are also most likely to be those with lack of computer and technical skills, setting in place a vicious cycle that perpetuates lack of capability, under development and poverty.

knowledge creation is evident by the devotion of financial capital to promoting public, private and individual learning. The disparity between the developed and the developing regions is evident in financial outlays for learning and research. For example, OECD economies invest nine times as much of their income in research and development and have about 17 times as many technicians and eight times as many scientists per capita as the economies of sub-Saharan Africa.[33]

Lack of education and technical skills widens the gap in economic and social opportunities, which stem from technology. Currently in most of the developing countries, a small group dominates the use of Internet and other ICTs—people with higher levels of educational attainment. For example, according to one estimate in Ethiopia, where 65 per cent of the adult population is illiterate, 98 per cent of Ethiopian Internet users had a university degree.[34]

The education access-divide compounds all other access divides. Those with low levels of literacy and formal education are also most likely to be those with lack of computer and technical skills, setting in place a vicious cycle that perpetuates lack of capability, under development and poverty. High levels of disparity in access and use of ICTs for learning within a country generate their own inequalities. Modern ICTs, especially computers, may worsen inequality since people with greater skills and education are also best able to use information technology.[35] Hence these newer technologies are likely to gravitate initially to those with the means and the skills. Further, in some countries "when a new technology is introduced into a social setting where scarce resources and opportunities are distributed asymmetrically those with more resources will employ them to gain additional ones, including ICTs."[36] The problem is compounded by the extent to which levels of human capital are much lower in many developing countries. These countries have fewer people with the capacity to work with and benefit from computers. The few who do are likely to benefit disproportionately from the information revolution. Meanwhile, the groups of disadvantaged individuals that have not had access even to basic levels of education are likely to be out of the race from the start.

In summary, the rapid integration of ICTs into education is exerting new demands and pressures on governments, which have yet to consolidate their education development programmes. A government that has inclusion as a goal will ensure that the immense potential benefits of ICT use in education are available to all.

The box on the next page presents a set of considerations when devising pro-access literacy and education policies. They have been culled from various sources.

Lack of access to relevant web language and content

In today's technology driven environment the importance of language has surpassed its being a tool for communication; it has become the means for opportunity and empowerment. The opportunity to use one's language on global information networks such as the Internet determines the extent to which he or she can participate in the emerging knowledge society.[37] At the same time, content adapted to the needs

Formulating pro-access literacy and education policies: some thoughts to keep in mind

- Universal literacy level is a problem facing many developing countries. The first step towards increasing access to ICTs is that governments should make *concerted efforts to increase the literacy levels.*
- *Capacity building should focus on teacher training.* Insofar as possible Internet access should be provided free to the schools to encourage more and more of them to incorporate e-education in their syllabuses.
- The government should *lift taxes on the import of computers for educational purposes.* Also, low fee training centres can be set up by governments to encourage more and more people to get computer training.
- Governments need to *pay extra attention to encourage women to join the ICT sector.* Promoting female literacy is an important aspect in this regard.

of various access groups such as women, disadvantaged, elderly, poor or those in the rural areas allows greater chances at learning and productivity. Relevant school curricula and information on health and agriculture are key instruments for ensuring greater access and socio-economic inclusion. Extracting full opportunities from a country's integration in the information society depends upon the development of an information infrastructure; the development of content that renders the information infrastructure an effective vehicle for change; and the distribution of content through programmes that promote universal access to the new technologies.

Information is one of the key reasons people log on to the Internet.[39] In the information age access to ICTs is the means to the end of greater information, better services and enhanced social interaction. Together these promote greater inclusion and well-being. In leading industrialized nations the Internet has become the first medium people turn to when seeking information. For example, a survey in the United States found that a large share of Internet users now say that they will begin by turning to the Internet when they next need information about health care or government services.[40] Half of all American adults have searched online for information on 16 health topics ranging from various diseases to smoking cessation strategies. Health information seekers go online to become informed, to prepare for appointments and surgery, to share data and to seek and provide support.[41]

However, at present two major barriers to seeking and accessing information exist. The first, the **language access-divide,** is created by the dominance of English as a main language of the WWW and the Internet. And the second, the **content access-divide,** stems from a scarcity of the type of information users want—the lack of relevant content on the Web for the user.

In the initial years of most Web development, content was written not only in the English language but with the advanced-language-skills user in mind. Furthermore, since most of the content has thus far been developed in the industrialized countries there is an inherent tilt towards western culture and values. The result

Content adapted to the needs of various access groups such as women, the disadvantaged, the elderly, the poor or those in the rural areas allows greater chances at learning and productivity

In the information age access to ICTs is the means to the end of greater information, better services and enhanced social interaction. Together these promote greater inclusion and well-being.

Two major barriers to seeking and accessing information exist. The first is the language access-divide, and the second is the content access-divide.

is a Web environment heavily tilted in favour of the English-speaking user with advanced educational skills in the developed world. In other words, the huge disparity in access to the WWW and the Internet spills over into the content in terms of the number of websites in developing countries, the amount of local language content and the use of online content by key sectors.[42] To compound the disparity, the majority of ICT and technical courses, books and manuals are also written in English.

As Figure 6.15 presents, there are a total of around 508 million native English speakers in the world and more than 10 times more (5.82 billion) English speakers whose mother tongue is not English.[43] English is native to only eight countries: the United States, the United Kingdom, Ireland, Canada, Australia, New Zealand, South Africa and the Philippines; and is used online in India. It is not widely understood in Japan, Germany, China, the Southern European countries or South and Central America. With the WWW content predominantly in English, the non-English speaking population (10 times greater than the number of native English speakers) that currently is not online either has to learn English or be excluded from the myriad of information on the Web.

With the WWW content predominantly in English, the non-English speaking population (10 times greater than the number of native English speakers) that currently is not online either has to learn English or be excluded from the myriad of information on the Web.

Figure 6.15.
English language domination

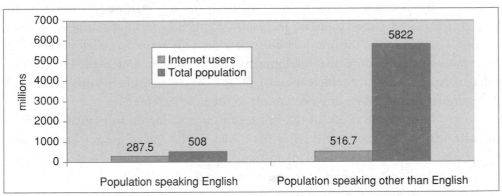

Source: Global Reach. http://global-reach.biz/globstats/index.php3

The English language is also the predominant choice of e-government worldwide. In 2003, the *UN Global e-government Survey* reported that English was available to some extent on 125 websites out of 173, either as the default site language or in addition to the native language. The 2004 survey re-affirmed the prevalence of English, with 128 out of the 175 country sites having some English content. Continuing the trend, this year's update found some content translated into—or by default in—English on 132 of the 177 national sites. In other words, 75 per cent of the national sites of all Member States have some English language content.

It is notable that as additional countries come online with a national site even more nations choose to provide site content in English. Specifically, the 2004 survey found two further countries online but three more offering English; likewise, this year two more countries appeared with a national site but four more offered some form of English. *Therefore, the establishment of English content outpaces national site presence growth.*

Table 6.10.

English language domination on national government websites

	National sites in English	Other native language country websites with English as:			
		Heavy	**Medium**	**Light**	**No English**
TOTAL	65	39	25	3	45
Per cent	37	22	14	2	25
Total number of countries with some English: 132					
Total number of countries with national sites surveyed: 177					

Heavy = 75–100 per cent of content in English; Medium = 25–74 per cent of the content in English; Light = below 25 per cent of the content in English.

Additionally, as last year, the amount of content being offered in English was assessed. Out of the 177 countries with national websites surveyed, 65 countries had English as the primary site language. Another 39 had "heavy" English language content, meaning that they offered approximately 75–100 per cent of native language content in English as well. Another 25 countries provided "medium" content in English, or roughly 25 to 75 per cent, while three countries had "light" English usage, i.e., below 25 per cent of site content (Table 6.10). Two countries, Oman and Syria, do not have a national site per se and were not included in this language assessment. It is notable though, that both have ministries that offer English in addition to Arabic.

Figure 6.16 and Table 6.11 present the number of English language websites by regions of the world. Except for those in Latin America and some regions of

Figure 6.16.

Websites with English language content

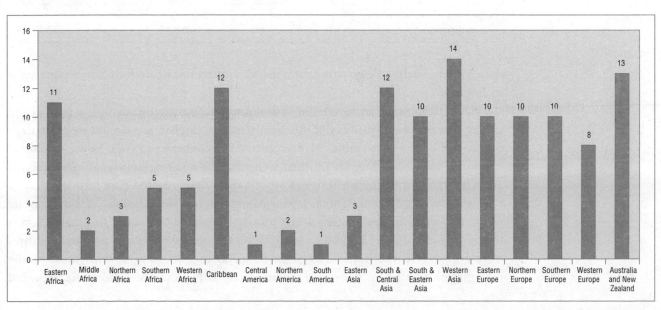

Table 6.11.

Regional classification of sites with any English language content

	Total number of countries with National Sites	Sites with any English	
		Number	Per cent
Africa (all)	**45**	**26**	**58**
Eastern Africa	15	11	73
Middle Africa	6	2	33
Northern Africa	5	3	60
Southern Africa	5	5	100
Western Africa	14	5	36
Americas (all)	**34**	**16**	**47**
Caribbean	12	12	100
Central America	8	1	13
Northern America	2	2	100
South America	12	1	8
Asia (all)	**43**	**39**	**91**
Eastern Asia	4	3	75
South and Central Asia	13	12	92
South and Eastern Asia	11	10	91
Western Asia	15	14	93
Europe (all)	**42**	**38**	**90**
Eastern Europe	10	10	100
Northern Europe	10	10	100
Southern Europe	13	10	77
Western Europe	9	8	89
Australia and New Zealand	13	13	100
Total national sites with any English	177	132	75

Africa the majority of e-government websites around the world have a heavy presence in English.

Among other factors, historical and cultural traditions play a part in the choice of web language. Many of the countries have English as a default web language on official sites. For example, 91 per cent of the countries in Asia, home to half of mankind, have *some* English on their websites while the default language of South and Central Asia is English. On the other hand, disaggregated data indicate that in Eastern Asia, comprising China, Japan, Mongolia and the Republic of Korea, none of the national sites use English as the primary language. However, to provide access to the vast majority of English-speaking Internet users worldwide, national websites were available in the English language either as mirror pages or with most of the information carried on the native language pages. For example, Mongolia provided heavy English content on its sites. Much the same was the case in Western Asia (comprised of Armenia, Azerbaijan, Bahrain, Cyprus, Georgia, Iraq, Israel, Jordan, Kuwait, Lebanon, Oman, Qatar, Saudi Arabia, Syrian Arab Republic, Turkey, United Arab Emirates and Yemen). While Kuwait and Turkey had no English on its various websites, Armenia, Azerbaijan, Bahrain and Cyprus had a heavy English presence.

Policies of social inclusion need to take into account the present disparities for a computer literate-online-native user who cannot benefit from the vast amount of information his/her government has put out in English, the government's preferred choice of online communication.

The overwhelmingly western content on the WWW is likely to pose additional barriers to the average person in a developing country who is likely to want to surf the Web in his/her own language. At present large populations around the world such as in India and China do not have the opportunity to access the Web, primarily due to lack of relevant language and content. Table 6.12 indicates that 68.4 per cent of the current web content is in English—a language spoken by 5.4 per cent of the world population. On the other hand, the content in Chinese is only about 3.9 per cent while the language is spoken by around 20 per cent of the world's population. Even though native Chinese is among the most widely spoken languages it does not have a significant share of web content, denying *de facto* access to millions.

With negligible content in one's own language an average user is unlikely to find much of interest online. Many surveys find that while users worldwide may

Policies of social inclusion need to take into account the present disparities for a computer literate-online-native user who cannot benefit from the vast amount of information his/her government has put out in English, the government's preferred choice of online communication.

The overwhelmingly western content on the WWW is likely to pose additional barriers to the average person in a developing country who is likely to want to surf the Web in his/her own language.

Table 6.12.

Content access-divide

	% of world population with primary language	% of web content written in each language
English	5.4	68.4
Non-English	94.6	32.6
Chinese	19.0	3.9
Hindi	5.8	—
Spanish	5.7	2.4
Arabic	4.6	—
Portuguese	2.8	1.4
Russian	2.6	1.9
Japanese	1.9	5.9
German	1.6	5.8
French	1.2	3.0
Turkish	1.0	—
Korean	0.7	1.3
Ukrainian	0.5	—

Source: Content data from *Global Reach*, http://global-reach.biz/globstats/refs.php3. Accessed 17 October 2005. Data on No. of speakers in each language from *Ethnologue*, http://www.ethnologue.com/country_index.asp.

Many surveys find that users worldwide may be conversant in English, but their interest in using the Internet is primarily in their own language.

be conversant in English, they are primarily interested in using the Internet in their own language. In an attempt to measure this interest, an online survey conducted by the ITU in May 2004 found that 53 per cent of those responding said that encouraging the development of content and technical conditions to facilitate the presence and use of all world languages on the Internet was very important.[44] However, at present the necessary tools are available in few languages, e.g., word-processors, spell-checkers, internet browsers and IT manuals. Thus, thousands of world languages remain absent from the Internet, denying millions the access and inclusion they need to become part of the information society. There is a danger that an Internet culture will develop in which people either come to accept it as natural to use a language other than their native one when using the Internet, or feel excluded because of their lack of fluency in another language.[45]

One rough measure representative of this exclusion in the everyday life of an average user can be gauged by checking the extent of web page availability on Google. A sample test was performed using a wild card (*) on Google to yield the number of documents in several languages, including English. As of 14 October 2005, there were 4.59 billion web pages on Google in English, 12.6 million in Arabic (or 0.3 per cent of English pages), 87.1 million in Chinese (or 2 per cent of English) and 1.25 million in Portuguese (or 0.02 per cent of English). A comparative assessment of the online population, number of native speakers and number of web pages available on Google for English, Arabic, Chinese and Portuguese, given in Figures 6.17 to 6.20, indicates the extent of disparity in online language resources among these four languages. This is indicative of the exclusion faced by the majority of non-English speaking users.

Figure 6.17.
English language domination

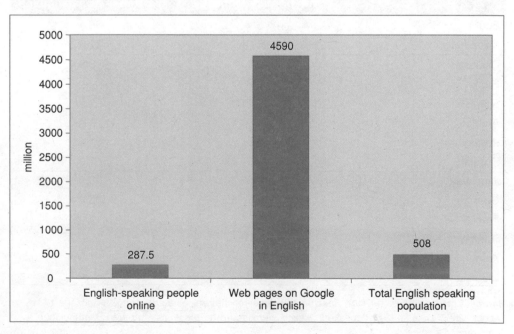

Figure 6.18.
Arabic language disparity

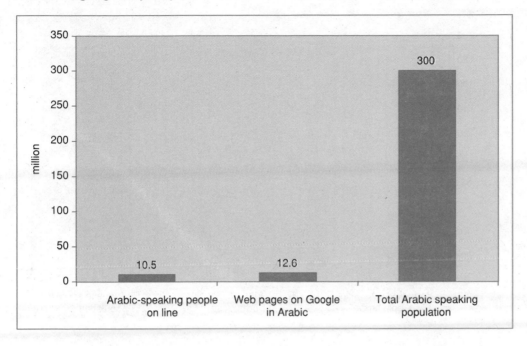

Content access-divide poses issues of exclusion. Lack of local language and content is consistently cited as a major constraint to usage in many countries. Moreover, with language domination, content and culture bias follow.

Figure 6.19.
Chinese language disparity

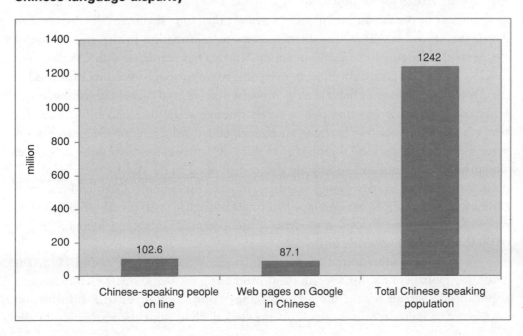

Figure 6.20.

Portuguese language disparity

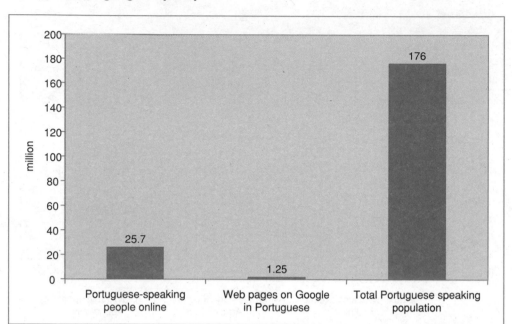

Many governments have taken note of the importance of language accessibility in the use of ICTs and are taking steps to develop websites, on-line news and local government information in local languages. In a bid to promote access many are following a two-pronged approach. On the one hand, given the predominance of English content on the WWW they are promoting English in schools nationally. On the other, they are investing in the development of local language content. For example, the Government of Azerbaijan has initiated a project that aims at content development in Azeri, the official language. To enhance access to information in the digitization of the Armenian language, the Government of Armenia has partnered with UNESCO to develop a Unicode-compatible font to overcome some current constraints in the use of the Armenian language in fields such as modern printing and digital publishing. Some other countries are promoting public access through telecentres and info. shops for two-way communication in far-flung areas. Such efforts will both provide greater information and encourage local solutions to making ICT-driven products more accessible. The private sector and civil society are also contributing to the development of appropriate content in many developing countries. In India for example, Chennai Interactive Business Services (CIBS) has developed an English-language web portal offering a wide range of local content directed at residents of and potential visitors to Chennai.[46] A few of these approaches are given in Box 26.

Among other initiatives worldwide, the World Summit Award (WSA) is an online global contest for selecting and promoting the world's best e-contents and applications. Set up within the ambit of the World Summit on the Information Society (WSIS), it sees the bridging of the digital divide and the narrowing of the

Box 26. Promoting web content in developing countries

Web Language development in Azerbaijan

The Government of Azerbaijan, with partners, has initiated the "Internet Access and Infrastructure Development for Research, Educational and Civil Society Development Purposes" project for ICT training and development. A key component of the project is content development in Azeri, the official language. A number of projects will be started under this umbrella:

An Internet Start-Up Kit. It aims to help individuals and organization create and publish Azerbaijani content on the Net. The list of its websites can be found at http://www.osi-az.org/links.shtml.

AzerWeb, Azerbaijan's largest NGO portal. Its main goal is to give NGOs the ability to publish information about their activities on a daily basis. More than 300 local and international organizations are registered on AzerWeb, which is functioning successfully and has become one of the most popular and visited sites for local and foreign non-governmental organizations.

Web content projects, such as www.saznet.org—Azerbaijan, a Web resources directory; www.webmail.aznet.org, a free mail server for IRTC users; and www.forum.aznet.org. The Web Content Development project aims to provide free hosting for NGOs and humanitarian content. It offers 30 MB of free space and an e-mail account, as well as free access to a Web Laboratory equipped with equipment and software to further encourage web content development.

Localization projects. Two projects, Azerbaijan Font Converter, http://convert.aznet.org, and Azerbaijan Language on the Net, http://www.azlang.info, have been established to help local webmasters to use the Azerbaijani language.

Source: http://www.aznet.org/content/index.html.

Promoting local content in India

The Chennai Interactive Business Services (CIBS) has developed an English-language web portal offering a wide range of local content directed at residents of and potential visitors to Chennai, India (formerly known as Madras). The expansive portal receives over 10,000 visitors daily and provides information on everything from recipes to railway reservations, links to government agencies and lists of government tenders. http://www.chennaionline.com/

CIBS also has what it calls the only Tamil language e-zine, covering a variety of different issues, and appealing primarily to the dispersed Tamil Diaspora. It uses technology to support the perseverance of this ancient language and maintain ties with community members long since emigrated. http://www.aaraamthinai.com/

Source: http://cyber.law.harvard.edu/readiness guide/examples.html.

Development of Armenian Unicode System

Together with UNESCO, the Matenadaran Institute in Yerevan, Armenia, has launched a project to enhance access to information in the digital environment for the Armenian language. Started in 2004, the project aims at developing a Unicode

---

Box 26 *(continued)*

compatible font to overcome some current constraints in the use of the Armenian language in fields such as modern printing and digital publishing.

At present there are many Armenian fonts that use non-standard encoding systems, which can make information exchange between users, such as e-mail, unreliable. Many of the available fonts have only limited styles and do not offer the possibility of recreating the rich detailed design features of the language, such as can be seen in older, traditional Armenian manuscripts. This poses certain challenges and limitations for publishers and contemporary digital graphic artists. The project will seek to address aesthetic, legal and standardization issues. Training will be provided for local font designers.

Today, some 3 million inhabitants of Armenia use the Armenian language. There is also a culturally aware Armenian Diaspora of around 4 million persons, many of whom still write and speak Armenian. It is expected that this initiative will facilitate online information exchanges and content creation in Armenian and contribute to the preservation and promotion of the Armenian culture in the digital environment.

El Salvador: Inclusion and content

Asociación Infocentros [AI] contributes to the development of El Salvador by enabling people's access to Internet technologies and by facilitating content generation and publication. http://www.infocentros.org.sv/nai/

The Web Portal, Infocentros.org.sv, has a modular design and its structure allows for the decentralized generation of content in different categories, such as local information, themes, communities and specialties. Members in 40 Infocentros and Telecentres nationwide generate and feed contents into the portal. In this way, local knowledge from around the region is shared easily.

Content creation in Singapore

To address the diversity of cultures in Singapore, a variety of government-sanctioned Internet-related projects have been created. Specifically, the Chinese, Tamil and Malay communities have created Internet portals that promote the use of these native languages in cyberspace. The key objective for each of the initiatives is to promote the creation and use of content for their respective communities.

Ameliorating content barriers in Thailand

With a penetration rate of just 29 per cent—limited to the most affluent Thais—Internet penetration in Thailand has not yet reached critical mass. The key barrier facing most potential Internet and ICT users in the country is the lack of Thai-centric content. To address this problem and help spur interest in the Internet, companies such as Microsoft, Terra Lycos and M-Web have begun initiatives to incorporate Thai into their programme and portal designs. M-Web in particular, by purchasing the most popular Thai portal, Sanook.com, intends to incorporate Thai content on its websites and browser software. Improving knowledge of the English language may also be a means for the government to increase accessibility.

Source: http://www.itu.int/osg/spu/wsis-themes/ict_stories/Themes/Content.html.

Source: http://www.wsis-award.org/index.php?folder=57.

For more information: see http://www.itu.int/ITUD/ict/cs/singapore/material/Singapore.pdf.

For more information: see http://www.itu.int/ITUD/ict/cs/thailand/material/THA%20CS.pdf.

content gap as its overall goal. It focuses on projects that help people develop the contents and applications they need to live a better life. Today it comprises representatives in 168 countries on each continent. Putting its focus on cultural identity and diversity, the WSA has developed a set of simple guidelines for e-content development, presented in Box 27.

Box 27. WSA guidelines for e-content and applications

1. Quality and comprehensiveness of content.

2. Ease of use: functionality, navigation and orientation.

3. Value added through interactivity and multimedia.

4. Quality of design (aesthetic value of graphics/music or sounds).

5. Quality of craftsmanship (technical realization).

6. Strategic importance for the global development of the Information Society.

7. Accessibility according to the W3C, (http://www.w3.org).

Source: http://www.wsis-award.org/index.php?folder=262.

Policies for social inclusion also need to be geared towards bridging the gap stemming from language and content inaccessibility. To make cyberspace more attractive for indigenous populations it has to be tailored to local needs, since the content on the website is one of the key factors that draw people. It is also important because targeted information helps in increasing productivity and efficiency. E-government and e-inclusion programmes need to take into account the potential benefits from, and opportunities for, the average citizen from promoting and developing language and indigenous content useful for the millions who are currently outside the ambit of access.

The following box presents a set of thoughts for consideration for language and content promoting policies and programmes.

Policies for social inclusion also need to be geared towards bridging the gap stemming from language and content inaccessibility.

Policies to promote indigenous language and content

- Governments need to ensure that *there is adequate awareness among the policy makers about the need to develop indigenous online local content and language capability.*

- *Capacity building and training for development of local content should be encouraged.*

- *To increase users' accessibility and capture the interest of the public,* governments should tailor the content of the websites to incorporate the demands of the indigenous people.

- The government should *encourage innovations in the local IT* sector so that software programming can take place within a country.

- *Greater policy coordination and coherence is required for the development of local content approaches at the community level.*

Gender access-divide

Information technology is a tool for providing access for all. But for women, who are often in the economically insecure, marginalized groups, it can be an especially potent tool for economic and social advancement. *Promoting gender access and inclusion to ICTs should be considered primarily an issue of opportunity since ICTs can help women enhance economic and social empowerment and achieve greater political participation.*

But who is the typical Internet user in the developing world? He is male, under 35 years of age, urban-based, speaks English and has a university education and a high income: he is a member of an elite minority.[47]

This perpetuates the existing lack of opportunities for women, which stems from their lesser endowment of income, education, skills and social equality, as well as other biases prevalent in the society. In many countries these biases are long-standing and structural. They often spill over into the ICT sector as women's access to and use of new technologies may not be promoted, given their stereotypical roles. The challenges to women's access to ICTs in many developing countries stem from such factors as lack of education, lack of income, social attitudes towards female usage of technology, women having to balance their roles of mother and worker, and lack of Internet content relative to women's needs. Ultimately this leads to lesser life chances and opportunities for the economic and social empowerment of women. "The intersection of gendered social relationships, gender discrimination and gender-blind ICT policy processes (those that do not specifically take into account different effects on women and men) undermine women's access to opportunities in the emerging information society and also diminish the potential of ICT to be an effective tool for the promotion of gender equality."[48] Box 28 gives some of the major causes of the lack of gender access to ICTs.

Box 28. Lack of gender access to ICTs derives from:

- lack of literacy and education among women compared to men;
- lesser ability and opportunity to use ICTs;
- social attitudes prevalent in many countries, which prevent girls from attaining education in science and mathematics;
- uneven and unaffordable access to ICT facilities and services;
- inadequate provision of relevant content and applications;
- lack of purchasing power to adopt new technologies;
- lack of gender awareness on the part of ICT decision-makers.

At present there is a gender divide in the access and use of ICTs around the world. For example, in Latin America only 38 per cent of Internet users with a computer are women. In Africa women users make up an even lesser proportion of the total population of Internet users. In Zambia, 36 per cent of the users are female, while in Senegal and Ethiopia women comprise 17 per cent and 14 per cent of the users, respectively.[49]

The Republic of Korea's Ministry of Gender Equality has assessed the extent of the gender digital divide between men and women. The Index of Women's Informatization (defined as the process by which information technologies have transformed economy and society) measured the impact of ICTs in terms of *awareness, access, utilization, skill* and *effects* on both men and women. Although women scored high on awareness, skills and effect, in terms of access and usage the situation of women was particularly deficient, with women having a gap of 22.9 per cent in "access" and 28.2 per cent in "use" of ICTs as compared to men (Table 6.13).

Table 6.13.

Digital divide between men and women

	Awareness	Access	Use	Capacity	Effects
Men	100.0	100.0	100.0	100.0	100.0
Women	95.8	77.1	71.8	97.3	95.9

Source: United Nations Division for the Advancement of Women (DAW), International Telecommunication Union (ITU), UN ICT Task Force Secretariat. *Information and Communication Technologies and their Impact on and use as an Instrument for the Advancement and Empowerment of Women.* Report of the Expert Group Meeting. Seoul, Republic of Korea, 11–14 November 2002, http://www.un.org/women watch/daw/egm/ict2002/reports/EGMFinalReport.pdf. P. 54. Accessed 10 October 2005.

Women make up 50 per cent or more of the world's population. However, benefits and opportunities accorded to women remain at less than their full share. *Inclusive governance requires that the gender-divide be addressed through cross-cutting approaches that take into account a nation's economic, social and cultural factors.* Digital illiteracy affects many women, including those belonging to affluent backgrounds, in most developing countries. Lack of inclusion in ICT and educational approaches is further widening women's life chances.

This Report takes the approach that *the key factor affecting women's life chances is a lack of adequate attention to the important interlinkages among women's education, access to ICTs and development.*

Women encounter disadvantages in access to ICT and education at all levels. For example, two out of three of the 110 million children in the world who do not attend school are girls and there are 42 million fewer girls than boys in primary school.[50]

There are gross gender disparities in education and ICT measures across the countries of the world. Most women in developing countries have little access to technologies. Table 6.14 shows key gender and ICT statistics for developed and developing countries. Whereas a direct causal link between gender and ICT is difficult to prove, it is certain that most developing countries are far behind the developed economies. Women as Internet users in the developing countries form a relatively small proportion of the total population compared to female users in the developed countries. For example, of the more than two thirds to three fourths of the population online in countries such as Iceland, the United States, Canada, Sweden and Australia, women make up around 50 per cent. On the other hand, in many developing countries, such as Brazil and Mexico, to begin with, only 12.3 per cent

Inclusive governance requires that gender-divide be addressed through cross-cutting approaches which take into account economic, social and cultural factors in a nation.

The key factor affecting women's life chances is a lack of adequate attention to the important interlinkages among women's education, access to ICTs and development.

Table 6.14.

Key gender and ICT indicators

	Women as % of Internet users	Internet users as % of total population	Female professionals & technical workers as % of total	Female literacy rate %
United States	51.1	68.6	55.0	99.0
Canada	51.0	63.8	54.0	99.0
Philippines	51.0	0.6	65.1	94.3
South Africa	51.0	9.9	46.7	83.2
Iceland	49.0	76.5	55.0	99.0
Thailand	49.0	12.8	52.0	92.8
Australia	48.0	68.2	55.0	99.0
Sweden	48.0	73.6	51.0	99.0
Chile	47.0	36.1	52.0	95.6
Brazil	42.0	12.3	62.0	88.6
Mexico	42.0	14.3	40.0	88.7
Croatia	42.0	29.2	52.0	97.1
Estonia	38.0	49.8	69.0	99.6
Russia	38.0	15.5	64.0	99.2
Zambia	37.5	2.1	31.9[a]	59.7
Uganda	31.5	0.7	—	59.2
China	30.4	7.9	45.1[a]	86.5
India	23.0	3.6	20.5[a]	47.8
Poland	18.7	27.8	61.0	99.7
Belarus	17.5	16.4	38.4[a]	99.4
Ethiopia	13.9	0.2	—	33.8
Czech Republic	12.0	46.9	52.0	99[a]
Slovakia	12.0	42.3	61.0	99.0
Senegal	12.0	4.5	—	29.2
Lithuania	10.0	28.2	70.0	99.6
Jordan	6.0	1.8	—	84.7

Note: a) = from LearnLink

Source: Nancy Hafkin and Nancy Taggart. *Gender, Information Technology and Developing Countries: an Analytical Study.* Learn Link http://learnlink.aed.org/Publications/Gender_Book/Home.htm. Accessed 12 February 2006.

Data on Internet users as per cent of total from Internet World Stats http://www.internetworld stats.com/stats.htm. Accessed 12 February 2006.

Data on female professional workers and literacy from UNDP *Human Development Report* http://hdr.undp.org/statistics/data/indicators.cfm?x=241&y=1&z=1. Accessed 12 February 2006.

and 14.3 per cent of the population, respectively, uses the Internet and women make up less than half of this small minority. In Jordan, 1.8 per cent of the total population uses the Internet of which women constitute a mere six per cent. These variations of female Internet use are shown in Figure 6.21.

Figure 6.21.

Women as percentage of Internet users, selected countries

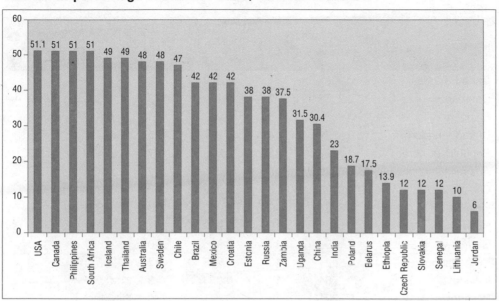

A major part of the problem is the lack of female education. Whereas all developed countries and many developing countries have universal female literacy there are still a number of developing countries where women's education is left behind. For example, as is shown in Table 6.14, India has an overall female literacy rate of 47.8 per cent and only 3.6 per cent of the total population uses the Internet, of which 23 per cent are women. This implies that only 1.8 per cent of all women in India are online. Similarly, Senegal has a 29.2 per cent literacy rate for women and 4.5 per cent of its population uses the Internet, of which 12 per cent are women. This implies that only 1.0 per cent of Senegal's female population are Internet users.

Research has indicated that there is a direct link between female literacy and a country's economic growth. Attainment of secondary education by females tends to lead to higher growth rates.[51] Lower access to education means lesser employment opportunities. In countries where women do not become a part of the labour force, productivity falls and consequently GNP is adversely affected. Thus a vicious circle is created in which lower access to female education leads to a lower standard of living and feeds into fewer socio-economic resources.

Table 6.15 presents the relationship between e-government readiness and gender development. The Gender Development Index (GDI) of the UNDP is a composite index reflecting a long and healthy life, as measured by life expectancy at birth; knowledge, as measured by the adult literacy rate and the combined primary, secondary and tertiary gross enrolment ratio; and a decent standard of living, as measured by estimated earned income (PPP US$).[52] The index is gender-sensitive inasmuch as it has been adjusted to reflect gender inequalities in the three dimensions.

Generally countries with high e-readiness are also countries which have ensured equality of opportunity for women, as can be seen in highly developed economies such as those of Norway, Sweden and Australia, in which the global e-government leaders also have higher levels of gender equality and gender development. On the other hand, in countries such as Estonia and Malta middle level

Generally countries with high e-readiness are also countries which have ensured equality of opportunity for women.

Table 6.15.

Interlinkages among gender, development and ICTs

	E-government Index		Gender Development Index		Gender Empowerment Index	
	Index	Rank	GDI	Rank	GEM	Rank
United States	0.9062	1	0.942	8	0.793	12
Denmark	0.9058	2	0.938	13	0.860	2
Sweden	0.8983	3	0.947	4	0.852	3
United Kingdom	0.8777	4	0.937	15	0.716	18
Republic of Korea	0.8727	5	0.896	27	0.479	59
Australia	0.8679	6	0.954	2	0.826	7
Canada	0.8425	8	0.946	5	0.807	10
Finland	0.8231	9	0.940	10	0.833	5
Norway	0.8228	10	0.960	1	0.928	1
Germany	0.8050	11	0.926	20	0.813	9
Netherlands	0.8021	12	0.939	12	0.814	8
Iceland	0.7794	15	0.953	3	0.834	4
Belgium	0.7381	18	0.941	9	0.828	6
Estonia	0.7347	19	0.852	35	0.595	35
Malta	0.7012	21	0.858	32	0.486	58
Chile	0.6963	22	0.846	38	0.475	61
Israel	0.6903	24	0.911	23	0.622	24
Mexico	0.6061	31	0.804	46	0.583	38
Latvia	0.6050	32	0.834	43	0.606	28
Slovakia	0.5887	36	0.847	37	0.597	33
Poland	0.5872	38	0.856	33	0.612	27
Uruguay	0.5387	49	0.836	42	0.504	50
Colombia	0.5221	54	0.780	55	0.500	52
Venezuela	0.5161	55	0.765	58	0.441	64
Peru	0.5089	56	0.745	67	0.511	48
Turkey	0.4960	60	0.742	70	0.285	76
El Salvador	0.4225	78	0.715	80	0.467	62
Saudi Arabia	0.4105	80	0.749	65	0.253	78
Botswana	0.3978	90	0.559	100	0.505	49
Iran (Islamic Republic of)	0.3813	98	0.719	78	0.316	75
Swaziland	0.3593	108	0.485	115	0.492	54
Republic of Moldova	0.3459	109	0.668	91	0.494	53
Namibia	0.3411	111	0.621	96	0.603	31
United Republic of Tanzania	0.3020	127	0.414	127	0.538	42
Cambodia	0.2989	128	0.567	99	0.364	73
Pakistan	0.2836	136	0.508	107	0.379	71
Yemen	0.2125	154	0.448	121	0.123	80
Bangladesh	0.1762	162	0.514	105	0.218	79

e-readiness is accompanied by a mid range ranking on gender development. Estonia is ranked 35th and Malta 32nd on the GDI.

Figure 6.22.

Female representation in professional and technical jobs, selected countries

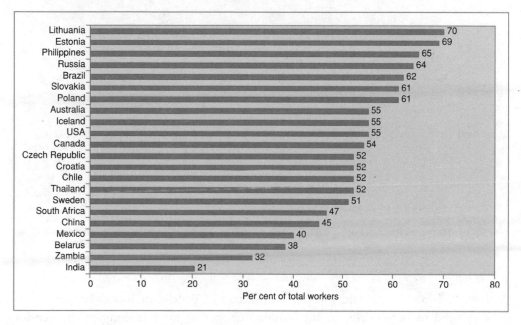

Per cent of total workers

There also appears to be a positive correlation between e-government readiness and gender empowerment. Focusing on women's opportunities rather than their capabilities, the Gender Empowerment Measure (GEM) captures gender inequality in three key areas: political participation and decision-making power, as measured by women's and men's percentage shares of parliamentary seats; economic participation and decision-making power, as measured by two indicators (women's and men's percentage share of legislators, senior officials and managerial positions, and women's and men's percentage shares of professional and technical positions); and power over economic resources, as measured by women's and men's estimated earned income (PPP US$).[53]

As the table shows, women are well represented in political participation and economic decision-making in developed countries such as Norway, Denmark, Sweden and Iceland. But many developing countries lag behind in women's political participation and empowerment. Figure 6.23 presents the positive relationship between e-government readiness and gender development in selected countries around the world. As can be seen, the e-government readiness index is positively correlated with the gender development index, implying that greater gender development goes together with improved e-government readiness in a country.

A key factor promoting the ability of women to have equal access to ICTs is the government's recognition of the importance of incorporating gender in ICTs as part of a wider policy of inclusion.

A key factor promoting the ability of women to have equal access to ICTs is the government's recognition of the importance of incorporating gender in ICTs as part of a wider policy of inclusion.

Figure 6.23.
E-government and gender development

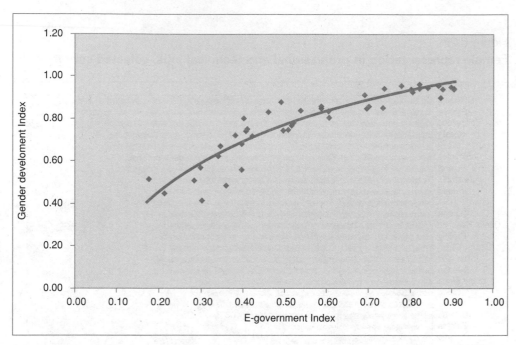

Towards this end the first imperative of gender-inclusion is that policy makers need to be sensitive to the looming danger of the widening of the **gender access-divide.** In this context, the governments need to ensure that an enabling environment is created that aims at removing gender-specific barriers to women's access to ICTs. Among other things, this includes extending information networks and physical infrastructure so as to take into account female users in particular. It also implies that policies and programmes of e-government and e-inclusion be geared towards promoting female literacy, education and technical skills.

ICTs can open up new frontiers for women. Providing access to women would enable them to fully utilize their talents and potentials. Products like online courses and training materials, knowledge of legal and political rights, and information on children's health and women's nutritional needs would increase awareness and contribute towards reducing gender disparity with regard to ICTs. Governments need to pay special attention to cultural and societal biases against gender use of ICTs. Government policies need to be geared towards encouraging women's access to careers in technology and decision-making processes.

In summary, governments need to ensure:

1. *awareness at all levels among ICT planners and policy makers of the importance of and need for gender-inclusion;*

2. *understanding that the impact of technology on women is not the same as it is on men* due to their incomes, time constraints, literacy, education, language and socio-cultural contexts;

3. *development of programmes and plans that explicitly take into account gender sensitive technology diffusion;*

> Governments need to ensure that an enabling environment is created which aims at removing gender-specific barriers to women's access to ICTs.

4. special attention to promoting *women's literacy, education and technical skills* for use of ICTs;

5. *promotion of wide awareness within society of the importance of gender inclusion to the information society.*

The following box presents a set of guidelines for consideration when devising gender sensitive inclusion policies. They have been culled from various expert group meetings and research on gender and ICT.

Preparing gender sensitive ICT policies: a rough "how to" guide[54]

- For removing social, cultural, economic and technological barriers to access, *gender sensitive development of an information society infrastructure is necessary.*

- Governments need to ensure that the *ICT infrastructure is affordable* to women belonging to every strata.

- *The location of the infrastructure should facilitate access for women.* Public access points need to be opened as an alternative to private online access. The location of the public access points should be gender sensitive to encourage female use.

- Since women lag behind men in technological fields, special emphasis needs to be placed on overcoming inequalities prevalent in the ICT sector. *Training should be provided to women for capacity building in ICTs, keeping in mind their low literacy and IT skill level.*

- Proper regulation of the ICT industry would *lower the prohibitively expensive costs of Internet access* in some countries, which adversely affects women in particular.

- *Greater policy coordination and coherence is required for gender inclusion strategies in education, work and at the community level.*

- Introducing a quota system to *encourage women to join the ICT sector* on both the collegiate and professional level is an effective way of achieving a critical mass of women in the ICT sector.

- Governments need to promote civil society and women's groups to play a *more active role at the national level to ensure gender equality.* Activism to include more women in the higher echelons of ICT decision- and policy-making is required.

- There is a need to design policies to remove the gender access-divide in accordance with local socio-economic factors. This translates into modelling *content and language to meet women's interests and demands.*

Lack of Web accessibility for marginalized people

In the Information Age the Web and the Internet are the gateways to the flow of all information. An important part of access-for-all is that no one be left behind when

An important part of access-for-all is that no one be left behind when it comes to accessing ICTs in general and the information and services on the Web in particular.

it comes to accessing ICTs in general and the information and services on the Web in particular. This requires a holistic approach towards incorporating all segments of a society so that life chances are equalized for each individual.

Currently there are many situations in which the Internet is not accessible to everyone or use of computers is difficult due to mental or physical impairment, advanced age or simply because network connections in a country are too slow. In many countries, for instance, people with disability (PWD) or older people may find their social functioning challenged due to changing vision, hearing, dexterity or memory. People with inadequate access to ICTs may also include those suffering from temporary disabilities, for example from an accident or illness. These groups have not been the focus of ICT access policies and programmes in the majority of countries.

Information technologies and e-government can play a major role in alleviating the disadvantages of a disability.

Information technologies and e-government can play a major role in alleviating the disadvantages of a disability. People with disability (PWD) and the elderly can gain tremendously from using ICTs to help overcome economic, social and political exclusion. If targeted properly, ICTs can enable PWD to communicate, educate and equip themselves with the right skills to become more independent and make effective contributions. ICT is the ultimate medium for providing opportunity. But this opportunity is predicated on the accessibility of technology.

The unique opportunity for access provided by the ICTs is that these technologies can help PWD by bringing service to the person.

The unique opportunity for access provided by the ICTs is that these technologies can help PWD by bringing service *to* the person. Using a computer, for example, can help people with disability receive information, conduct transactions, find jobs and lodge concerns via the Web. The accessibility barriers to print, audio and visual media can be much more easily overcome through web technologies.[55] E-government solutions for PWD are especially valuable inasmuch as ICTs and use of online services alleviate the traditional need for physical mobility. These people need not be treated as a marginalized group with no access to the world as afforded by newer technologies.

These populations are aware of the unique opportunities ICTs hold in store for them. Table 6.16 presents the results of a U.S. survey that enquired about the impact of the Internet on the well-being of people, including PWD. It found that

Table 6.16.

Impact of Internet on the quality of life of the disabled

		Disabled	Non-disabled
Going online significantly increased quality of life		48	27
Internet helped receipt of better information about the world		52	39
Internet increased ability to reach out to people with similar interests	Severely disabled	Less severely disabled	
	34	52	34

Doria Pilling, Paul Barrett and Mike Floyd. *Disabled people and the Internet Experiences, Barriers and Opportunities*. City University, 2004. http://www.jrf.org.uk/bookshop/eBooks/1859351867.doc. Accessed 5 October 2005.

48 per cent of Americans with disabilities who connected to the Internet said that going online significantly increased their quality of life, compared with 27 per cent of non-disabled people. In a similar survey, 54 per cent of PWD considered Internet access essential, as opposed to only six per cent of the general population. Fifty-six per cent of the disabled population considered a home computer essential.[56]

Despite compelling reasons, access for PWD remains compromised in many of the developing countries. There are estimates of around 500 to 600 million people in the world who have one form or another of disability.[57] Of these, an estimated 400 million are in the developing world—and at risk of exclusion.[58] This forms a sizeable population whose needs for access to the information society must be taken into account.

Lack of data on PWD and the elderly and their use of ICTs is a serious problem. In any study of access for these groups, gathering such data constitutes the first step towards a systematic understanding and provision of access to ICTs.

Many developing countries have no firm data on PWD or the elderly due to wide differences in definitions or simply because these groups lack priority and data has not been collected on them. The situation is compounded by societal norms in some cultures where impairment is often not publicized or even acknowledged. Traditionally, in many developing countries disability rates were reported to be very low. More recently this has begun to change. For example, Brazil's 1991 census reported a 1-2 per cent disability rate; but in its 2001 census, which used a revised definition of disability, the rate was reported to be 14.5 per cent. Similar jumps in the measured rate of disability have occurred in Turkey (12.3 per cent) and Nicaragua (10.1 per cent).[59]

Defining disability is not a simple task. It is a multidimensional concept with subjective and objective characteristics and needs to be viewed within the context of social and economic disadvantages or the discrimination a person faces due to being disabled.[60] The World Health Organization defines disability as "any restriction or lack (resulting from an impairment) of ability to perform an activity in a manner or within the range considered normal for a human being."[61] A new paradigm of disability posits that the notion of disability should be construed as a product of an interaction between characteristics of the individual (e.g., impairments or functional status) and characteristics of his/her cultural and social environments.[62] A consensus is emerging on a more holistic approach to disability that is broader in scope, including impairments as well as less then full social functioning due to old age or restrictions. According to the International Classification of Functioning, Disability and Health (ICF), disability serves as an umbrella term for impairments, activity limitations or participation restrictions.[63] This definition provides a multi-perspective approach to disability, describing it as an evolutionary concept affecting different people in different ways. A person's disability or functioning is conceived of as a dynamic interaction between health conditions (diseases, disorders, injuries, traumas etc.) and contextual factors. The latter include both personal and environmental factors.[64]

Disability, then, is a physical, mental or social limitation of the functional capacities and talents of a person that prevents him/her from participating in the activities of a society in a normal manner. In line with the broader concept of social inclusion presented in this Report, the onus of responsibility is on the government and the society to provide to all of its citizens, facilities that would enable them to lead fulfilling lives.

Lack of access to ICTs constitutes a real barrier to the inclusion of PWD. According to Amartaya Sen, not only do PWD have lower incomes (the earnings gap), they also suffer from the "conversion gap," the disadvantage a disabled person has in converting money into a good living.[65] In other words, a poor disabled person is doubly poor, lacking extra resources to compensate for not having hands, feet, a voice etc., and is unable to live at a level equivalent to that of an able bodied person at the same income level. As an example, a study in the United Kingdom found that the poverty rate for disabled people was 23.1 per cent compared to 17.9 per cent for non-disabled people; but that when extra expenses associated with being disabled were considered, the poverty rate for people with disabilities shot up to 47.4 per cent.[66] In most instances "people with physical or mental disability are not only the most deprived human beings they are the most neglected."[67]

PWD are disadvantaged in many aspects of social inclusion. They may not be able to attain the desired degree of education, which then leads to a lesser level of earnings. The same is the case with the elderly, who are at a stage in life when earnings are reduced. In many instances this contributes to poverty and lack of a full social life. Disability in a family is likely to adversely affect the incomes and opportunities of all members of a household. For example, it may have a negative effect on the schooling pattern of children if they are needed to take care of one or more family members. Poverty would compound this pattern.

Lack of access and opportunity for disabled children is most stark in many developing countries, which do not have the resources needed to provide for special access. According to one estimate, of the 100 million or more children who are out of school in the world, 40 million or so have disabilities of one kind or another.[68] Compounding the lack of financial resources is the frequent lack of awareness of how to deal with children who have a disability. With countries often struggling to provide the required budget to the education sector special minority needs are habitually overlooked.

Some advanced countries have already put into place programmes to ensure that educational and informational facilities are easily accessible to all. Leading among these are the United States and countries of the European Union. Among the various initiatives within the private sector and the government to widen the tools of accessibility in the United States, one such effort focuses on the State Libraries for the Blind in Colorado, Delaware, Illinois, New Hampshire and Oregon. Along with the National Library Service for the Blind and Physically Handicapped (NLS), part of the Library of Congress, they have partnered to launch an innovative digital audio book service for visually impaired users.[69] *Unabridged* http://www.unabridged.info/, enables blind patrons to check out and download digital, spoken word audio books directly to their computers. The digital audio books can then be played back on a PC, transferred to a portable MP3 playback device or burned onto CDs.

E-accessibility is the effort to include people with disability in the European Union i2010 Information Society for All.[70] The European Union is addressing the issue

> Lack of access to ICTs constitutes a real barrier to the inclusion of the PWDs.

of e-accessibility through a mix of research and stimulation measures to make ICT systems easier to use for a wider range of people.[71] In an attempt to remove the difficulties that PWD and others experience when trying to use electronic products or services such as computers, mobile phones or the Internet, the European Commission launched a public consultation on how to make the benefits of ICTs available to the widest possible range of citizens, including to older people and people with disabilities.

There is growing awareness of the importance of providing ICT access for PWD and the elderly. In many developing countries partnerships between the international organizations, the NGOs, and in some cases the private sector, have resulted in establishing projects aimed at capacity building among these groups. For example, The International Telecommunication Union (ITU) and the United Nations Educational, Scientific and Cultural Organization (UNESCO) have established a computer training centre in Ethiopia, the "Adaptive Technology Centre for the Blind," to assist the blind and visually impaired members of the community to gain access to information and communication technologies through computer training.[72] The Trust for the Americas, affiliated with the Organization of American States (OAS), in partnership with the World Bank, is strengthening the capacity of local NGOs to provide job training to PWD, including women, to enhance their employment prospects in four Central American countries—Guatemala, El Salvador, Honduras and Nicaragua.[73] The Bangladesh Protibandhi Kallyan Somity (BPKS) has launched an innovative project to assist people with disabilities in gaining employment and becoming part of the development process.

Box 29. ICT accessibility for persons with disabilities: an example of good practices of BPKS in Bangladesh

Bangladesh Protibandhi Kallyan Somity (BPKS) is an organization of, and by, disabled persons focusing on holistic development efforts of people with disabilities. It assists people with disabilities to gain employment and become part of the development process.

The ICT training unit of BPKS runs a two-month long training course for PWD from the grassroots level as part of its capacity-building initiative for the disabled.

The training course teaches basic computer operating systems and programmes and how to adapt technology to overcome disabilities. The basic components of the course include an introduction to computers and operating systems as well as Microsoft Word, Microsoft Excel, Microsoft PowerPoint, Photo Editor and connections to fax, e-mail, Internet and Web browsing. The participants have not had previous computer experience due to a lack of infrastructure and ICT development, including electricity, at the village level.

The BPKS course is unique in Dhaka, Bangladesh, in that it is a residential, no-fee-paying course. BPKS believes this support is necessary to provide opportunities to gain employment for people with disabilities and also to demonstrate to society the capacity and skills of people with disabilities.

Source: BPKS website, http://www.bpksbd.org/.

A few developing country governments are in the vanguard of providing opportunities for special access to the PWDs.

A few developing country governments are also in the vanguard of providing opportunities for special access to PWD. The government of South Africa launched a national accessibility portal in 2004 to make ICT available to PWD. The portal aims to improve access to information to 4 million South Africans with disabilities, contribute towards their empowerment and ensure that they live independent lifestyles. Phase One of the project was completed in 2004 and a follow-up project will be rolled out in three phases over a five-year period.

Box 30. South Africa's National Accessibility Portal

The South African National Accessibility Portal (NAP) will be a one-stop information, services and communications channel that will support persons with disabilities, caregivers, the medical profession and those offering services in this domain. NAP services will be accessible from anywhere in the country, including from home, as well as from specific, specially-equipped service centres and access points located in schools, clinics, hospitals and multi-purpose community centres, linking up where possible with existing government, private sector and Disabled Peoples' Organizations' structures. Usage by unskilled people will be facilitated by interpreters and helpers trained in ICT and disabilities (expected to include people with disabilities themselves).

Technical challenges that are being tackled include research and development in Text-to-Sign-Language, support for South African Languages, development of quality Open Source technologies including Text-To-Speech screen readers and measures to enable Disabled Persons' Organizations (DPOs) to operate the portal.

The project was conceptualized and developed by the Council for Scientific and Industrial Research (CSIR) in partnership with a representative group of DPOs and the Office on the Status of Disabled Persons (OSDP) in the Presidency.

Source: http://www.africafiles.org/article.asp?ID=8691&ThisURL=/.southern.asp&URLName=S.

However, issues of the high costs associated with special equipment and facilities aimed at providing access to PWD arise for many developing countries. For example, computer equipment that includes special features for the visually impaired is higher in cost than standard equipment. Connecting libraries with special facilities will require scarce resources.

Promoting accessibility to the Web for all: a special focus

Accessibility is about ensuring that online content can be read and navigated by everyone, regardless of experience, circumstances or type of technology being used to access it.[74] Web accessibility means access to the Web for everyone. According to the World Wide Web Consortium (W3C), this encompasses promoting access not only to PWD but to anyone with a slow connection; allowing those who have lacked opportunities for training to become proficient in the use of web technologies; and creating for those whose access has been limited, a social environment that encourages high-bandwidth connections or even regular Web access and use. A few of the factors that may adversely affect Web accessibility are presented in Box 31.

Box 31. Lack of Web accessibility implies:

- lack of accessible mainstream Web technologies (such as browsers and authoring tools);
- lack of effective, up-to-date assistive technologies;
- lack of opportunities for training to become proficient in using Web technologies;
- limited access to a social environment that encourages Web use;
- limited access to high-bandwidth connections, or even to regular Web access.

Source: W3C. Web Accessibility Initiative. "Social Factors in Developing a Web Accessibility Business Case for Your Organization," http://www.w3.org/WAI/bcase/soc. Accessed 6 October 2005.

ICT accessibility encompasses different technical aspects. Among these, access to the Web involves the ability to read and understand a web page and, where necessary, use adaptive technologies.[75] This implies that computer programmes need to have built-in features that ensure that everyone can access the Web to gain information and that being disabled does not constitute a barrier to gaining such access. Common adaptive technologies include programmes that read or describe the information on the screen, programmes that enlarge or change the colour of screen information, and special pointing or input devices. Adaptive technologies are modifications or upgrades to a computer's hardware and software that provide alternative methods of input and output.[76]

Internet accessibility allows for a much larger participating audience. Increasing the accessibility of web pages, for example, opens up a site's potential audience to the millions who are disabled, or who have slow connections. In 1998, the World Wide Web Consortium (W3C) launched the Web Accessibility Initiative (WAI), which focuses on expanding the protocols and data formats to make the WWW more accessible.[77] According to the W3C Web Accessibility Initiative, "Web accessibility means that people with disabilities can use the Web. More specifically, Web accessibility means that people with disabilities can perceive, understand, navigate and interact with the Web, and that they can contribute to the Web. Web accessibility also benefits others, including older people with changing abilities due to aging."[78] Thus, the Web Accessibility Initiative covers all disabilities that affect Web access, including visual, auditory, physical, speech, cognitive and neurological ones. It includes sites and applications that PWD can perceive, understand and navigate and with which they can interact; Web browsers and media players that can be used effectively by people with disabilities and that work well with the assistive technologies that some people with disabilities use to access the Web; and Web authoring tools and evolving Web technologies that support production of accessible Web content and websites, and that can be used effectively by people with disabilities.[79]

To promote inclusion,
some advanced
economies have
already taken steps to
promote accessibility
of the PWD.

To promote inclusion, some advanced economies have already taken steps to promote accessibility by PWD. In the United States, among the world's most advanced societies for ICTs, the "Americans with Disabilities Act" requires reasonable accommodation for employees with disabilities and that requirement extends to website accessibility.[80]

Box 32 presents some of the initiatives being undertaken for improving Web accessibility worldwide.

Box 32. Accessibility technologies and programmes

The Trace R&D Center has won recognition and many awards for its continuing work in accessible technology development. Its two on-line databases, ABLEDATA and TraceBase, list more than 18,000 products for people with disabilities. These databases can be found at http://tracecenter.org.

Microsoft corporation has an Accessibility and Disabilities page that lists accessibility aids that are compatible with its products, http://www.microsoft.com/enable/products/aids.htm.

The Yuri Rubinsky Insight Foundation also provides features on adaptive technologies in its WebAble site at http://www.yuri.org/webable.

The Web Accessibility Initiative (WAI) "Page Authoring Guidelines of the WWW" reflect the accessibility improvements in the "HTML 4.0 Recommendation." Alternative text, the description of pictures when graphics are turned off in a browser, is now required for images. HTML 4.0 also enables more detailed textual description of image maps, tables and frames. The W3C HTML Validator Service at http://validator.w3.org/ is one service to help developers get into the habit of creating ALT (alternative content) tags, among other enhancements.

CAST or Center for Applied Special Technology is a non-profit organization whose mission is to expand opportunities for all through innovative uses of computer technology. Its free Web-based service, and downloadable Validator programme, can analyze a web page and describe areas for improvement. The four-star system has been replaced by a single "Bobby Approved!" emblem that is mostly based on the HTML 4.0 Recommendation, http://www.cast.org/bobby.

The Web Access Project of the National Center for Accessible Media or NCAM, located at http://ncam.wgbh.org/webaccess, allows sites to display its Web access symbol if a reasonable effort is made to comply with the Web Accessibility Initiative (WAI) Page-Authoring Guidelines.

The Government of Canada Internet Guide includes guidelines for Universal Accessibility that can be used as an accessibility checklist for Web designers. This initiative follows a successful Canadian Access Working Group workshop entitled "Persons with Disabilities and the Use of Electronic Networks." The Public Service Commission of Canada, which runs an Employment Equity Positive Measures Programme, built a Web Page Accessibility Evaluation Self-Test for Web page authors. It runs on Javascript and can also be downloaded as a text file.

Source: Leo Valdes. "Accessibility on the Internet," http://www.un.org/esa/socdev/enable/disacc00.htm. Accessed 5 October 2005.

UN Global E-government Survey 2005
Accessibility Measurement

As e-government services expand to provide greater access, website accessibility becomes a more important issue for a larger number of people. While the major obstacle to real access is often the ICT infrastructure, or lack thereof, even those who possess the necessary prerequisites for going online at broadband speed can encounter limitations due to a disability. In a special focus this year the *UN Global E-government Report 2005* assessed the Member States online to determine which ones provided website accessibility.

Accessibility evaluation

Website accessibility means that access to a site should be available to everyone, regardless of disability.

The *UN Global Survey 2005* evaluated all Member States' National Site homepages or their equivalent for standard, Priority 1, accessibility compliance as defined by the World Wide Web Consortium's (W3C) Web Accessibility Initiative's (WAI) Web Content Accessibility Guidelines (WCAG).[81] The guidelines are divided into three levels of priority, with Priority 1 representing the basic level of accessibility compliance. The test was carried out using Watchfire's free online evaluation tool, WebXACT, to measure the National Sites for compliance with the current accessibility standards.[82]

National Site compliance is especially important because it is the entry point for the entire country and serves as a gateway to government ministries and services. Specifically, non-compliance at this most basic level of e-government would limit many online users with various disabilities from accessing a country's most basic information, which should be available to them.

Compliance with Priority 1 is determined to be a basic requirement. Otherwise, according to the W3C, one or more groups could find it impossible to access information at the site. Specifically, while full compliance is beneficial for everyone, it is arguably especially important for people with disabilities. For example, someone who relies on screen-reader software to access information on a page could be severely limited in navigating and interpreting a site in non-compliance.

It should, however, be noted that the accessibility test findings presented here, because of the tool's technical automation, should be interpreted with caution. For example, the U.S. Government's FirstGov portal, http://www.firstgov.gov, is deemed by the tool as not being in compliance with Priority 1 because the user receives an error message noting, "Use a descriptive D link in addition to LONGDESC." Meanwhile, Mali's national gateway, http://www.sgg.gov.ml, which consists of brief, rudimentary text, is—perhaps not surprisingly—in full compliance.

This underscores two points. First, the automated tool does not take into account the quality of a site. This may have an unintended consequence: large, cutting-edge sites with a complex structure could fail the test because of a minor infraction while simple one-page sites with only brief text could pass, even though they might be of little or no value. Secondly, while the tool's reporting service specifies the number and types of errors on a site, the assessment's final verdict simply determines whether the site is either in full compliance or fails. Consequently, sites that fail the test might do so because of one minor infraction (as in the U.S. case) or could have four serious errors with any number of associated instances. Even so, the automated tool is useful for gauging site accessibility at a glance because the fact remains that sites in noncompliance do, at some level, remain inaccessible to certain groups.

The accessibility assessment reveals that, in general, there is currently relatively little accessibility compliance on the National Site homepages.[83] Specifically, only 20 per cent of all sites surveyed passed the test without any errors. Passing the test without errors implies that the site was "accessible" for PWD. The box below gives the countries which had "accessible" national websites.

> The accessibility assessment reveals that there is currently relatively little accessibility compliance on the National Site homepages.

Countries with Priority I website accessibility 2005

Antigua and Barbuda, Australia, Austria, Azerbaijan, Botswana, Cambodia, Canada, Chile, Czech Republic, Dominica, Eritrea, Finland, France, Iceland, Ireland, Japan, Mali, Micronesia (Federated States of), Morocco, Nauru, Netherlands, New Zealand, Norway, Republic of Korea, Saint Kitts and Nevis, Saudi Arabia, Slovakia, Slovenia, Sweden, Switzerland, The Former Yugoslav Republic of Macedonia, Tonga, United Arab Emirates, United Kingdom of Great Britain and Northern Ireland, and Yemen.

National site download time

Promoting access and inclusion is especially important for users who do not possess high-speed Internet service, either because the country infrastructure does not allow it or because the user simply cannot afford it. In many developing countries and areas broadband connection is not available and users would access e-government information and services via dial-up modems. In this case the site design and loading time is a key factor affecting access. A long download time for the National Site would unnecessarily limit many dial-up users from accessing basic information in a timely manner and might actually work to discourage use of the site. If a site takes too long to access the user may give up.

The *UN Global E-government Report 2005* used Watchfire's free online evaluation tool, WebXACT, to evaluate the loading time of all National Site homepages surveyed.[84] It revealed that the average download time on a 56.6 connection for all countries is just about 21 seconds; however, there is wide discrepancy because 131 countries are below the average while 41 are above it.[85] Additionally, nine countries had a download time of more than one minute (60 seconds): Greece,

Guatemala, Guyana, India, Jamaica, Nicaragua, Sierra Leone, Togo and the United Republic of Tanzania.

Table 6.17.
Assessing accessibility of national sites

Mean download time on 56.6 kps in seconds	21
No. of countries above the mean	41
No. of countries below the mean	131
Median download time in seconds	11

Wireless access

While dial-up download time can serve as a proxy for access at the basic end of the spectrum, top tier and future access may very well be measured by the ability to access the National Site using a wireless device, such as a cell phone or Personal Digital Assistant (PDA). A wireless access alternative, sometimes referred to as mobile government or simply m-government, enables citizens to be instantly connected to government information, anywhere and at any time. For leading e-ready countries such a feature constitutes a value added service that complements and enhances the overall e-government experience. In fact, given the enormous wireless technology penetration among the population of countries in the vanguard of ICT use, some form of a wireless access alternative to the National Site should be a natural step.

As was pointed out in last year's report, with ever evolving e-government initiatives as well as technological change, it is the task of the survey instrument to remaining constant while also incorporating change. Therefore, with the developing trend of m-government, the core instrument this year evaluated whether a wireless access alternative was available at the National Site level. As usual, the measurement only surveyed whether any such feature was available; it did not evaluate the content or quality of the feature. In the end, only eight countries were found to provide citizens with some form of m-government, namely Canada, France, Ireland, Japan, Malta, Norway, Philippines and Slovenia. It is interesting to note that not only is the list very small, with key developed economies missing, but that a few developing countries are on it. This list is sure to grow as development of m-government will only expand access to citizens—no matter where they are.

Governments need to devise programmes aimed at improving accessibility for the disabled and the elderly. Devising adequate legislation and setting standards for products and services for access is required. Governments' e-government services should aim at creating public websites that are accessible to the disabled and the elderly, to allow full social integration. Box 33 presents a set of guidelines for inclusion of PWD prepared by the Information Society Project Office (ISPO) of the European Commission.

> ## Box 33. Guidelines for promoting access for PWD
>
> *Availability.* Wide availability of equipment and online services is a prerequisite to assisting people with disabilities. Initiatives must, therefore, define ways to ensure that individuals have access to equipment and connections, and that service providers are encouraged to provide useful and desirable services.
>
> *Awareness.* One major barrier to inclusive approaches is the lack of awareness in public policy making, in industry, and in other sectors, such as education, of the needs of disabled people and the ways in which these needs can be satisfied. Potential users must also be aware of possibilities and opportunities.
>
> *Accessibility.* Disability initiatives must give the highest priority to the promotion and implementation of design for all to ensure that everyone can have access.
>
> *Affordability.* Public funding is important because disabled people often have low incomes and many older people are still at risk of poverty. Therefore, initiatives must actively address the financial dimension and ensure that lack of income does not exclude the participation of those who could benefit the most.
>
> *Appropriateness.* The appropriateness (or usefulness) of applications in particular circumstances is important. One way to assess appropriateness is with the involvement of end-users. Initiatives must include social assessment as a central dimension.
>
> *Acceptability.* Finally, a key ingredient of usage is whether the user accepts the product for what it is.
>
> **Source:** PROMISE, "Promoting an Information Society for Everyone. Equal Opportunities and Good Practice for Older People and Disabled People in the Information Society," Report of the *PROMISE Colloquium*, http://www.stakes.fi/promise/colloq/prcolloq.htm#c2. Accessed 7 October 2005.

The box on the following page presents a set of recommendations for consideration when devising accessibility-promoting policies. They have been culled from various expert group meetings and state-of-the-art research on promoting Web accessibility in general, and on ICT use and access for people with disability and the elderly in particular.

Urban and rural access-divide

Access to, and use of, ICTs should be the first imperative in promoting inclusion of the rural communities. It is a crucial element in not only bridging the access-divide but for promoting long-term sustainable development. Access and inclusion of rural communities through ICTs also provides the opportunity to broaden awareness about the benefits of the new technologies in education, health and agriculture. Feedback from rural communities is an effective way for engendering participation. ICTs can connect the millions of poor and marginalized farmers in the developing countries to the world's economic and social opportunities.

ICTs can connect the millions of poor and marginalized farmers in the developing countries to the world's economic and social opportunities.

Promoting Web accessibility in ICT policies and programmes: A rough "how to" guide[86]

- Encourage the *development of web content* that is relevant and useful for people with disability and the elderly. Promote the application of Web-accessibility principles in web design to enable equal access to information.

- *Encourage the use of ICT* to ensure the right of expression of disadvantaged groups, including training of trainers to teach women with disabilities.

- *Promulgate and enforce laws,* policies and programmes to monitor and protect the right of persons with disabilities to information and communication—for instance, legislation providing copyright exemptions to organizations that make information content accessible to persons with disabilities; and incentives, including exemption of duties for ICT devises used by persons with disabilities and provision of subsidies for assistive technology equipment.

- *Raise awareness* concerning disability issues, including disabled persons' accessibility needs, capabilities and aspirations to be productive members of society through training for ICT policy-makers and regulatory agency representatives as well as technical personnel of private ICT companies.

- *Recognize efforts of private companies and organizations* to promote ICT access and use for persons with disabilities; presentation of awards should be promoted.

- Support *improved localization of assistive technologies,* including the resources and specific technologies needed to support their effective operation.

- Identify measurable indicators *to monitor and assess the progress* and impact, including social aspects, of ICT policies and programmes in improving the quality of life of disadvantaged groups.

- *Support the creation and strengthening of networks,* including cooperatives, of consumers with disabilities at the national, regional and international levels in order to increase bargaining and buying power for ICT products and services, which are generally expensive to buy individually.

ICTs have a particular role to play in rural areas. Access to timely information for farmers, often unaware of the price trends in the big cities, could boost their income and productivity. Advance knowledge of weather forecasts will enable many to smooth out the fluctuations of weather and other natural disasters. Information and communication technologies can improve the quality of life in rural areas through increased inclusion in the national economy, greater access to government services online and an enhanced sense of belonging.[87]

However, in many countries rural areas lack the resources and infrastructure for ICTs, which gravitate in initial stages to the centres of highest concentrations of income, physical infrastructure, educational skills and industry. For example, 26 of the 53 countries in Africa have Point of Presence in only one city while just 15 have a nationwide dial-up service.[88] Digital centralization replicates existing eco-

In many countries rural areas lack the resources and infrastructure for ICTs, which gravitate in initial stages to the centres of highest concentrations of income, physical infrastructure, educational skills and industry.

nomic, political and infrastructure centralization.[89] In this way traditional inequities of income, education and resources are mapped onto ICTs as well.

The population living in rural areas is mostly engaged in the agricultural sector, where incomes are low as compared to those in industrialized urban areas. A rural resident is generally an individual with *relatively less* income, a lesser amount of education, fewer skills and a lower standard of living. He/she also lacks awareness of the usefulness and relevance of newer technologies. The relatively high cost of ICTs is another factor limiting their use in rural areas since, in many countries, regulated telecommunication markets limit the expansion of telecommunications networks to these areas.

Compounding the traditional inequalities of the urban-rural divide are the ICTs themselves. Around the world, initial patterns of ICT diffusion indicate a concentration in and around large urban metropolises that are hubs of established economic activity. Information technologies gravitate to urban centres with greater income, education and skills.

Figure 6.24 presents the declining access to and use of the Internet in the European countries by area. As can be seen, whereas Internet use was close to 42 per cent among the population of the metropolitan areas, it declined to 29 per cent in rural areas.

> Compounding the traditional modes of inequalities between the urban-rural divide are the ICTs.

Figure 6.24.
Centre periphery gap

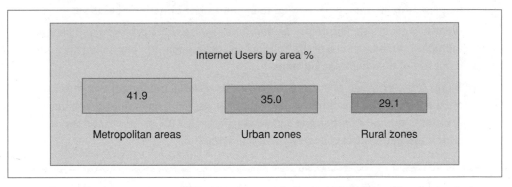

Source: European commission staff Working Paper. *e-Inclusion: The Information Society's potential for social inclusion in Europe,* http://europa.eu.int/comm/employment_social/knowledge_society/eincl_en.pdf.
Accessed 18 October 2005.

Viewed within a spectrum of educational facilities, the above identifies a particular area of concern. A study that used data from the Canadian portion of the Second International Technology in Education Study to measure the use of technological resources in schools found that rural schools appeared to face various disadvantages in comparison to urban schools. They had less access to educational software and fewer types of specialized and subject-specific software. They were also less likely to have different types of technical training for computer teachers.[90] These differences are likely to be compounded in the case of developing countries.

There are no comparable data for the number of villages across the world. Part of the problem is the variation in the definition of what constitutes a rural area.

According to one estimate, the top ten developing countries with the largest rural populations have as many as 2.7 million villages.[91]

Though rural areas in most developing countries are already connected with electricity and fixed telephone lines, for the most part, extensive access of all to telephones remains limited. Although with mobile telephony the access and coverage has theoretically expanded, prohibitively high costs in many countries do not allow its pervasive use. Furthermore, access to newer technologies such as computers, and to the Internet, is scant. For example, only 0.11 per cent of the homes in the rural areas of Nepal had private phone access compared to 10.4 per cent in the urban areas, making the urban areas 100 times richer in private telephones than the rural areas.[92] The ratio of urban to rural on the other side of the world, in Panama, was slightly better, at six to one. Overall, there are almost four times as many telephone lines per 100 people in the largest city of lower middle-income countries as in their rural areas.[93] These **urban and rural access-divides** are significant since more than 50 per cent of the population in the poorest countries lives in rural areas.

The situation is worse in Africa, which is the least e-ready region. Figure 6.25 presents the presence of electricity, radio and TVs in four African countries.[94] As can be seen, the percentage of rural households with a radio (which needs only batteries) was high, but in Ghana, only 20 per cent of rural households had electricity and 12 per cent had TV. The same ratios were even lower in Namibia and Mozambique. Because of a lack of electricity, access to newer technologies is one of the key challenges of ICT-led development in the far-flung and remote areas in most developing countries.

Figure 6.25.
Rural households with electricity, radio and TV

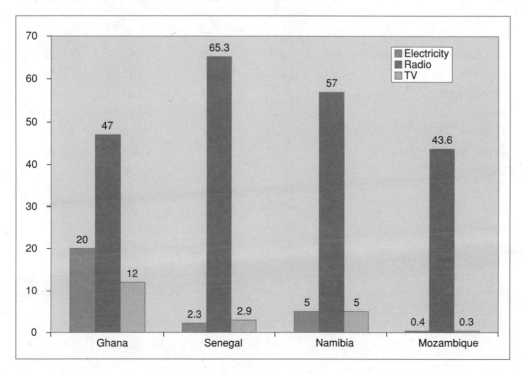

To assess the magnitude of the problem of lack of access to rural areas, Table 6.18 presents the urban and rural population for a select few of the developing countries in 2000 and their estimated projections for 2025. A glance at the table indicates that the rural populations in many developing countries remain high. For example, in 2000 Bhutan had 92 per cent of its population living in rural areas; Ethiopia, 85 per cent; and Ukraine, 88 per cent. For many of the countries these high proportions are likely to remain the same over the next two decades. For example, of India's projected 2025 population of 1.44 billion, 62 per cent or around 878 million people are expected to still be living in the rural areas. The same is the case in many other large developing countries. The sheer numbers of people highlight the importance of inclusive policies, which would allow for the use of ICTs to integrate these populations into mainstream economic and social activities.

Table 6.18.
Urban and rural population

	2000		2025 Projected	
	Urban %	Rural %	Urban %	Rural %
Afghanistan	22	78	38	62
Bhutan	8	92	17	83
Burundi	9	91	20	80
Cambodia	17	83	33	67
Chad	24	76	38	62
China	36	64	57	43
Ethiopia	15	85	25	75
India	28	72	38	62
Lao People's Democratic Republic	19	81	34	66
Lesotho	18	82	27	74
Madagascar	26	74	37	63
Malawi	15	85	28	72
Pakistan	33	67	46	54
Papua New Guinea	13	87	18	82
Somalia	33	67	50	50
Sri Lanka	21	79	27	73
Swaziland	23	77	33	67
Tajikistan	26	74	29	71
Thailand	31	69	43	57
Ukraine	12	88	18	82

Source: United Nations. Department of Economic and Social Affairs, http://unstats.un.org/unsd/cdb/cdb_advanced_data_extract.asp.
Accessed 18 October 2005.

The urban-rural access divide should be viewed in light of the economic and social costs of the opportunities lost due to the lack of ICT access to the millions who live in the rural areas.

Most developed countries are in the vanguard of recognizing the importance of the centre-periphery divide. The Swedish Government is increasing its infrastructure investment for sparsely populated areas by giving tax reductions for higher capacity network connections.[95] The Irish Development Plan 2000–2006 promotes advanced communications and e-commerce infrastructure in the less developed regions. In France, a new legal framework for regional development facilitates promotes ICT investment in less favoured areas, while Greece is prioritizing the development of local access network infrastructure in small towns and remote areas.[96]

Realizing the necessity of access to ICTs, many developing countries are also taking steps to promote them in the rural areas. Some countries in Latin America have successfully experimented with "audio visual pedagogy," a participatory approach to agricultural development that empowers local communities.[97] The project links the needs of the rural population, sources of information and experts who can respond to requirements by producing documentaries and training presentations.[98] Among other countries, Brazil has introduced public Internet access points.

Box 34. *Acessa São Paulo*—Promoting digital inclusion in Brazil

Enhancing outreach of ICTs is important in Brazil. Since its inception the *Programme Acessa São Paulo* (PASP) has implemented 123 Community Access Points, called *Infocentros,* with the capacity to receive 1,750,000 accesses a year, making this programme a very effective instrument for reducing the digital exclusion in São Paulo. *PASP* objectives are to provide Internet access to low-income citizens through the Infocentros. By doing so, these communities can define their own priorities, including how the equipment donated by the provincial government will be used.

Source: http://www.icamericas.net/modules/DownloadsPlus/uploads/Awards_Application/AcessaSaoPaulo-integr-Portuguese.pdf.

The government of Uganda is implementing a project titled "Electronic Delivery of Agricultural Information to Rural Communities in Uganda," aimed at disseminating data regarding access to agricultural information to the rural communities. A combination of traditional media such as printed materials and new ICTs like video, television, e-mail and CD-ROMS, along with the Internet, are being used to increase agricultural production.[99] To make ICTs accessible and relevant, a key priority of the programme is to develop local content and focus on the needs of women and youth. In India, one NGO is taking ICTs to the rural poor in an attempt to alleviate poverty while bringing them the benefits of emerging and frontier technologies (Box 35).

The urban-rural access divide should be viewed in light of the economic and social costs of the opportunities lost due to the lack of access of ICTs to the millions who live in the rural areas.

> ## Box 35. Reaching the poor in the rural areas: ICTs in Pondicherry, India
>
> With a grant from the Canadian government, the M.S. Swaminathan Research Foundation (MSSRF) has established an ICT project for the rural poor as part of its programme to take the benefits of emerging and frontier technologies to this group. Out of a population of 22,000, around 4500 or approximately 20 per cent of the rural families in the area are officially classified as living below the poverty line, and half the population has a total family income equivalent to less than US$25 per month.
>
> The Foundation provided the villagers with computers, a printer, a wireless device, a solar panel, specially designed websites in the local language and training programmes for the villagers. The Local Area Network (LAN) hub of the wireless system was installed in Villianur. The hub connects to the Internet through dial-up telephone lines.
>
> Information is sourced from the Web, as well as from local people, and national and international sources. It is collected by operators, often female, translated into the local language, Tamil, and fed into the system via an ISDN connection to the Internet. Village volunteers have been trained to input material in Tamil using the standard QWERTY English keyboard.
>
> The Foundation worked in partnership with the villagers right from the beginning, developing content that is relevant to the people and that takes into account their daily needs, their culture and their language. As a result, farmers are getting the right prices for their farm produce and wage-labourers are getting the right wages from their employers.
>
> **Source:** http://www.tve.org/ho/doc.cfm?aid=1393&lang=English.

One solution to promoting community access, especially in the rural areas, is the establishment of Public Access Points and or telecentres. These are public places where the Internet may be used, such as community halls, libraries and Internet cafes equipped with computers with Internet connections.

In the past few years, many countries, often in partnership with the private sector, have set up public Internet access points (PIAPs) as part of their e-government strategy. Telecentres have been seen as a means of addressing the lack of ICTs throughout Africa and of assisting in providing universal access to both telephony and other forms of ICTs.[100] Senegal is the African country with the largest number of telecentres: more than 9000. The telecentres have been supported by Sonatel, the telephone company, which has helped set up these *"telecentres privés"* (private telecentres) instead of pay phones. The telecentres started in 1992 and there are now about 6000 in Dakar—one on almost every street corner—and they are increasingly spreading to rural areas. To promote access in far-flung areas, the International Telecommunication Union, UNESCO and the Canadian International Development Research Centre (IDRC) have jointly established major centres in Mali, Uganda, Mozambique and South Africa offering a range of telephony, computing, Internet and information services.[101]

In summary, it is important to create local capacities for access and use of ICTs. Creating opportunities for connecting rural communities to the global information and communication network is important. There is a need to study and set up village information centres, which would dispense relevant and needed information, such as on micro-credit, providing new economic and social opportunities for the villagers.

For the propagation of ICTs in the far-flung and rural areas, a coherent policy is needed to accommodate specific needs in these areas, including expansion of infrastructure and promoting awareness regarding the benefits of ICTs. ICTs are the means to achieve an end. The following box presents a set of thoughts for consideration when devising rural area inclusion policies. They have been culled from several sources.

Promoting access and inclusion of rural areas in ICT policies and programmes

- A coherent holistic policy needs to be developed to use ICTs for the inclusion of the remote areas.

- Capacity building of the local population has to be taken into account to ensure that a vast number of people can benefit from the ICTs.

- There is a need to provide affordable ICT resources and bandwidth to rural areas through community access points such as telecentres and other such facilities.

- Particular attention should be paid to the integration of ICTs to meet the needs of low income rural and urban people.

- Strategies to promote awareness of ICT to rural people could include use of broadcasting media and demonstrations of their benefits through exhibitions and other fora.

- Encouraging public media to reorient their mission to accommodate educational, scientific and cultural needs of remote areas, especially as they relate to the use of information technologies, would be useful.

- To encourage their use in communities and areas not familiar with technology, the Internet and other new communication technologies should not be presented as technological gimmicks or marvels but as resources that are useful in day-to-day life.

- Care has to be taken in developing content that is relevant to the needs and demands of the local population. The content should be in a language that is comprehensible to the reader. Words should be simple, in keeping with readers' reading capacity.

Notes

1   Governance is defined as the sum of the many ways individuals and institutions, public and private, manage their common affairs. (*Our Global Neighborhood. The Report of the Commission on Global Governance*. UN. Chapter 1.) It is the exercise of political, economic and administrative decision-making. UNDP. *Governance for Sustainable Human Development*. A UNDP Policy document. January 1997. P. iv.

2   Mark Warschauer. *Reconceptualising the Digital Divide.* http://www.gse.uci.edu/markw/papers.html. Accessed 7 September 2005.

3   Mark Warschauer. "Demystifying the Digital Divide." *Scientific American.* August 2003. P. 47.

4   i2010—"A European Information Society for Growth and Employment." http://europa.eu.int/information_society/eeurope/i2010/docs/communications/com_229_i2010_310505_fv_en.doc. Accessed 8 October 2005.

5   Ruth Levitas. *The Idea of Social Inclusion.* http://www.ccsd.ca/events/inclusion/papers/rlevitas.htm. Accessed 15 September 2005.

6   http://www.socialinclusion.sa.gov.au/site/page.cfm. Accessed 15 September 2005.

7   Christina Freiler. *From Experiences of Exclusion to a Vision of Inclusion: What Needs to Change?* Laidlaw Foundation. http://www.ccsd.ca/subsites/inclusion/bp/cf2.htm.

8   http://www.cpa.ie/facts_jargon.html#S Accessed 15 September 2005.

9   This concept draws on the work of the following: Laidlaw Foundation. http://www.ccsd.ca/subsites/inclusion/bp/index.htm, including "A New Way of thinking? Towards a Vision of Social Inclusion" http://www.ccsd.ca/subsites/inclusion/bp/cf2.htm; Mark Warschauer. *Reconceptualising the Digital Divide* http://www.firstmonday.org/issues/issue7_7/warschauer/w4. Accessed 21 October 2005.; EU "Participation for all in the Knowledge-based Society." European Union. http://europa.eu.int/information_society/soccul/eincl/index_en.htm. Accessed 8 October 2005; Peter Evans. *Collective Capabilities, Culture, and Amartya Sen's Development as Freedom.* http://sociology.berkeley.edu/faculty/evans/evans_pdf/Collective_Capabilities.pdf. Accessed 21 October 2005.

10   *Universal Declaration of Human Rights.* http://www.un.org/millennium/declaration/ares552e.htm.

11   Martha Nussbaum. *Sex and Social Justice.* Oxford University Press. 1999.

12   Marvyn Novick. *Social Inclusion: The Foundation of a National Policy Agenda.* http://www.ccsd.ca/subsites/inclusion/bp/mn.htm. Accessed 15 September 2005.

13   Ibid.

14   See Amartaya Sen. *Development as Freedom.* Oxford University Press, 1999; Peter Evans. *Collective Capabilities, Culture, and Amartya Sen's Development as Freedom.* http://sociology.berkeley.edy/faculty/EVANS/evans_pdf/Collecice_Capabilities.pdf. Accessed 16 September, 2005; Mark Warschauer. *Reconceptualising the Digital Divide* http://www.firstmonday.org/issues/issue7_7/warschauer/w4. Accessed 21 October 2005.

15   Peter Evans. *Collective Capabilities, Culture, and Amartya Sen's Development as Freedom.* http://sociology.berkeley.edu/faculty/evans/evans_pdf/Collective_Capabilities.pdf. Accessed 21 October 2005.

16   Ibid.

17   Ibid.

18   Pippa Norris. *Digital Divide, Civic Engagement, Information Poverty and the Internet Worldwide.* 2002.

19   Francisco Rodríguez and Ernest J. Wilson, III. *Are Poor Countries Losing the Information Revolution?* InfoDev Working Paper. May 2000.

20   UNCTAD. *The Digital Divide: ICT development Indices 2004.* P.5.

21   The World Bank. *Telecommunications and Information Services for the Poor: Towards a Strategy for Universal Access.* April 2002. P. ix.

22   Based on data from Internet world stats. http://www.internetworldstats.com/stats.htm.

23   UNCTAD. *The Digital Divide: ICT development Indices 2004.* P. 10.

24   Internet World Stats. http://www.internetworldstats.com/top20.htm. Accessed 25 August 2005.

25   Source: Mathew Clarke. *E-development? Development and the New Economy.* UNU World Institute for Development Economics Research (UNU-WIDER) policy paper. http://www.wider.unu.edu/publications/pb7.pdf. P.15. Accessed 26 August 2005.

26   Mathew Clarke. *E-development? Development and the New Economy.* UNU World Institute for Development Economics Research (UNU-WIDER) policy paper. http://www.wider.unu.edu/publications/pb7.pdf. P.15. Accessed 26 August 2005.

27   Countries not online in each region are not included in the average regional index.

28   Taken from: *World Information and Communication for Development 200: Trends and Policies for the Information Society,* www.wbln0018.worldbank.org/ict/projects.nsf; *The Wireless Internet Opportunity for Developing Countries,* http://www.infodev.org/files/1061_file_The_Wireless_Internet_Opportunity.pdf. Accessed Sept. 2005.

29   *UNESCO and an Information Society for All.* http://www.unesco.org/webworld/telematics/gis.htm. Accessed 3 October 2005.

30   Ibid.

31   International Telecommunication Union. *World Telecommunication Development Report 2003.* P. 53.

32   Aref Adamali et al. "Trends in National e-Strategies: A review of Forty Countries." *World Information and Communication for Development 2006.* Draft. P.18.

33   Francisco Rodríguez and Ernest J. Wilson, III. *Are Poor Countries Losing the Information Revolution?* INFODEV Working Paper. Annex. http://wbln0018.worldbank.org/ict/resources.nsf/ a693f575e01ba5f385256b500062af05/45a738b8c7305beb85256da400504c12/$FILE/_patkmos rfdoj54rr4e9kmetb5f8_.doc. Accessed 2 October 2005.

34   Kenny Charles et al. *ICTs and Poverty.* The World Bank. 2000. P. 22.

35   Francisco Rodríguez and Ernest J. Wilson, III. *Are Poor Countries Losing the Information Revolution?* INFODEV Working Paper. P. 32. http://wbln0018.worldbank.org/ict/resources.nsf/ a693f575e01ba5f385256b500062af05/45a738b8c7305beb85256da400504c12/$FILE/_ patkmosrfdoj54rr4e9kmetb5f8_.doc. Accessed 2 October 2005.

36   Ibid.

37   UNESCO. http://portal.unesco.org/ci/ev.php?URL_ID=1536&URL_DO=DO_TOPIC&URL_ SECTION=201&reload=1085145184.

38   Silvana Rubino-Hallman. *E-Government in Latin America and the Caribbean: Reinventing Governance in the Information Age.* http://www.cnti.ve/cnti_docmgr/sharedfiles/gobierno electronico8.pdf. P. 3.

39   S. Nanthikesan. *Trends in Digital Divide.* November 2000. P. 19.

40   http://www.pewinternet.org/PPF/r/80/report_display.asp.

41   http://www.pewinternet.org/PPF/c/5/topics.asp.

42   Madanmohan Rao. *Struggling with the Digital Divide: Internet Infrastructure, Content, and Culture: Is a Progressive Internet Environment Enough to Close the Gap between North and South?* http://www.isoc.org/oti/articles/1000/rao.html.

43   Data from Global Reach. Source: Global Reach. http://global-reach.biz/globstats/index.php3.

44   International Telecommunication Union. http://www.itu.int/newsroom/wtd/2004/survey/results.asp.

45   *Linguistic Diversity on the Internet: Assessment of the Contribution of Machine Translation.* http://www.europarl.eu.int/stoa/publi/99-12-01/default_en.htm. Accessed 19 October 2005.

46   http://cyber.law.harvard.edu/readinessguide/examples.html.

47   *Women and Information Technology: Fast Facts 2005;* http://www.umbc.edu/cwit/fastfacts.html; http://www.learningpartnership.org/facts/tech.phtml. December 2004

48   Source: United Nations Division for the Advancement of Women (DAW), International Telecommunication Union (ITU), UN ICT Task Force Secretariat. *Information and Communication Technologies and Their Impact on and use as an Instrument for the Advancement and Empower-ment of Women.* Report of the Expert Group Meeting, Seoul, Republic of Korea, 11–14 November 2002. http://www.un.org/womenwatch/daw/egm/ict2002/reports/EGMFinalReport.pdf. P. 3. Accessed 10 October 2005.

49   Kenny Charles et al. *ICTs and Poverty.* The World Bank, 2000. P. 22.

50   Sophia Huyer. *Gender, ICT and Education.* June 2003. http://www.wigsat.org/engenderedICT.pdf. Accessed August 2005.

51   Dollar, David and Gatti, Robert (1999). "Gender Inequality, Income and Growth: Are Good Times Good for Women?" *Policy Research Report on Gender and Development.* Working Paper Series, No. 1. The World Bank. May. http://siteresources.worldbank.org/INTGENDER/ Resources/wp1.pdf. Accessed August 2005.

52   Gender development index is prepared by the United Nations Development Programme (UNDP) annually for the *Human Development Report.* http://hdr.undp.org/ reports/view_reports.cfm?type=1.

53   Gender empowerment measure is prepared annually by the United Nations Development Programme (UNDP) for the *Human Development Report.* http://hdr.undp.org/reports/.

54   The recommendations are culled from the following: United Nations. Division for the Advance-ment of Women (DAW); *Report of Expert Group Meeting on Information and Communication Technologies and their Impact on and use as an Instrument for the Advancement and Empower-ment of Women.* Seoul, Republic of Korea, 11–14 November 2002. Source: http://www.un.org/

womenwatch/daw/egm/ict2002/reports/Paper-NHafkin.PDF; Strategies for Inclusion, Gender and the Information Society (SIGIS). www.rcss.ed.ac.uk/sigis/index.php. accessed Sept 2005; Forum on ICTs and Gender http://www.globalknowledge.org/gender2003/index.cfm?menuid=27.

55   W3C. Web Accessibility Initiative. *Social Factors in Developing a Web Accessibility Business Case for Your Organization.* http://www.w3.org/WAI/bcase/soc. Accessed 6 October 2005.

56   Leonard Cheshire (Knight et al., 2002) quoted in *Disabled People and the Internet Experiences, Barriers and Opportunities.* Doria Pilling, Paul Barrett and Mike Floyd. http://www.jrf.org.uk/bookshop/eBooks/1859351867.doc. Accessed 20 Sept 2005

57   *Greater Equity for Disabled People.* James Wolfensohn. http://www1.worldbank.org/devoutreach/july05/article.asp?id=309. Accessed Sept. 2005.

58   Amartya Sen. "Disability and Justice," Keynote Speech at conference, "Disability and Inclusive Development: Sharing, Learning and Building Alliances," organized by the World Bank, Washington, 30 November–1 December 2004. http://siteresources.worldbank.org/DISABILITY/214576-1092421729901/20291152/Amartya_Sen_Speech.doc. Accessed 2 October 2005.

59   "Disability and Development and The World Bank." A Briefing Summary on 2 February 2005. http://siteresources.worldbank.org/DISABILITY/Resources/Overview/DD_and_WB_Briefing_Summary.doc. Accessed 5 October 2005.

60   http://www.sdc.gc.ca/asp/gateway.asp?hr=/en/hip/odi/documents/Definitions/Definitions009.shtml&hs=pyp.

61   Ibid.

62   "The New Paradigm of Disability," www.accessiblesociety.org/topicsemogarphics-identity/newparadigm.htm. Accessed 20 September 2005.

63   http://www3.who.int/icf/intros/ICF-Eng-Intro.pdf.

64   ICF Introduction. http://www3.who.int/icf/intros/ICF-Eng-Intro.pdf.

65   Amartya Sen. "Disability and Justice." Keynote Speech at conference "Disability and Inclusive Development: Sharing, Learning and Building Alliances," organized by the World Bank, Washington, 30 November–1 December 2004. http://siteresources.worldbank.org/DISABILITY/214576-1092421729901/20291152/Amartya_Sen_Speech.doc. Accessed 2 October 2005.

66   Ibid.

67   Ibid.

68   Ibid.

69   http://i-newswire.com/pr2127.html.

70   "i2010–A European Information Society for Growth and Employment." http://europa.eu.int/information_society/eeurope/i2010/docs/communications/com_229_i2010_310505_fv_en.doc. Accessed 8 October 2005.

71   Ibid.

72   International Telecommunication Union. *Disability success stories.* http://www.itu.int/osg/spu/wsis-themes/ict_stories/Cross-Cutting/Disabilities.html. Accessed 7 October 2005.

73   Ibid.

74   http://www.becta.org.uk/page_documents/industry/advice/accessibility/full.doc.

75   Leo Valdes. "Accessibility on the Internet." http://www.un.org/esa/socdev/enable/disacc00.htm.

76   Leo Valdes. "Accessibility on the Internet." http://www.un.org/esa/socdev/enable/disacc00.htm. Accessed 5 October 2005.

77   Ibid.

78   W3C. Web Accessibility Initiative. http://www.w3.org/WAI/intro/accessibility.php. Accessed 6 October 2005.

79   W3C. Web Accessibility Initiative. http://www.w3.org/Talks/WAI-Intro/slide3-0.html. Accessed 06 October 2005

80   http://www.un.org/esa/socdev/enable/disacc00.htm.

81   More information on the World Wide Web Consortium's (W3C) Web Accessibility Initiative (WAI) can be found at http://www.w3.org/WAI/.

82   Watchfire's WebXACT is available at http://webxact.watchfire.com/.

83   The assessment covered the 177 countries that had some form of national site presence; at the time of the evaluation, which was conducted 9–16 September, three countries' national sites did not work or were unavailable. Additionally, Belgium and Denmark utilized a technical back-end implementation, which made it technically infeasible to assess them using the online tool. They are consequently excluded from the evaluation. The figures given represent the remaining 172 countries.

84   Watchfire's WebXACT is available at http://webxact.watchfire.com/.

85   See Endnote 84.

86   From *Disability Information Resources*. http://www.dinf.ne.jp/doc/english/asia/resource/z00ap/vol5no2/recommend.htm and *ICTs in the Service of People with Disabilities: Recommendations of UNESCO Experts Group Meeting, Paris 2003* http://portal.unesco.org/ci/en/file_download.php/27b60ea2f1f733ee007bb0dc85f7ae81Recommendations+of+the+UNESCO+Expert+Meeting.doc.

87   http://www.itu.int/itunews/issue/2002/04/ict-minding.html.

88   S. Nanthikesan. *Trends in Digital Divide*. Harvard Center for Population and Development Studies. November 2000. P. 33.

89   Ibid.

90   http://www.statcan.ca/Daily/English/030623/d030623b.htm.

91   The World Bank. *World Information and Communication for Development 2006: Trends and Policies for the Information Society*. Draft. P. 5. Accessed 24 August 2005.

92   *The Networking Revolution: Opportunities and Challenges for Developing Countries*. InfoDev Working Paper. June 2000. P. 17. Accessed 24 August 2005. http://wbln0018.worldbank.org/ict/resources.nsf/a693f575e01ba5f385256b500062af05/e32c6ac01ae044db85256e7c006a28c5/$FILE/NetworkingRevolution.pdf.

93   Ibid.

94   Data from International Telecommunication Union. *World Telecommunication Development Report 2003*. P. 14.

95   http://europa.eu.int/comm/employment_social/knowledge_society/eincl_en.pdf.

96   Ibid

97   *Information and Communication Technologies for Rural Development and Food Security: Lessons from Field Experience in Developing Countries*. http://www.fao.org/sd/cddirect/CDre0055b.htm.

98   Ibid.

99   *Information and Communication Technologies for Rural Development and Food Security: Lessons from Field Experience in Developing Countries*. http://www.fao.org/sd/cddirect/CDre0055b.htm.

100   Peter Benjamin. *African Experience with Telecenters*. http://www.isoc.org/oti/articles/1100/benjamin.html. Accessed 19 October 2005.

101   Ibid.

Chapter VII
Conclusions and recommendations

Trends in e-government development in 2005 indicate that a consciousness of the benefits of the information society is gaining currency. Many developing country governments around the world are promoting awareness of their policies and programmes, as well as their approaches and strategies, to the citizen on their e-government websites. They are making an effort to engage multi-stakeholders in participatory decision-making—in some cases through the use of innovative e-government initiatives aimed at greater access and inclusion.

Approaches to e-government programme offerings differ from country to country. The "how" of what countries choose to display on their websites is a function of "what" they want to focus on and "why" they want to focus on the issue(s). Whereas some countries closely follow the model of an integrated and multifaceted approach to a portal others may spin off separate portals from one national site. Political ideology, economic and social systems, level of development, resource availability, human and technological infrastructure, institutional framework and cultural patterns all have a bearing on how, and how well, both e-government and ICT-for-development initiatives are utilized.

E-government development appears to have a strong correlation with income per capita. Whereas part of the reason for the high e-readiness in most of the developed economies is past investment in, and development of, telecommunications infrastructure, resource availability appears to be a critical factor inhibiting e-government initiatives in many developing countries.

Despite steady progress in e-government development across the globe, lack of access to ICTs remains a major challenge for the world. One of the central obstacles in the march towards an information society for the future in developing countries is the huge disparity that exists in both access to and use of ICTs.

Inclusive policies, which would include the majority of the populations in the ambit of ICTs, are not the norm in the developing world.

Across the world the access-divide exists not only between the developed and the developing countries where it is commonly perceived to be, but between the rich and the poor in a country, between men and women, between the educated and the illiterate, between the urban and the rural, and between those with capabilities and persons with disability.

The analysis in this Report suggests that the extent of this access-divide is huge and unlikely to be bridged any time soon.

As the *UN Global E-government Readiness Reports* have stated before, utilization of the full potential of e-government is yet to materialize in the majority of the countries of the world.

- The access-divide is multi-faceted and stems from disparities, first and foremost, in income per capita and the level of development. The developed countries are far more advanced in their ICT

Many developing country governments around the world are promoting awareness about policies and programmes, and approaches and strategies to the citizen on their e-government websites.

Approaches to e-government programme offerings differ from country to country. The "how" of what countries choose to display on the websites is a function of the "what" they want to focus on and "why" they want to focus on the issue.

Inclusive policies, which would include the majority of the populations in the ambit of ICTs, are not the norm in the developing world.

The access-divide exists not only across the world, between the developed and the developing countries where commonly perceived to be, but between the rich and the poor in a country, between men and women, between the educated and the illiterate; between the urban and the rural and between those with capabilities and persons with disability.

infrastructure, e-government offerings and programmes for access and inclusion of the disadvantaged groups than the majority of developing countries.

Recent patterns of ICT diffusion around the world indicate a concentration of newer technologies in developing countries around those with higher incomes, more technical skills, and living in the urban areas.

The likelihood of many developing countries and vast groups of populations around the globe being excluded from the benefits of ICT-led development is real.

Of particular concern are the countries belonging to the regions of South and Central Asia and Africa, which together, house one third of humanity.

Exploring the issue of social inclusion illustrates that the majority of the developing country populations face a grave challenge from the new technological revolution.

- Recent patterns of ICT diffusion around the world indicate a concentration of newer technologies in developing countries around those with higher incomes, more technical skills, and living in the urban areas. This has accentuated existing disparities in these countries, where only the rich have access to opportunity—something that needs to be addressed for improving access and inclusion.

- For broader citizen inclusion through the use of ICTs and e-government programmes, progress is uneven and mostly limited to a handful of developed economies. The likelihood of many developing countries and vast groups of populations around the globe being excluded from the benefits of ICT-led development is real.

- Of particular concern are the countries belonging to the regions of South and Central Asia and Africa, which together, house one third of humanity. The 32 least e-ready countries show little relative progress compared to the developed countries. Access to, and use of, ICTs for development is at a rudimentary level, relegating millions of people to an existence outside the inclusive net of the ICTs.

- Lack of telecommunications infrastructure and education are the key factors limiting both access and inclusion of societies in the developing world.

- *Exploring the issue of social inclusion illustrates that the majority of the developing country populations face a grave challenge from the new technological revolution. Whereas some of the developing countries that have in place the right mix of reforms, institutions and programmes will no doubt benefit from the ICTs, most are likely to be mired in a cycle of low income, poverty and a growing disparity in access to modern technology.*

The overwhelming evidence of the current gap in access to, and use of, ICTs between and within countries, should not be a cause for inaction. ICTs provide a unique opportunity for leapfrogging traditional development patterns in developing countries. However, the hope of achieving higher standards of living and greater economic and social empowerment for the millions of disadvantaged around the world requires a new set of complementary and comprehensive approaches to reaching the vision of an information society.

Recommendations

The first imperative is to *recognize the importance of providing equal opportunity for participation in the information society.* Governments need to fully understand the vast potential of ICTs as a tool, and the benefits and opportunities that can accrue in the current age if ICTs are effectively applied to human development.

Second, *commitment and leadership for an ICT-led development agenda for equality is a prerequisite*. This requires political commitment to ensure that each step taken towards meeting the goals and objectives of the country is inclusive of the values of the majority of the society, including those at its fringes.

Third, there is *need for a vision to develop a socially inclusive development strategy, which aims at the empowerment of each according to his or her capabilities*. A vision grounded in the reality of the level of development and the availability of physical and human infrastructure and financial resources should allow the setting of objectives for the economy and the society in a way that reorients and maximizes the public value.

Fourth, *a country needs to have a resolve to harness the potential of the information society*. The policies and programmes of the government need to be restructured with the role of ICTs blended and integrated into governance systems and development plans.

Fifth, *the formulation of a development strategy based on effective and indigenously appropriate utilization of the ICTs in each sector is required so that the market, the government and the citizen have a mutually beneficial and equitable role to play*. This requires rethinking the interaction between the state and the citizen towards a partnership that actively promotes participatory decision-making. It includes redefining institutions, processes and mechanisms whereby information is supplied and information is demanded. A national strategy is needed, based on a realistic diagnosis of the economic, financial and human resource availability, and the infrastructure, human capital, financial and social needs required to attain the objectives—but one based on the holistic concept of e-inclusion and actively aimed at promoting access for all.

The set of policy recommendations given below provides a way forward for thinking about how to approach this agenda of access and inclusion.

The way forward: a policy agenda

- The *importance of information technology as a tool for socio-economic development needs to be fully embraced* by developing countries. ICTs usher in changes not often readily accepted by traditional societies.

- Information dissemination should be carried out by the governments to *increase the level of awareness regarding the benefits of ICTs*. Campaigns targeted at making the local population realize the importance and advantages of becoming a part of the Information Society are needed.

- The foremost responsibility of the government in ensuring that all its citizens have equal access to ICTs is to *have a coherent and strategic policy geared towards the propagation of ICTs*. Preparing, creating and managing a policy and programme of access and inclusion require visionary and committed leadership. To ensure an equitable development of all the regions, a coordinated policy is needed at the national, regional and local level.

- Governments, especially in the developing world, need to realize the importance of ICTs as the engine of economic and social growth. In this context, *infrastructure needs to be strengthened* to both increase the level and reduce the cost of connectivity, which in some countries is prohibitively expensive.

- Governments can play the role of a catalyst in generating ICT demand in their country by creating an *enabling environment for the growth of ICTs.* They should invest in research & development to encourage the production of low-cost ICTs to enable the vast majority of people to have access.

- *Promoting literacy and education and technical skills should receive the highest priority.*

- To promote equitable development, *special attention needs to be given to capacity building* at both the donor and the recipient level. Human resource development is a key here. Computer literacy should be promoted by setting up national computer training programmes providing free or subsidized training in IT skills.

- *Skills training is an essential tool to encourage users.* In this context, instructions should be kept simple, keeping in mind the literacy level of the user, and step-by-step guidance should be provided at the access points to facilitate learning by the users.

- To promote access to marginalized communities like PWD and women in developing countries, the government can benefit from *forging Public-Private Partnerships.* Such partnerships not only increase the resource pool of talent but also initiate knowledge transfer and are cost effective. To bring the rural and far-flung areas into the fold of ICTs and take computer literacy to the grassroots level, building partnerships with NGOs can prove to be extremely useful.

- To bridge the access-divide in gender, governments need to *design gender sensitive policies.* Promoting women's and girls' education deserves special attention. The number of women in the higher levels of decision-making at the national level should be increased to ensure that the new ICT policies being designed are not gender blind.

- There is a need to invest in the development of appropriate online content and services, which would include *supporting local communities for the development of online services and networks,* in particular in disadvantaged urban neighbourhoods and less-favoured rural and peripheral areas. *Content indigenization should be encouraged.* The government needs to formulate a well-thought-out and coherent strategy to promote content development according to the local culture and values.

- Governments need to devise new strategies to *increase the accessibility of people with disabilities to ICTs.* New laws also need to be formulated to protect the rights and interests of PWD and ensure that they do not loose out through the changes being brought about by the ICT revolution.

- Creating opportunities for connecting rural communities to the global information and communication network is important. For the propagation of ICTs in the far-flung and rural areas, a coherent policy is needed to accommodate specific needs in these areas, including *expansion of infrastructure and promoting awareness regarding the benefits of ICTs.* ICTs are the means to achieve an end. To encourage their use in communities and areas not familiar with technology, the Internet and other new communication technologies should not be presented as technological gimmicks or marvels but as something that is useful in day-to-day life.

Annex One

Annex Tables

Table 1.
E-government Readiness Index 2005

	Country	Index
1	United States	0.9062
2	Denmark	0.9058
3	Sweden	0.8983
4	United Kingdom	0.8777
5	Republic of Korea	0.8727
6	Australia	0.8679
7	Singapore	0.8503
8	Canada	0.8425
9	Finland	0.8231
10	Norway	0.8228
11	Germany	0.8050
12	Netherlands	0.8021
13	New Zealand	0.7987
14	Japan	0.7801
15	Iceland	0.7794
16	Austria	0.7602
17	Switzerland	0.7548
18	Belgium	0.7381
19	Estonia	0.7347
20	Ireland	0.7251
21	Malta	0.7012
22	Chile	0.6963
23	France	0.6925
24	Israel	0.6903
25	Italy	0.6794
26	Slovenia	0.6762
27	Hungary	0.6536
28	Luxembourg	0.6513
29	Czech Republic	0.6396
30	Portugal	0.6084
31	Mexico	0.6061
32	Latvia	0.6050
33	Brazil	0.5981
34	Argentina	0.5971
35	Greece	0.5921
36	Slovakia	0.5887
37	Cyprus	0.5872
38	Poland	0.5872
39	Spain	0.5847
40	Lithuania	0.5786

Table 1.   *(continued)*

	Country	Index
41	Philippines	0.5721
42	United Arab Emirates	0.5718
43	Malaysia	0.5706
44	Romania	0.5704
45	Bulgaria	0.5605
46	Thailand	0.5518
47	Croatia	0.5480
48	Ukraine	0.5456
49	Uruguay	0.5387
50	Russian Federation	0.5329
51	Belarus	0.5318
52	Mauritius	0.5317
53	Bahrain	0.5282
54	Colombia	0.5221
55	Venezuela	0.5161
56	Peru	0.5089
57	China	0.5078
58	South Africa	0.5075
59	Jamaica	0.5064
60	Turkey	0.4960
61	Barbados	0.4920
62	Qatar	0.4895
63	Seychelles	0.4884
64	Panama	0.4822
65	Kazakhstan	0.4813
66	Trinidad and Tobago	0.4768
67	Bahamas	0.4676
68	Jordan	0.4639
69	T.F.Y.R.Macedonia	0.4633
70	Costa Rica	0.4612
71	Lebanon	0.4560
72	Saint Kitts and Nevis	0.4492
73	Brunei Darussalam	0.4475
74	Saint Lucia	0.4467
75	Kuwait	0.4431
76	Kyrgyzstan	0.4417
77	Maldives	0.4321
78	El Salvador	0.4225
79	Uzbekistan	0.4114
80	Saudi Arabia	0.4105

Table 1. *(continued)*

	Country	Index
81	Fiji	0.4081
82	Dominican Republic	0.4076
83	Georgia	0.4034
84	Bosnia and Herzegovina	0.4019
85	Bolivia	0.4017
86	Antigua and Barbuda	0.4010
87	India	0.4001
88	Saint Vincent and the Grenadines	0.4001
89	Guyana	0.3985
90	Botswana	0.3978
91	Samoa	0.3977
92	Ecuador	0.3966
93	Mongolia	0.3962
94	Sri Lanka	0.3950
95	Grenada	0.3879
96	Indonesia	0.3819
97	Belize	0.3815
98	Iran (Islamic Republic of)	0.3813
99	Egypt	0.3793
100	Guatemala	0.3777
101	Azerbaijan	0.3773
102	Albania	0.3732
103	Cuba	0.3700
104	Tonga	0.3680
105	Viet Nam	0.3640
106	Armenia	0.3625
107	Paraguay	0.3620
108	Swaziland	0.3593
109	Republic of Moldova	0.3459
110	Suriname	0.3449
111	Namibia	0.3411
112	Oman	0.3405
113	Nicaragua	0.3383
114	Lesotho	0.3373
115	Honduras	0.3348
116	Cape Verde	0.3346
117	Tajikistan	0.3346
118	Iraq	0.3334
119	Dominica	0.3334
120	Zimbabwe	0.3316

Table 1.   *(continued)*

	Country	Index
121	Tunisia	0.3310
122	Kenya	0.3298
123	Algeria	0.3242
124	San Marino	0.3110
125	Uganda	0.3081
126	Nepal	0.3021
127	United Republic of Tanzania	0.3020
128	Cambodia	0.2989
129	Myanmar	0.2959
130	Bhutan	0.2941
131	Gabon	0.2928
132	Syrian Arab Republic	0.2871
133	Ghana	0.2866
134	Congo	0.2855
135	São Tomé and Principe	0.2837
136	Pakistan	0.2836
137	Malawi	0.2794
138	Morocco	0.2774
139	Nigeria	0.2758
140	Solomon Islands	0.2669
141	Madagascar	0.2641
142	Papua New Guinea	0.2539
143	Rwanda	0.2530
144	Timor-Leste	0.2512
145	Cameroon	0.2500
146	Mozambique	0.2448
147	Lao People's Democratic Republic	0.2421
148	Monaco	0.2404
149	Djibouti	0.2381
150	Sudan	0.2370
151	Benin	0.2309
152	Togo	0.2274
153	Senegal	0.2238
154	Yemen	0.2125
155	Comoros	0.1974
156	Serbia and Montenegro	0.1960
157	Eritrea	0.1849
158	Angola	0.1840
159	Andorra	0.1836
160	Côte d'Ivoire	0.1820

Table 1.   *(continued)*

	Country	Index
161	Liechtenstein	0.1789
162	Bangladesh	0.1762
163	Gambia	0.1736
164	Mauritania	0.1723
165	Vanuatu	0.1664
166	Burundi	0.1643
167	Sierra Leone	0.1639
168	Afghanistan	0.1490
169	Chad	0.1433
170	Guinea	0.1396
171	Ethiopia	0.1360
172	Burkina Faso	0.1329
173	Mali	0.0925
174	Niger	0.0661
175	Palau	0.0564
176	Micronesia (Federated States of)	0.0532
177	Marshall Islands	0.0440
178	Tuvalu	0.0370
179	Nauru	0.0357
	World Average	0.4267

Table 2.
E-government Readiness Data 2005

	Country	Web Measure Index	Infrastructure Index	Human Capital Index	E-government Readiness Index
1	United States	1.0000	0.7486	0.9700	0.9062
2	Denmark	0.9731	0.7642	0.9800	0.9058
3	Sweden	0.8654	0.8395	0.9900	0.8983
4	United Kingdom	0.9962	0.6471	0.9900	0.8777
5	Republic of Korea	0.9769	0.6713	0.9700	0.8727
6	Australia	0.9038	0.7098	0.9900	0.8679
7	Singapore	0.9962	0.6448	0.9100	0.8503
8	Canada	0.8923	0.6552	0.9800	0.8425
9	Finland	0.8269	0.6524	0.9900	0.8231
10	Norway	0.7962	0.6823	0.9900	0.8228
11	Germany	0.8423	0.6226	0.9500	0.8050
12	Netherlands	0.7346	0.6815	0.9900	0.8021
13	New Zealand	0.8038	0.6021	0.9900	0.7987
14	Japan	0.8154	0.5850	0.9400	0.7801
15	Iceland	0.6077	0.7704	0.9600	0.7794
16	Austria	0.7423	0.5784	0.9600	0.7602
17	Switzerland	0.6038	0.7105	0.9500	0.7548
18	Belgium	0.7115	0.5127	0.9900	0.7381
19	Estonia	0.6962	0.5281	0.9800	0.7347
20	Ireland	0.7115	0.5037	0.9600	0.7251
21	Malta	0.7923	0.4413	0.8700	0.7012
22	Chile	0.9115	0.2773	0.9000	0.6963
23	France	0.6115	0.5060	0.9600	0.6925
24	Israel	0.7308	0.4002	0.9400	0.6903
25	Italy	0.6269	0.4812	0.9300	0.6794
26	Slovenia	0.5923	0.4762	0.9600	0.6762
27	Hungary	0.7038	0.3069	0.9500	0.6536
28	Luxembourg	0.4000	0.6439	0.9100	0.6513
29	Czech Republic	0.5885	0.4102	0.9200	0.6396
30	Portugal	0.4269	0.4283	0.9700	0.6084
31	Mexico	0.8192	0.1491	0.8500	0.6061
32	Latvia	0.4846	0.3805	0.9500	0.6050
33	Brazil	0.7500	0.1644	0.8800	0.5981
34	Argentina	0.6577	0.1737	0.9600	0.5971
35	Greece	0.5115	0.3148	0.9500	0.5921
36	Slovakia	0.5385	0.3176	0.9100	0.5887
37	Cyprus	0.4615	0.4101	0.8900	0.5872
38	Poland	0.5115	0.2901	0.9600	0.5872

Table 2. *(continued)*

	Country	Web Measure Index	Infrastructure Index	Human Capital Index	E-government Readiness Index
39	Spain	0.3923	0.3919	0.9700	0.5847
40	Lithuania	0.5231	0.2528	0.9600	0.5786
41	Philippines	0.7423	0.0840	0.8900	0.5721
42	United Arab Emirates	0.6115	0.3639	0.7400	0.5718
43	Malaysia	0.5769	0.3048	0.8300	0.5706
44	Romania	0.6423	0.1889	0.8800	0.5704
45	Bulgaria	0.5192	0.2522	0.9100	0.5605
46	Thailand	0.6654	0.1299	0.8600	0.5518
47	Croatia	0.4423	0.3018	0.9000	0.5480
48	Ukraine	0.5808	0.1161	0.9400	0.5456
49	Uruguay	0.4500	0.2261	0.9400	0.5387
50	Russian Federation	0.4538	0.1947	0.9500	0.5329
51	Belarus	0.4885	0.1571	0.9500	0.5318
52	Mauritius	0.6288	0.1762	0.7900	0.5317
53	Bahrain	0.4192	0.3152	0.8500	0.5282
54	Colombia	0.6154	0.1110	0.8400	0.5221
55	Venezuela	0.5769	0.1113	0.8600	0.5161
56	Peru	0.5577	0.1091	0.8600	0.5089
57	China	0.5692	0.1241	0.8300	0.5078
58	South Africa	0.5692	0.1234	0.8300	0.5075
59	Jamaica	0.4885	0.2008	0.8300	0.5064
60	Turkey	0.5231	0.1648	0.8000	0.4960
61	Barbados	0.2154	0.3107	0.9500	0.4920
62	Qatar	0.3269	0.3116	0.8300	0.4895
63	Seychelles	0.3308	0.2343	0.9000	0.4884
64	Panama	0.4885	0.0980	0.8600	0.4822
65	Kazakhstan	0.4500	0.0638	0.9300	0.4813
66	Trinidad and Tobago	0.3635	0.1969	0.8700	0.4768
67	Bahamas	0.2923	0.2304	0.8800	0.4676
68	Jordan	0.4346	0.0971	0.8600	0.4639
69	T.F.Y.R. Macedonia	0.3962	0.1237	0.8700	0.4633
70	Costa Rica	0.2538	0.2596	0.8700	0.4612
71	Lebanon	0.3423	0.1857	0.8400	0.4560
72	Saint Kitts and Nevis	0.1115	0.2562	0.9800	0.4492
73	Brunei Darussalam	0.2462	0.2264	0.8700	0.4475
74	Saint Lucia	0.2865	0.1737	0.8800	0.4467
75	Kuwait	0.2500	0.2694	0.8100	0.4431
76	Kyrgyzstan	0.3654	0.0398	0.9200	0.4417
77	Maldives	0.3115	0.0748	0.9100	0.4321
78	El Salvador	0.4269	0.0906	0.7500	0.4225

Table 2. *(continued)*

	Country	Web Measure Index	Infrastructure Index	Human Capital Index	E-government Readiness Index
79	Uzbekistan	0.2731	0.0510	0.9100	0.4114
80	Saudi Arabia	0.3769	0.1445	0.7100	0.4105
81	Fiji	0.2808	0.0836	0.8600	0.4081
82	Dominican Republic	0.3115	0.0912	0.8200	0.4076
83	Georgia	0.2115	0.1086	0.8900	0.4034
84	Bosnia and Herzegovina	0.2731	0.0926	0.8400	0.4019
85	Bolivia	0.2885	0.0568	0.8600	0.4017
86	Antigua and Barbuda	0.1577	0.2454	0.8000	0.4010
87	India	0.5827	0.0277	0.5900	0.4001
88	Saint Vincent and the Grenadines	0.2538	0.1763	0.7700	0.4001
89	Guyana	0.1846	0.1209	0.8900	0.3985
90	Botswana	0.3692	0.0640	0.7600	0.3978
91	Samoa	0.2654	0.0377	0.8900	0.3977
92	Ecuador	0.2500	0.0899	0.8500	0.3966
93	Mongolia	0.2308	0.0679	0.8900	0.3962
94	Sri Lanka	0.3192	0.0359	0.8300	0.3950
95	Grenada	0.0885	0.2254	0.8500	0.3879
96	Indonesia	0.2962	0.0494	0.8000	0.3819
97	Belize	0.2538	0.1407	0.7500	0.3815
98	Iran (Islamic Republic of)	0.2962	0.1079	0.7400	0.3813
99	Egypt	0.4462	0.0717	0.6200	0.3793
100	Guatemala	0.4346	0.0484	0.6500	0.3777
101	Azerbaijan	0.1808	0.0712	0.8800	0.3773
102	Albania	0.1615	0.0680	0.8900	0.3732
103	Cuba	0.1500	0.0499	0.9100	0.3700
104	Tonga	0.1269	0.0472	0.9300	0.3680
105	Viet Nam	0.2231	0.0489	0.8200	0.3640
106	Armenia	0.1115	0.0759	0.9000	0.3625
107	Paraguay	0.1654	0.0706	0.8500	0.3620
108	Swaziland	0.2923	0.0456	0.7400	0.3593
109	Republic of Moldova	0.0538	0.1138	0.8700	0.3459
110	Suriname	0.0500	0.1148	0.8700	0.3449
111	Namibia	0.1654	0.0678	0.7900	0.3411
112	Oman	0.1731	0.1385	0.7100	0.3405
113	Nicaragua	0.2500	0.0348	0.7300	0.3383
114	Lesotho	0.2385	0.0135	0.7600	0.3373
115	Honduras	0.2231	0.0412	0.7400	0.3348
116	Cape Verde	0.1731	0.0808	0.7500	0.3346
117	Tajikistan	0.0615	0.0422	0.9000	0.3346

Table 2. *(continued)*

	Country	Web Measure Index	Infrastructure Index	Human Capital Index	E-government Readiness Index
118	Iraq	0.0538	0.0164	0.9300	0.3334
119	Dominica	0.0692	0.1709	0.7600	0.3334
120	Zimbabwe	0.1654	0.0395	0.7900	0.3316
121	Tunisia	0.1538	0.0993	0.7400	0.3310
122	Kenya	0.2308	0.0187	0.7400	0.3298
123	Algeria	0.2462	0.0365	0.6900	0.3242
124	San Marino	0.2846	0.6482	0.0000	0.3110
125	Uganda	0.2154	0.0090	0.7000	0.3081
126	Nepal	0.4000	0.0063	0.5000	0.3021
127	United Republic of Tanzania	0.2750	0.0110	0.6200	0.3020
128	Cambodia	0.2308	0.0060	0.6600	0.2989
129	Myanmar	0.1538	0.0040	0.7300	0.2959
130	Bhutan	0.3846	0.0175	0.4800	0.2941
131	Gabon	0.0923	0.0662	0.7200	0.2928
132	Syrian Arab Republic	0.0654	0.0458	0.7500	0.2871
133	Ghana	0.1885	0.0214	0.6500	0.2866
134	Congo	0.1346	0.0119	0.7100	0.2855
135	São Tomé and Principe	0.0115	0.0797	0.7600	0.2837
136	Pakistan	0.4269	0.0238	0.4000	0.2836
137	Malawi	0.1731	0.0053	0.6600	0.2794
138	Morocco	0.2385	0.0637	0.5300	0.2774
139	Nigeria	0.2231	0.0143	0.5900	0.2758
140	Solomon Islands	0.1000	0.0206	0.6800	0.2669
141	Madagascar	0.1846	0.0075	0.6000	0.2641
142	Papua New Guinea	0.1615	0.0302	0.5700	0.2539
143	Rwanda	0.1154	0.0035	0.6400	0.2530
144	Timor-Leste	0.1135	0.0000	0.6400	0.2512
145	Cameroon	0.0962	0.0139	0.6400	0.2500
146	Mozambique	0.2788	0.0057	0.4500	0.2448
147	Lao People's Democratic Republic	0.0788	0.0074	0.6400	0.2421
148	Monaco	0.2192	0.5021	0.0000	0.2404
149	Djibouti	0.1731	0.0211	0.5200	0.2381
150	Sudan	0.1615	0.0293	0.5200	0.2370
151	Benin	0.2385	0.0142	0.4400	0.2309
152	Togo	0.0308	0.0313	0.6200	0.2274
153	Senegal	0.2538	0.0275	0.3900	0.2238
154	Yemen	0.0962	0.0413	0.5000	0.2125
155	Comoros	0.0538	0.0082	0.5300	0.1974
156	Serbia and Montenegro	0.4462	0.1417	0.0000	0.1960

Table 2. *(continued)*

	Country	Web Measure Index	Infrastructure Index	Human Capital Index	E-government Readiness Index
157	Eritrea	0.0577	0.0069	0.4900	0.1849
158	Angola	0.1654	0.0066	0.3800	0.1840
159	Andorra	0.2519	0.2990	0.0000	0.1836
160	Côte d'Ivoire	0.0538	0.0223	0.4700	0.1820
161	Liechtenstein	0.1731	0.3637	0.0000	0.1789
162	Bangladesh	0.0731	0.0055	0.4500	0.1762
163	Gambia	0.0962	0.0248	0.4000	0.1736
164	Mauritania	0.0692	0.0278	0.4200	0.1723
165	Vanuatu	0.0500	0.0293	0.4200	0.1664
166	Burundi	0.0385	0.0043	0.4500	0.1643
167	Sierra Leone	0.0962	0.0056	0.3900	0.1639
168	Afghanistan	0.1769	0.0020	0.2680	0.1490
169	Chad	0.0077	0.0023	0.4200	0.1433
170	Guinea	0.0385	0.0102	0.3700	0.1396
171	Ethiopia	0.0154	0.0027	0.3900	0.1360
172	Burkina Faso	0.2327	0.0060	0.1600	0.1329
173	Mali	0.0615	0.0060	0.2100	0.0925
174	Niger	0.0115	0.0069	0.1800	0.0661
175	Palau	0.1692	0.0000	0.0000	0.0564
176	Micronesia (Federated States of)	0.1077	0.0519	0.0000	0.0532
177	Marshall Islands	0.0904	0.0416	0.0000	0.0440
178	Tuvalu	0.0269	0.0841	0.0000	0.0370
179	Nauru	0.0577	0.0495	0.0000	0.0357
	Countries with no web presence in 2005				
180	Central African Republic	0.0000	0.0028	0.4300	0.1443
181	Democratic People's Republic of Korea	0.0000	0.0057	0.0000	0.0019
182	Democratic Republic of the Congo	0.0000	0.0021	0.5100	0.1707
183	Equatorial Guinea	0.0000	0.0254	0.7600	0.2618
184	Guinea-Bissau	0.0000	0.0107	0.3900	0.1336
185	Haiti	0.0000	0.0157	0.5200	0.1786
186	Kiribati	0.0000	0.0253	0.0000	0.0084
187	Liberia	0.0000	0.0032	0.0000	0.0011
188	Libyan Arab Jamahiriya	0.0000	0.0573	0.8700	0.3091
189	Somalia	0.0000	0.0073	0.0000	0.0024
190	Turkmenistan	0.0000	0.0375	0.9300	0.3225
191	Zambia	0.0000	0.0230	0.6800	0.2343

Table 3.
Web Measure Assessment 2005

	Country	Web Measure
1	Afghanistan	0.1769
2	Albania	0.1615
3	Algeria	0.2462
4	Andorra	0.2519
5	Angola	0.1654
6	Antigua and Barbuda	0.1577
7	Argentina	0.6577
8	Armenia	0.1115
9	Australia	0.9038
10	Austria	0.7423
11	Azerbaijan	0.1808
12	Bahamas	0.2923
13	Bahrain	0.4192
14	Bangladesh	0.0731
15	Barbados	0.2154
16	Belarus	0.4885
17	Belgium	0.7115
18	Belize	0.2538
19	Benin	0.2385
20	Bhutan	0.3846
21	Bolivia	0.2885
22	Bosnia and Herzegovina	0.2731
23	Botswana	0.3692
24	Brazil	0.7500
25	Brunei Darussalam	0.2462
26	Bulgaria	0.5192
27	Burkina Faso	0.2327
28	Burundi	0.0385
29	Cambodia	0.2308
30	Cameroon	0.0962
31	Canada	0.8923
32	Cape Verde	0.1731
33	Central African Republic	0.0000
34	Chad	0.0077
35	Chile	0.9115
36	China	0.5692
37	Colombia	0.6154
38	Comoros	0.0538
39	Congo	0.1346
40	Costa Rica	0.2538

Table 3. *(continued)*

	Country	Web Measure
41	Côte d'Ivoire	0.0538
42	Croatia	0.4423
43	Cuba	0.1500
44	Cyprus	0.4615
45	Czech Republic	0.5885
46	Democratic People's Republic of Korea	0.0000
47	Democratic Republic of the Congo	0.0000
48	Denmark	0.9731
49	Djibouti	0.1731
50	Dominica	0.0692
51	Dominican Republic	0.3115
52	Ecuador	0.2500
53	Egypt	0.4462
54	El Salvador	0.4269
55	Equatorial Guinea	0.0000
56	Eritrea	0.0577
57	Estonia	0.6962
58	Ethiopia	0.0154
59	Fiji	0.2808
60	Finland	0.8269
61	France	0.6115
62	Gabon	0.0923
63	Gambia	0.0962
64	Georgia	0.2115
65	Germany	0.8423
66	Ghana	0.1885
67	Greece	0.5115
68	Grenada	0.0885
69	Guatemala	0.4346
70	Guinea	0.0385
71	Guinea-Bissau	0.0000
72	Guyana	0.1846
73	Haiti	0.0000
74	Honduras	0.2231
75	Hungary	0.7038
76	Iceland	0.6077
77	India	0.5827
78	Indonesia	0.2962
79	Iran (Islamic Republic of)	0.2962
80	Iraq	0.0538

Table 3. *(continued)*

	Country	Web Measure
81	Ireland	0.7115
82	Israel	0.7308
83	Italy	0.6269
84	Jamaica	0.4885
85	Japan	0.8154
86	Jordan	0.4346
87	Kazakhstan	0.4500
88	Kenya	0.2308
89	Kiribati	0.0000
90	Kuwait	0.2500
91	Kyrgyzstan	0.3654
92	Lao People's Democratic Republic	0.0788
93	Latvia	0.4846
94	Lebanon	0.3423
95	Lesotho	0.2385
96	Liberia	0.0000
97	Libyan Arab Jamahiriya	0.0000
98	Liechtenstein	0.1731
99	Lithuania	0.5231
100	Luxembourg	0.4000
101	Madagascar	0.1846
102	Malawi	0.1731
103	Malaysia	0.5769
104	Maldives	0.3115
105	Mali	0.0615
106	Malta	0.7923
107	Marshall Islands	0.0904
108	Mauritania	0.0692
109	Mauritius	0.6288
110	Mexico	0.8192
111	Micronesia (Federated States of)	0.1077
112	Monaco	0.2192
113	Mongolia	0.2308
114	Morocco	0.2385
115	Mozambique	0.2788
116	Myanmar	0.1538
117	Namibia	0.1654
118	Nauru	0.0577
119	Nepal	0.4000
120	Netherlands	0.7346

Table 3.   *(continued)*

	Country	Web Measure
121	New Zealand	0.8038
122	Nicaragua	0.2500
123	Niger	0.0115
124	Nigeria	0.2231
125	Norway	0.7962
126	Oman	0.1731
127	Pakistan	0.4269
128	Palau	0.1692
129	Panama	0.4885
130	Papua New Guinea	0.1615
131	Paraguay	0.1654
132	Peru	0.5577
133	Philippines	0.7423
134	Poland	0.5115
135	Portugal	0.4269
136	Qatar	0.3269
137	Republic of Korea	0.9769
138	Republic of Moldova	0.0538
139	Romania	0.6423
140	Russian Federation	0.4538
141	Rwanda	0.1154
142	Saint Kitts and Nevis	0.1115
143	Saint Lucia	0.2865
144	Saint Vincent and the Grenadines	0.2538
145	Samoa	0.2654
146	San Marino	0.2846
147	São Tomé and Principe	0.0115
148	Saudi Arabia	0.3769
149	Senegal	0.2538
150	Serbia and Montenegro	0.4462
151	Seychelles	0.3308
152	Sierra Leone	0.0962
153	Singapore	0.9962
154	Slovakia	0.5385
155	Slovenia	0.5923
156	Solomon Islands	0.1000
157	Somalia	0.0000
158	South Africa	0.5692
159	Spain	0.3923
160	Sri Lanka	0.3192

Table 3.   *(continued)*

	Country	Web Measure
161	Sudan	0.1615
162	Suriname	0.0500
163	Swaziland	0.2923
164	Sweden	0.8654
165	Switzerland	0.6038
166	Syrian Arab Republic	0.0654
167	Tajikistan	0.0615
168	Thailand	0.6654
169	T.F.Y.R. Macedonia	0.3962
170	Timor-Leste	0.1135
171	Togo	0.0308
172	Tonga	0.1269
173	Trinidad and Tobago	0.3635
174	Tunisia	0.1538
175	Turkey	0.5231
176	Turkmenistan	0.0000
177	Tuvalu	0.0269
178	Uganda	0.2154
179	Ukraine	0.5808
180	United Arab Emirates	0.6115
181	United Kingdom	0.9962
182	United Republic of Tanzania	0.2750
183	United States	1.0000
184	Uruguay	0.4500
185	Uzbekistan	0.2731
186	Vanuatu	0.0500
187	Venezuela	0.5769
188	Viet Nam	0.2231
189	Yemen	0.0962
190	Zambia	0.0000
191	Zimbabwe	0.1654

Table 4.
Internet Users and PCs Index 2005 (per 100 persons)

	Country	Internet data	Internet users Index	PCs	PC Index
1	Afghanistan	0.1	0.001	0	0
2	Albania	1.000	0.015	1.200	0.015
3	Algeria	1.600	0.024	0.800	0.010
4	Andorra	11.900	0.176	0.000	0.000
5	Angola	0.300	0.004	0.200	0.002
6	Antigua and Barbuda	12.800	0.190	0.000	0.000
7	Argentina	11.200	0.166	8.200	0.100
8	Armenia	3.700	0.055	2.600	0.032
9	Australia	56.700	0.840	60.200	0.736
10	Austria	46.200	0.684	37.400	0.457
11	Azerbaijan	3.700	0.055	0.000	0.000
12	Bahamas	26.500	0.393	0.000	0.000
13	Bahrain	21.600	0.320	15.900	0.194
14	Bangladesh	0.200	0.003	0.800	0.010
15	Barbados	37.100	0.550	10.400	0.127
16	Belarus	14.100	0.209	0.000	0.000
17	Belgium	38.600	0.572	31.800	0.389
18	Belize	10.900	0.161	12.700	0.155
19	Benin	1.000	0.015	0.400	0.005
20	Bhutan	2.000	0.030	1.400	0.017
21	Bolivia	3.200	0.047	2.300	0.028
22	Bosnia and Herzegovina	2.600	0.039	0.000	0.000
23	Botswana	3.500	0.052	4.100	0.050
24	Brazil	8.200	0.121	7.500	0.092
25	Brunei Darussalam	10.230	0.152	7.700	0.094
26	Bulgaria	20.600	0.305	5.200	0.064
27	Burkina Faso	0.400	0.006	0.200	0.002
28	Burundi	0.200	0.003	0.200	0.002
29	Cambodia	0.300	0.004	0.200	0.002
30	Cameroon	0.400	0.006	0.600	0.007
31	Canada	51.300	0.760	48.700	0.595
32	Cape Verde	4.400	0.065	7.800	0.095
33	Central African Republic	0.100	0.001	0.200	0.002
34	Chad	0.200	0.003	0.200	0.002
35	Chile	27.200	0.403	11.900	0.145
36	China	6.300	0.093	2.800	0.034
37	Colombia	5.300	0.079	4.900	0.060
38	Comoros	0.600	0.009	0.600	0.007
39	Congo	0.400	0.006	0.400	0.005
40	Costa Rica	28.800	0.427	21.800	0.267
41	Côte d'Ivoire	1.400	0.021	0.900	0.011
42	Croatia	23.200	0.344	17.400	0.213

Table 4. *(continued)*

	Country	Internet data	Internet users Index	PCs	PC Index
43	Cuba	0.900	0.013	2.400	0.029
44	Cyprus	33.700	0.499	27.000	0.330
45	Czech Republic	30.800	0.456	17.700	0.216
46	Democratic People's Rep. of Korea	0.000	0.000	0.000	0.000
47	Democratic Rep. of the Congo	0.100	0.001	0.000	0.000
48	Denmark	54.100	0.801	57.700	0.705
49	Djibouti	1.000	0.015	2.200	0.027
50	Dominica	16.300	0.241	9.000	0.110
51	Dominican Republic	10.200	0.151	0.000	0.000
52	Ecuador	4.600	0.068	3.200	0.039
53	Egypt	4.400	0.065	2.900	0.035
54	El Salvador	8.300	0.123	3.300	0.040
55	Equatorial Guinea	0.400	0.006	0.700	0.009
56	Eritrea	0.700	0.010	0.300	0.004
57	Estonia	44.400	0.658	44.000	0.538
58	Ethiopia	0.100	0.001	0.200	0.002
59	Fiji	6.700	0.099	5.100	0.062
60	Finland	53.400	0.791	44.200	0.540
61	France	36.600	0.542	34.700	0.424
62	Gabon	2.600	0.039	1.900	0.023
63	Gambia	1.900	0.028	1.400	0.017
64	Georgia	2.400	0.036	3.500	0.043
65	Germany	47.300	0.701	48.500	0.593
66	Ghana	0.800	0.012	0.400	0.005
67	Greece	15.000	0.222	8.200	0.100
68	Grenada	16.900	0.250	13.200	0.161
69	Guatemala	3.300	0.049	1.400	0.017
70	Guinea	0.500	0.007	0.600	0.007
71	Guinea-Bissau	1.500	0.022	0.000	0.000
72	Guyana	14.220	0.211	2.700	0.033
73	Haiti	1.800	0.027	0.900	0.011
74	Honduras	4.000	0.059	1.500	0.018
75	Hungary	23.200	0.344	10.800	0.132
76	Iceland	67.500	1.000	45.100	0.551
77	India	1.800	0.027	0.700	0.009
78	Indonesia	3.800	0.056	1.200	0.015
79	Iran (Islamic Republic of)	7.200	0.107	9.100	0.111
80	Iraq	0.100	0.001	0.800	0.010
81	Ireland	31.700	0.470	42.100	0.515
82	Israel	30.100	0.446	24.300	0.297
83	Italy	33.700	0.499	23.100	0.282
84	Jamaica	22.800	0.338	5.400	0.066
85	Japan	48.300	0.716	38.200	0.467

Table 4.   *(continued)*

·	Country	Internet data	Internet users Index	PCs	PC Index
86	Jordan	8.100	0.120	4.500	0.055
87	Kazakhstan	1.600	0.024	0.000	0.000
88	Kenya	1.300	0.019	0.700	0.009
89	Kiribati	2.300	0.034	1.100	0.013
90	Kuwait	22.800	0.338	16.100	0.197
91	Kyrgyzstan	3.800	0.056	1.400	0.017
92	Lao People's Democratic Republic	0.300	0.004	0.400	0.005
93	Latvia	40.400	0.599	18.800	0.230
94	Lebanon	14.300	0.212	10.000	0.122
95	Lesotho	1.400	0.021	0.000	0.000
96	Liberia	0.000	0.000	0.000	0.000
97	Libyan Arab Jamahiriya	2.900	0.043	2.300	0.028
98	Liechtenstein	59.100	0.876	0.000	0.000
99	Lithuania	20.200	0.299	11.000	0.134
100	Luxembourg	37.600	0.557	62.000	0.758
101	Madagascar	0.400	0.006	0.500	0.006
102	Malawi	0.300	0.004	0.200	0.002
103	Malaysia	34.400	0.510	16.700	0.204
104	Maldives	5.300	0.079	7.100	0.087
105	Mali	0.240	0.004	0.100	0.001
106	Malta	30.300	0.449	25.500	0.312
107	Marshall Islands	2.600	0.039	5.600	0.068
108	Mauritania	0.400	0.006	1.100	0.013
109	Mauritius	12.300	0.182	14.900	0.182
110	Mexico	12.000	0.178	8.300	0.101
111	Micronesia (Federated States of)	9.300	0.138	0.000	0.000
112	Monaco	49.100	0.727	16.200	0.198
113	Mongolia	5.800	0.086	7.700	0.094
114	Morocco	3.300	0.049	2.000	0.024
115	Mozambique	0.300	0.004	0.500	0.006
116	Myanmar	0.100	0.001	0.600	0.007
117	Namibia	3.400	0.050	9.900	0.121
118	Nauru	2.600	0.039	0.000	0.000
119	Nepal	0.300	0.004	0.400	0.005
120	Netherlands	52.200	0.773	46.700	0.571
121	New Zealand	52.600	0.779	41.400	0.506
122	Nicaragua	1.700	0.025	2.900	0.035
123	Niger	1.300	0.019	0.100	0.001
124	Nigeria	0.600	0.009	0.700	0.009
125	Norway	34.600	0.513	52.800	0.645
126	Oman	7.100	0.105	3.700	0.045
127	Pakistan	1.000	0.015	0.400	0.005
128	Palau	0.000	0.000	0.000	0.000

Table 4.   (continued)

	Country	Internet data	Internet users Index	PCs	PC Index
129	Panama	6.200	0.092	3.800	0.046
130	Papua New Guinea	1.400	0.021	5.900	0.072
131	Paraguay	2.000	0.030	3.500	0.043
132	Peru	10.400	0.154	4.300	0.053
133	Philippines	4.400	0.065	2.800	0.034
134	Poland	23.200	0.344	14.200	0.174
135	Portugal	19.400	0.287	13.400	0.164
136	Qatar	19.900	0.295	16.400	0.200
137	Republic of Korea	61.000	0.904	55.800	0.682
138	Republic of Moldova	8.000	0.119	2.100	0.026
139	Romania	18.400	0.273	9.700	0.119
140	Russian Federation	4.100	0.061	8.900	0.109
141	Rwanda	0.300	0.004	0.000	0.000
142	Saint Kitts and Nevis	21.300	0.316	19.100	0.233
143	Saint Lucia	8.240	0.122	15.000	0.183
144	Saint Vincent and the Grenadines	6.000	0.089	12.000	0.147
145	Samoa	2.200	0.033	0.700	0.009
146	San Marino	53.600	0.794	81.800	1.000
147	São Tomé and Principe	9.900	0.147	0.000	0.000
148	Saudi Arabia	6.700	0.099	13.700	0.167
149	Senegal	2.200	0.033	2.100	0.026
150	Serbia and Montenegro	7.900	0.117	2.700	0.033
151	Seychelles	14.500	0.215	15.500	0.189
152	Sierra Leone	0.200	0.003	0.200	0.002
153	Singapore	50.900	0.754	62.200	0.760
154	Slovakia	25.600	0.379	23.600	0.289
155	Slovenia	40.100	0.594	32.500	0.397
156	Solomon Islands	0.500	0.007	4.000	0.049
157	Somalia	0.900	0.013	0.400	0.005
158	South Africa	6.800	0.101	7.300	0.089
159	Spain	23.900	0.354	19.600	0.240
160	Sri Lanka	1.300	0.019	1.700	0.021
161	Sudan	0.900	0.013	0.600	0.007
162	Suriname	4.400	0.065	4.600	0.056
163	Swaziland	2.600	0.039	2.900	0.035
164	Sweden	57.300	0.849	62.100	0.759
165	Switzerland	39.900	0.591	70.900	0.867
166	Syrian Arab Republic	1.300	0.019	1.900	0.023
167	Tajikistan	0.100	0.001	0.000	0.000
168	Thailand	11.100	0.164	4.000	0.049
169	T.F.Y.R. Macedonia	4.850	0.072	0.000	0.000
170	Timor-Leste	0.000	0.000	0.000	0.000
171	Togo	4.200	0.062	3.200	0.039

Table 4.   *(continued)*

	Country	Internet data	Internet users Index	PCs	PC Index
172	Tonga	2.920	0.043	2.000	0.024
173	Trinidad and Tobago	10.600	0.157	8.000	0.098
174	Tunisia	6.400	0.095	4.000	0.049
175	Turkey	8.500	0.126	4.300	0.053
176	Turkmenistan	0.200	0.003	0.500	0.006
177	Tuvalu	18.800	0.279	5.900	0.072
178	Uganda	0.500	0.007	0.400	0.005
179	Ukraine	1.900	0.028	2.000	0.024
180	United Arab Emirates	27.500	0.407	12.000	0.147
181	United Kingdom	42.300	0.627	40.600	0.496
182	United Republic of Tanzania	0.700	0.010	0.600	0.007
183	United States	55.600	0.824	66.000	0.807
184	Uruguay	11.900	0.176	11.000	0.134
185	Uzbekistan	1.900	0.028	0.300	0.004
186	Vanuatu	3.600	0.053	1.500	0.018
187	Venezuela	6.000	0.089	6.100	0.075
188	Viet Nam	4.300	0.064	1.000	0.012
189	Yemen	0.500	0.007	0.700	0.009
190	Zambia	0.600	0.009	0.900	0.011
191	Zimbabwe	4.300	0.064	5.300	0.065

Source: International Telecommunication Union. Accessed 19 July 2005.
http://unstats.un.org/unsd/cdb/cdb_advanced_data_extract.asp.

Note: Data is for the latest year available.

Table 5.
Telephone and Cellular Index 2005

	Country	Telephone data	Telephone Index	Cellular data	Cellular Index
1	Afghanistan	0.1000	0.0010	0.1000	0.0008
2	Albania	8.3000	0.0798	35.8000	0.2999
3	Algeria	6.9300	0.0666	4.5400	0.0380
4	Andorra	43.8000	0.4212	35.8000	0.2999
5	Angola	0.6700	0.0064	0.9300	0.0078
6	Antigua and Barbuda	48.7800	0.4690	48.9800	0.4103
7	Argentina	21.8800	0.2104	17.7600	0.1488
8	Armenia	14.8300	0.1426	3.0100	0.0252
9	Australia	54.2300	0.5214	71.9500	0.6027
10	Austria	48.0700	0.4622	87.8800	0.7361
11	Azerbaijan	11.4300	0.1099	12.8100	0.1073
12	Bahamas	41.5300	0.3993	36.6700	0.3072
13	Bahrain	26.7600	0.2573	63.8400	0.5348
14	Bangladesh	0.5500	0.0053	1.0100	0.0085
15	Barbados	49.6800	0.4777	51.9100	0.4348
16	Belarus	31.1100	0.2991	11.3200	0.0948
17	Belgium	48.9200	0.4704	79.2800	0.6641
18	Belize	11.2700	0.1084	20.4600	0.1714
19	Benin	0.9500	0.0091	3.3600	0.0281
20	Bhutan	3.4300	0.0330	1.0900	0.0091
21	Bolivia	7.2300	0.0695	15.2100	0.1274
22	Bosnia and Herzegovina	24.4800	0.2354	27.4000	0.2295
23	Botswana	7.4900	0.0720	29.7100	0.2489
24	Brazil	22.2900	0.2143	26.3600	0.2208
25	Brunei Darussalam	25.5700	0.2459	40.0600	0.3356
26	Bulgaria	38.0500	0.3659	46.6400	0.3907
27	Burkina Faso	0.5300	0.0051	1.8500	0.0155
28	Burundi	0.3400	0.0033	0.9000	0.0075
29	Cambodia	0.2600	0.0025	3.5200	0.0295
30	Cameroon	0.7000	0.0067	6.6200	0.0555
31	Canada	65.1400	0.6263	41.9000	0.3510
32	Cape Verde	15.6300	0.1503	11.6300	0.0974
33	Central African Republic	0.2300	0.0022	0.9700	0.0081
34	Chad	0.1500	0.0014	0.8000	0.0067
35	Chile	22.1000	0.2125	51.1400	0.4284
36	China	20.9000	0.2010	21.4800	0.1799
37	Colombia	17.9300	0.1724	14.1300	0.1184
38	Comoros	1.6600	0.0160	0.2500	0.0021
39	Congo	0.2000	0.0019	9.4300	0.0790
40	Costa Rica	27.7700	0.2670	18.1200	0.1518
41	Côte d'Ivoire	1.4300	0.0138	7.7000	0.0645
42	Croatia	41.7200	0.4012	58.3700	0.4889
43	Cuba	6.4000	0.0615	0.3100	0.0026
44	Cyprus	57.1900	0.5499	74.4000	0.6232

Table 5.   *(continued)*

	Country	Telephone data	Telephone Index	Cellular data	Cellular Index
45	Czech Republic	36.0300	0.3464	96.4600	0.8080
46	D.P.R. Korea	0.0000	0.0000	0.0000	0.0000
47	D.R. Congo	0.0200	0.0002	1.8900	0.0158
48	Denmark	66.9300	0.6436	88.3200	0.7398
49	Djibouti	1.5200	0.0146	3.4400	0.0288
50	Dominica	30.3900	0.2922	12.0000	0.1005
51	Dominican Republic	11.5400	0.1110	27.1600	0.2275
52	Ecuador	12.2400	0.1177	18.9200	0.1585
53	Egypt	12.7300	0.1224	8.4500	0.0708
54	El Salvador	11.3400	0.1090	17.3200	0.1451
55	Equatorial Guinea	1.7700	0.0170	7.6400	0.0640
56	Eritrea	0.9200	0.0088	0.0000	0.0000
57	Estonia	34.1200	0.3281	77.7400	0.6512
58	Ethiopia	0.6300	0.0061	0.1400	0.0012
59	Fiji	12.3500	0.1188	13.3100	0.1115
60	Finland	49.2000	0.4731	90.9600	0.7619
61	France	56.6000	0.5442	69.5900	0.5829
62	Gabon	2.8700	0.0276	22.4400	0.1880
63	Gambia	2.8900	0.0278	7.5300	0.0631
64	Georgia	13.4300	0.1291	14.5400	0.1218
65	Germany	65.7300	0.6320	78.5200	0.6577
66	Ghana	1.3500	0.0130	3.5600	0.0298
67	Greece	45.3900	0.4364	90.2300	0.7558
68	Grenada	29.0400	0.2792	37.6300	0.3152
69	Guatemala	7.0500	0.0678	13.1500	0.1102
70	Guinea	0.3400	0.0033	1.4400	0.0121
71	Guinea-Bissau	0.8200	0.0079	0.1000	0.0008
72	Guyana	9.1500	0.0880	9.9300	0.0832
73	Haiti	1.6800	0.0162	3.8400	0.0322
74	Honduras	4.8700	0.0468	5.5300	0.0463
75	Hungary	34.8600	0.3352	76.8800	0.6440
76	Iceland	65.9900	0.6345	96.5600	0.8088
77	India	4.6300	0.0445	2.4700	0.0207
78	Indonesia	3.9400	0.0379	8.7400	0.0732
79	Iran (Islamic Republic of)	21.9700	0.2113	5.0900	0.0426
80	Iraq	2.8000	0.0269	0.1000	0.0008
81	Ireland	49.1300	0.4724	87.9600	0.7368
82	Israel	45.8200	0.4406	96.0700	0.8047
83	Italy	48.4000	0.4654	101.7600	0.8524
84	Jamaica	16.9200	0.1627	68.0500	0.5700
85	Japan	47.1900	0.4538	67.9000	0.5688
86	Jordan	11.3600	0.1092	24.1900	0.2026
87	Kazakhstan	14.0700	0.1353	6.4300	0.0539
88	Kenya	1.0400	0.0100	5.0200	0.0421
89	Kiribati	5.1000	0.0490	0.6000	0.0050

Table 5. *(continued)*

	Country	Telephone data	Telephone Index	Cellular data	Cellular Index
90	Kuwait	19.6000	0.1885	57.1600	0.4788
91	Kyrgyzstan	7.6100	0.0732	2.6600	0.0223
92	Lao P.D.R.	1.2300	0.0118	1.9800	0.0166
93	Latvia	28.5400	0.2744	52.5800	0.4404
94	Lebanon	20.0000	0.1923	23.4300	0.1963
95	Lesotho	1.6100	0.0155	4.6700	0.0391
96	Liberia	0.2000	0.0019	0.1000	0.0008
97	Libya	13.5600	0.1304	2.3000	0.0193
98	Liechtenstein	58.3000	0.5606	33.3000	0.2789
99	Lithuania	23.9200	0.2300	62.9700	0.5275
100	Luxembourg	79.7500	0.7668	119.3800	1.0000
101	Madagascar	0.3600	0.0035	1.7400	0.0146
102	Malawi	0.8100	0.0078	1.2900	0.0108
103	Malaysia	18.1600	0.1746	44.2000	0.3702
104	Maldives	10.2000	0.0981	14.9100	0.1249
105	Mali	0.5300	0.0051	2.2500	0.0188
106	Malta	52.0700	0.5007	72.5000	0.6073
107	Marshall Islands	8.2000	0.0788	1.1100	0.0093
108	Mauritania	1.3900	0.0134	12.7500	0.1068
109	Mauritius	28.5200	0.2742	26.7000	0.2237
110	Mexico	15.9700	0.1536	29.4700	0.2469
111	Micronesia (Federated States of)	8.7000	0.0837	1.5000	0.0126
112	Monaco	104.0000	1.0000	45.9000	0.3845
113	Mongolia	5.6200	0.0540	12.9800	0.1087
114	Morocco	4.0500	0.0389	24.4300	0.2046
115	Mozambique	0.4600	0.0044	2.2800	0.0191
116	Myanmar	0.6800	0.0065	0.1200	0.0010
117	Namibia	6.6200	0.0637	11.6300	0.0974
118	Nauru	16.0000	0.1538	13.0000	0.1089
119	Nepal	1.5700	0.0151	0.2100	0.0018
120	Netherlands	61.4300	0.5907	76.7600	0.6430
121	New Zealand	44.8500	0.4313	64.8300	0.5431
122	Nicaragua	3.7400	0.0360	8.5100	0.0713
123	Niger	0.1900	0.0018	0.6200	0.0052
124	Nigeria	0.6900	0.0066	2.5500	0.0214
125	Norway	71.3500	0.6861	90.8900	0.7614
126	Oman	8.8400	0.0850	22.8300	0.1912
127	Pakistan	2.6600	0.0256	1.7500	0.0147
128	Palau	0.0000	0.0000	0.0000	0.0000
129	Panama	12.2000	0.1173	26.7600	0.2242
130	Papua New Guinea	1.1300	0.0109	0.2700	0.0023
131	Paraguay	4.6100	0.0443	29.8500	0.2500
132	Peru	6.7100	0.0645	10.6100	0.0889
133	Philippines	4.1200	0.0396	26.9500	0.2257
134	Poland	31.8700	0.3064	45.0900	0.3777

Table 5.   *(continued)*

	Country	Telephone data	Telephone Index	Cellular data	Cellular Index
135	Portugal	41.1100	0.3953	89.8500	0.7526
136	Qatar	26.1200	0.2512	53.3100	0.4466
137	Republic of Korea	53.8300	0.5176	70.0900	0.5871
138	Republic of Moldova	21.9300	0.2109	13.2000	0.1106
139	Romania	19.9400	0.1917	32.4200	0.2716
140	Russia	25.2700	0.2430	24.9300	0.2088
141	Rwanda	0.2800	0.0027	1.6000	0.0134
142	Saint Kitts and Nevis	50.0000	0.4808	10.6400	0.0891
143	Saint Lucia	31.9500	0.3072	8.9500	0.0750
144	Saint Vincent and the Grenadines	27.2500	0.2620	52.8700	0.4429
145	Samoa	7.2900	0.0701	5.7600	0.0482
146	San Marino	76.3000	0.7337	62.1000	0.5202
147	São Tomé and Principe	4.5900	0.0441	3.1700	0.0266
148	Saudi Arabia	15.5400	0.1494	32.1100	0.2690
149	Senegal	2.2100	0.0213	5.5600	0.0466
150	Serbia and Montenegro	24.2700	0.2334	33.7800	0.2830
151	Seychelles	25.6000	0.2462	59.4700	0.4982
152	Sierra Leone	0.4800	0.0046	1.3500	0.0113
153	Singapore	45.0300	0.4330	85.2500	0.7141
154	Slovakia	24.0800	0.2315	68.4200	0.5731
155	Slovenia	40.6800	0.3912	87.0900	0.7295
156	Solomon Islands	1.3100	0.0126	0.3100	0.0026
157	Somalia	1.0000	0.0096	0.3000	0.0025
158	South Africa	10.6600	0.1025	36.3600	0.3046
159	Spain	42.9100	0.4126	91.6100	0.7674
160	Sri Lanka	4.9000	0.0471	7.2700	0.0609
161	Sudan	2.7000	0.0260	1.9500	0.0163
162	Suriname	15.1700	0.1459	32.0300	0.2683
163	Swaziland	4.4300	0.0426	8.4300	0.0706
164	Sweden	73.5700	0.7074	98.0500	0.8213
165	Switzerland	72.7500	0.6995	84.3400	0.7065
166	Syrian Arab Republic	12.2600	0.1179	6.7500	0.0565
167	Tajikistan	3.7500	0.0361	0.7300	0.0061
168	Thailand	10.4900	0.1009	39.4200	0.3302
169	T.F.Y.R. Macedonia	27.1300	0.2609	17.7000	0.1483
170	Timor-Leste	0.0000	0.0000	0.0000	0.0000
171	Togo	1.2100	0.0116	4.4000	0.0369
172	Tonga	11.2900	0.1086	3.3800	0.0283
173	Trinidad and Tobago	24.9800	0.2402	39.9100	0.3343
174	Tunisia	11.7700	0.1132	19.6900	0.1649
175	Turkey	26.7500	0.2572	39.4400	0.3304
176	Turkmenistan	7.7300	0.0743	0.1700	0.0014
177	Tuvalu	6.8000	0.0654	0.0000	0.0000
178	Uganda	0.2400	0.0023	3.0300	0.0254
179	Ukraine	23.3400	0.2244	13.5900	0.1138

Table 5.   *(continued)*

	Country	Telephone data	Telephone Index	Cellular data	Cellular Index
180	United Arab Emirates	28.1100	0.2703	73.5700	0.6163
181	United Kingdom	59.0600	0.5679	91.1700	0.7637
182	United Republic of Tanzania	0.4200	0.0040	2.5200	0.0211
183	United States	62.3800	0.5998	54.5800	0.4572
184	Uruguay	27.9600	0.2688	19.2600	0.1613
185	Uzbekistan	6.7000	0.0644	1.2500	0.0105
186	Vanuatu	3.1500	0.0303	3.7600	0.0315
187	Venezuela	11.0600	0.1063	27.3000	0.2287
188	Viet Nam	5.4100	0.0520	3.3700	0.0282
189	Yemen	2.7800	0.0267	3.4700	0.0291
190	Zambia	0.7900	0.0076	2.1500	0.0180
191	Zimbabwe	2.5600	0.0246	3.2200	0.0270

Source: International Telecommunication Union.
http://www.itu.int/ITU-D/ict/statistics/at_glance/main03.pdf.
Accessed 19 July 2005.

Table 6.
TV and Online population Index 2005 *(per 100 persons)*

	Country	TV	TV Index	Online population data	Online population Index
1	Afghanistan	1.400	0.015	0.000	0.000
2	Albania	14.600	0.151	0.340	0.005
3	Algeria	10.700	0.111	0.570	0.008
4	Andorra	44.000	0.456	36.260	0.519
5	Angola	1.500	0.016	0.570	0.008
6	Antigua and Barbuda	49.300	0.511	7.520	0.108
7	Argentina	32.600	0.338	10.380	0.149
8	Armenia	24.100	0.250	0.900	0.013
9	Australia	71.600	0.742	54.380	0.779
10	Austria	52.600	0.545	45.200	0.648
11	Azerbaijan	25.700	0.266	0.320	0.005
12	Bahamas	24.300	0.252	5.620	0.081
13	Bahrain	44.600	0.462	21.360	0.306
14	Bangladesh	0.700	0.007	0.110	0.002
15	Barbados	29.000	0.301	2.190	0.031
16	Belarus	33.100	0.343	4.080	0.058
17	Belgium	53.200	0.551	36.620	0.525
18	Belize	18.300	0.190	6.840	0.098
19	Benin	4.400	0.046	0.370	0.005
20	Bhutan	0.600	0.006	0.020	0.000
21	Bolivia	11.800	0.122	0.980	0.014
22	Bosnia and Herzegovina	11.200	0.116	1.140	0.016
23	Botswana	2.100	0.022	0.760	0.011
24	Brazil	33.300	0.345	7.770	0.111
25	Brunei Darussalam	63.700	0.660	9.970	0.143
26	Bulgaria	42.900	0.445	7.590	0.109
27	Burkina Faso	1.100	0.011	0.200	0.003
28	Burundi	1.500	0.016	0.090	0.001
29	Cambodia	0.900	0.009	0.080	0.001
30	Cameroon	3.400	0.035	0.280	0.004
31	Canada	70.000	0.725	52.790	0.756
32	Cape Verde	0.500	0.005	2.940	0.042
33	Central African Republic	0.600	0.006	0.050	0.001
34	Chad	0.100	0.001	0.040	0.001
35	Chile	24.000	0.249	20.020	0.287
36	China	29.100	0.302	3.580	0.051
37	Colombia	27.900	0.289	2.810	0.040
38	Comoros	0.400	0.004	0.410	0.006
39	Congo	1.300	0.013	0.020	0.000
40	Costa Rica	22.900	0.237	10.010	0.143
41	Côte d'Ivoire	6.500	0.067	0.000	0.000
42	Croatia	28.600	0.296	11.070	0.159
43	Cuba	24.800	0.257	1.070	0.015

Table 6.   *(continued)*

	Country	TV	TV Index	Online population data	Online population Index
44	Cyprus	15.400	0.160	19.550	0.280
45	Czech Republic	48.700	0.505	26.210	0.376
46	Democratic People's Republic of Korea	5.500	0.057	0.000	0.000
47	Democratic Republic of the Congo	0.200	0.002	0.000	0.000
48	Denmark	77.600	0.804	62.730	0.899
49	Djibouti	4.800	0.050	0.700	0.010
50	Dominica	23.200	0.240	2.800	0.040
51	Dominican Republic	9.600	0.099	2.130	0.031
52	Ecuador	21.300	0.221	2.440	0.035
53	Egypt	17.000	0.176	0.850	0.012
54	El Salvador	19.100	0.198	0.650	0.009
55	Equatorial Guinea	11.600	0.120	0.220	0.003
56	Eritrea	1.600	0.017	0.220	0.003
57	Estonia	56.700	0.588	34.700	0.497
58	Ethiopia	0.500	0.005	0.020	0.000
59	Fiji	11.000	0.114	1.750	0.025
60	Finland	64.300	0.666	51.890	0.743
61	France	62.000	0.642	28.390	0.407
62	Gabon	25.100	0.260	1.240	0.018
63	Gambia	0.300	0.003	1.240	0.018
64	Georgia	51.600	0.535	0.500	0.007
65	Germany	58.100	0.602	38.910	0.557
66	Ghana	11.500	0.119	0.200	0.003
67	Greece	48.000	0.497	13.150	0.188
68	Grenada	37.600	0.390	5.830	0.084
69	Guatemala	6.100	0.063	1.500	0.021
70	Guinea	4.700	0.049	0.190	0.003
71	Guinea-Bissau	3.600	0.037	0.300	0.004
72	Guyana	7.000	0.073	13.610	0.195
73	Haiti	0.500	0.005	0.420	0.006
74	Honduras	9.500	0.098	0.640	0.009
75	Hungary	44.700	0.463	11.870	0.170
76	Iceland	50.500	0.523	69.800	1.000
77	India	7.500	0.078	0.670	0.010
78	Indonesia	14.300	0.148	1.930	0.028
79	Iran (Islamic Republic of)	15.400	0.160	0.630	0.009
80	Iraq	8.200	0.085	0.050	0.001
81	Ireland	40.600	0.421	33.720	0.483
82	Israel	32.800	0.340	17.120	0.245
83	Italy	49.200	0.510	33.370	0.478
84	Jamaica	19.100	0.198	3.730	0.053
85	Japan	71.900	0.745	44.100	0.632
86	Jordan	8.300	0.086	3.990	0.057

Table 6.   *(continued)*

	Country	TV	TV Index	Online population data	Online population Index
87	Kazakhstan	24.000	0.249	0.600	0.009
88	Kenya	2.200	0.023	1.610	0.023
89	Kiribati	2.300	0.024	1.090	0.016
90	Kuwait	48.000	0.497	9.470	0.136
91	Kyrgyzstan	4.900	0.051	1.100	0.016
92	Lao People's Democratic Republic	1.000	0.010	0.170	0.002
93	Latvia	75.700	0.784	13.080	0.187
94	Lebanon	35.500	0.368	8.380	0.120
95	Lesotho	1.600	0.017	0.230	0.003
96	Liberia	2.600	0.027	0.010	0.000
97	Libya	13.900	0.144	0.240	0.003
98	Liechtenstein	46.900	0.486	0.000	0.000
99	Lithuania	42.200	0.437	8.230	0.118
100	Luxembourg	59.900	0.621	22.860	0.328
101	Madagascar	2.300	0.024	0.210	0.003
102	Malawi	0.300	0.003	0.330	0.005
103	Malaysia	17.400	0.180	25.150	0.360
104	Maldives	3.800	0.039	1.990	0.029
105	Mali	1.300	0.013	0.260	0.004
106	Malta	54.900	0.569	24.910	0.357
107	Marshall Islands	0.000	0.000	1.220	0.017
108	Mauritania	9.500	0.098	0.250	0.004
109	Mauritius	24.800	0.257	0.130	0.002
110	Mexico	27.200	0.282	3.380	0.048
111	Micronesia (Federated States of)	2.000	0.021	1.500	0.021
112	Monaco	75.800	0.785	0.000	0.000
113	Mongolia	5.800	0.060	1.480	0.021
114	Morocco	16.500	0.171	1.280	0.018
115	Mozambique	0.500	0.005	0.080	0.001
116	Myanmar	0.700	0.007	0.020	0.000
117	Namibia	3.800	0.039	2.470	0.035
118	Nauru	0.100	0.001	0.000	0.000
119	Nepal	0.600	0.006	0.230	0.003
120	Netherlands	54.000	0.560	60.830	0.871
121	New Zealand	51.600	0.535	52.700	0.755
122	Nicaragua	6.900	0.072	0.420	0.006
123	Niger	1.500	0.016	0.110	0.002
124	Nigeria	6.900	0.072	0.080	0.001
125	Norway	65.300	0.677	59.200	0.848
126	Oman	57.500	0.596	4.420	0.063
127	Pakistan	10.500	0.109	0.850	0.012
128	Palau	0.000	0.000	0.000	0.000
129	Panama	19.200	0.199	1.600	0.023

Table 6. *(continued)*

	Country	TV	TV Index	Online population data	Online population Index
130	Papua New Guinea	1.300	0.013	2.740	0.039
131	Paraguay	20.500	0.212	0.360	0.005
132	Peru	14.700	0.152	10.730	0.154
133	Philippines	11.000	0.114	7.770	0.111
134	Poland	38.700	0.401	16.570	0.237
135	Portugal	56.700	0.588	43.600	0.625
136	Qatar	86.600	0.897	9.750	0.140
137	Republic of Korea	36.400	0.377	53.800	0.771
138	Republic of Moldova	29.700	0.308	0.340	0.005
139	Romania	31.200	0.323	4.480	0.064
140	Russian Federation	53.800	0.558	12.420	0.178
141	Rwanda	0.000	0.000	0.270	0.004
142	Saint Kitts and Nevis	25.600	0.265	5.150	0.074
143	Saint Lucia	36.800	0.381	1.920	0.028
144	Saint Vincent and the Grenadines	23.000	0.238	3.030	0.043
145	Samoa	5.600	0.058	1.680	0.024
146	San Marino	87.500	0.907	0.000	0.000
147	São Tomé and Principe	22.900	0.237	5.280	0.076
148	Saudi Arabia	26.300	0.273	2.500	0.036
149	Senegal	4.100	0.042	0.940	0.013
150	Serbia and Montenegro	27.700	0.287	2.810	0.040
151	Seychelles	21.400	0.222	11.240	0.161
152	Sierra Leone	1.300	0.013	0.380	0.005
153	Singapore	34.100	0.353	51.840	0.743
154	Slovakia	41.800	0.433	12.940	0.185
155	Slovenia	36.200	0.375	31.130	0.446
156	Solomon Islands	1.600	0.017	1.700	0.024
157	Somalia	1.400	0.015	0.000	0.000
158	South Africa	13.800	0.143	7.030	0.101
159	Spain	55.500	0.575	19.690	0.282
160	Sri Lanka	10.200	0.106	0.630	0.009
161	Sudan	17.300	0.179	0.150	0.002
162	Suriname	24.100	0.250	3.320	0.048
163	Swaziland	11.200	0.116	1.250	0.018
164	Sweden	96.500	1.000	67.810	0.971
165	Switzerland	55.400	0.574	52.700	0.755
166	Syrian Arab Republic	6.800	0.070	0.350	0.005
167	Tajikistan	32.800	0.340	0.030	0.000
168	Thailand	27.400	0.284	1.960	0.028
169	T.F.Y.R. Macedonia	27.300	0.283	4.900	0.070
170	Timor-Leste	0.000	0.000	0.000	0.000
171	Togo	2.200	0.023	0.950	0.014
172	Tonga	6.100	0.063	0.980	0.014

Table 6.   *(continued)*

	Country	TV	TV Index	Online population data	Online population Index
173	Trinidad and Tobago	33.700	0.349	10.310	0.148
174	Tunisia	19.000	0.197	4.080	0.058
175	Turkey	32.800	0.340	3.710	0.053
176	Turkmenistan	19.800	0.205	0.040	0.001
177	Tuvalu	0.900	0.009	0.000	0.000
178	Uganda	2.800	0.029	0.240	0.003
179	Ukraine	43.300	0.449	1.540	0.022
180	United Arab Emirates	30.900	0.320	36.790	0.527
181	United Kingdom	66.100	0.685	57.240	0.820
182	United Republic of Tanzania	2.100	0.022	0.810	0.012
183	United States	84.400	0.875	59.100	0.847
184	Uruguay	53.100	0.550	13.610	0.195
185	Uzbekistan	28.000	0.290	0.590	0.008
186	Vanuatu	1.200	0.012	1.580	0.023
187	Venezuela	18.500	0.192	5.350	0.077
188	Viet Nam	18.400	0.191	0.490	0.007
189	Yemen	28.600	0.296	0.090	0.001
190	Zambia	14.500	0.150	0.250	0.004
191	Zimbabwe	3.500	0.036	0.880	0.013

Source: For TV data: *United Nations, Department of Economic & Social Affairs Statistics Division.* http://unstats.un.org/unsd/cdb/cdb_advanced_data_extract_fm.asp?HYrID=1999&HCrID=all& HSrID=25720&yrID=1999&continue=Continue+%3E%3E. Accessed 2 August 2005

For online population: Data is for the latest available year during the period 1999–2002, *NUA Internet Surveys.* http://www.nua.com/surveys/how_many_online/.

Definition: "How Many Online" figures represent both adults and children who have accessed the Internet at least once during the three months prior to being surveyed. Where these figures are not available, figures are for users who have gone online in the past six months, past year, or ever.

Table 7.
Infrastructure Index 2005

	Country	Telecommunication Infrastructure Index
1	Afghanistan	0.002
2	Albania	0.068
3	Algeria	0.037
4	Andorra	0.299
5	Angola	0.007
6	Antigua and Barbuda	0.245
7	Argentina	0.174
8	Armenia	0.076
9	Australia	0.710
10	Austria	0.578
11	Azerbaijan	0.071
12	Bahamas	0.230
13	Bahrain	0.315
14	Bangladesh	0.005
15	Barbados	0.311
16	Belarus	0.157
17	Belgium	0.513
18	Belize	0.141
19	Benin	0.014
20	Bhutan	0.018
21	Bolivia	0.057
22	Bosnia and Herzegovina	0.093
23	Botswana	0.064
24	Brazil	0.164
25	Brunei Darussalam	0.226
26	Bulgaria	0.252
27	Burkina Faso	0.006
28	Burundi	0.004
29	Cambodia	0.006
30	Cameroon	0.014
31	Canada	0.655
32	Cape Verde	0.081
33	Central African Republic	0.003
34	Chad	0.002
35	Chile	0.277
36	China	0.124
37	Colombia	0.111
38	Comoros	0.008
39	Congo	0.012
40	Costa Rica	0.260

Table 7.   *(continued)*

	Country	Telecommunication Infrastructure Index
41	Côte d'Ivoire	0.022
42	Croatia	0.302
43	Cuba	0.050
44	Cyprus	0.410
45	Czech Republic	0.410
46	D.P.R. Korea	0.006
47	D. R. Congo	0.002
48	Denmark	0.764
49	Djibouti	0.021
50	Dominica	0.171
51	Dominican Republic	0.091
52	Ecuador	0.090
53	Egypt	0.072
54	El Salvador	0.091
55	Equatorial Guinea	0.025
56	Eritrea	0.007
57	Estonia	0.528
58	Ethiopia	0.003
59	Fiji	0.084
60	Finland	0.652
61	France	0.506
62	Gabon	0.066
63	Gambia	0.025
64	Georgia	0.109
65	Germany	0.623
66	Ghana	0.021
67	Greece	0.315
68	Grenada	0.225
69	Guatemala	0.048
70	Guinea	0.010
71	Guinea-Bissau	0.011
72	Guyana	0.121
73	Haiti	0.016
74	Honduras	0.041
75	Hungary	0.307
76	Iceland	0.770
77	India	0.028
78	Indonesia	0.049
79	Iran (Islamic Republic of)	0.108
80	Iraq	0.016

Table 7. *(continued)*

	Country	Telecommunication Infrastructure Index
81	Ireland	0.504
82	Israel	0.400
83	Italy	0.481
84	Jamaica	0.201
85	Japan	0.585
86	Jordan	0.097
87	Kazakhstan	0.064
88	Kenya	0.019
89	Kiribati	0.025
90	Kuwait	0.269
91	Kyrgyzstan	0.040
92	Lao P. D. R.	0.007
93	Latvia	0.381
94	Lebanon	0.186
95	Lesotho	0.013
96	Liberia	0.003
97	Libyan Arab Jamahiriya	0.057
98	Liechtenstein	0.364
99	Lithuania	0.253
100	Luxembourg	0.644
101	Madagascar	0.008
102	Malawi	0.005
103	Malaysia	0.305
104	Maldives	0.075
105	Mali	0.006
106	Malta	0.441
107	Marshall Islands	0.042
108	Mauritania	0.028
109	Mauritius	0.176
110	Mexico	0.149
111	Micronesia (Federated States of)	0.052
112	Monaco	0.502
113	Mongolia	0.068
114	Morocco	0.064
115	Mozambique	0.006
116	Myanmar	0.004
117	Namibia	0.068
118	Nauru	0.049
119	Nepal	0.006
120	Netherlands	0.682

Table 7.   *(continued)*

	Country	Telecommunication Infrastructure Index
121	New Zealand	0.602
122	Nicaragua	0.035
123	Niger	0.007
124	Nigeria	0.014
125	Norway	0.682
126	Oman	0.138
127	Pakistan	0.024
128	Palau	0.000
129	Panama	0.098
130	Papua New Guinea	0.030
131	Paraguay	0.071
132	Peru	0.109
133	Philippines	0.084
134	Poland	0.290
135	Portugal	0.428
136	Qatar	0.312
137	Republic of Korea	0.671
138	Republic of Moldova	0.114
139	Romania	0.189
140	Russian Federation	0.195
141	Rwanda	0.004
142	Saint Kitts and Nevis	0.256
143	Saint Lucia	0.174
144	Saint Vincent and the Grenadines	0.176
145	Samoa	0.038
146	San Marino	0.648
147	São Tomé and Principe	0.080
148	Saudi Arabia	0.145
149	Senegal	0.028
150	Serbia and Montenegro	0.142
151	Seychelles	0.234
152	Sierra Leone	0.006
153	Singapore	0.645
154	Slovakia	0.318
155	Slovenia	0.476
156	Solomon Islands	0.021
157	Somalia	0.007
158	South Africa	0.123
159	Spain	0.392
160	Sri Lanka	0.036

Table 7.   *(continued)*

	Country	Telecommunication Infrastructure Index
161	Sudan	0.029
162	Suriname	0.115
163	Swaziland	0.046
164	Sweden	0.840
165	Switzerland	0.711
166	Syrian Arab Republic	0.046
167	Tajikistan	0.042
168	Thailand	0.130
169	T.F.Y.R. Macedonia	0.124
170	Timor-Leste	0.000
171	Togo	0.031
172	Tonga	0.047
173	Trinidad and Tobago	0.197
174	Tunisia	0.099
175	Turkey	0.165
176	Turkmenistan	0.037
177	Tuvalu	0.084
178	Uganda	0.009
179	Ukraine	0.116
180	United Arab Emirates	0.364
181	United Kingdom	0.647
182	United Republic of Tanzania	0.011
183	United States	0.749
184	Uruguay	0.226
185	Uzbekistan	0.051
186	Vanuatu	0.029
187	Venezuela	0.111
188	Viet Nam	0.049
189	Yemen	0.041
190	Zambia	0.023
191	Zimbabwe	0.039

Table 8.
Education Index 2005

	Country	Education Index
1	Afghanistan	0.27
2	Albania	0.89
3	Algeria	0.69
4	Andorra	0.00
5	Angola	0.38
6	Antigua and Barbuda	0.80
7	Argentina	0.96
8	Armenia	0.90
9	Australia	0.99
10	Austria	0.96
11	Azerbaijan	0.88
12	Bahamas	0.88
13	Bahrain	0.85
14	Bangladesh	0.45
15	Barbados	0.95
16	Belarus	0.95
17	Belgium	0.99
18	Belize	0.75
19	Benin	0.44
20	Bhutan	0.48
21	Bolivia	0.86
22	Bosnia and Herzegovina	0.84
23	Botswana	0.76
24	Brazil	0.88
25	Brunei Darussalam	0.87
26	Bulgaria	0.91
27	Burkina Faso	0.16
28	Burundi	0.45
29	Cambodia	0.66
30	Cameroon	0.64
31	Canada	0.98
32	Cape Verde	0.75
33	Central African Republic	0.43
34	Chad	0.42
35	Chile	0.90
36	China	0.83
37	Colombia	0.84
38	Comoros	0.53
39	Congo	0.71
40	Costa Rica	0.87

Table 8. *(continued)*

	Country	Education Index
41	Côte d'Ivoire	0.47
42	Croatia	0.90
43	Cuba	0.91
44	Cyprus	0.89
45	Czech Republic	0.92
46	D.P.R. Korea	0.00
47	D.R. Congo	0.51
48	Denmark	0.98
49	Djibouti	0.52
50	Dominica	0.76
51	Dominican Republic	0.82
52	Ecuador	0.85
53	Egypt	0.62
54	El Salvador	0.75
55	Equatorial Guinea	0.76
56	Eritrea	0.49
57	Estonia	0.98
58	Ethiopia	0.39
59	Fiji	0.86
60	Finland	0.99
61	France	0.96
62	Gabon	0.72
63	Gambia	0.40
64	Georgia	0.89
65	Germany	0.95
66	Ghana	0.65
67	Greece	0.95
68	Grenada	0.85
69	Guatemala	0.65
70	Guinea	0.37
71	Guinea-Bissau	0.39
72	Guyana	0.89
73	Haiti	0.52
74	Honduras	0.74
75	Hungary	0.95
76	Iceland	0.96
77	India	0.59
78	Indonesia	0.80
79	Iran (Islamic Republic of)	0.74
80	Iraq	0.93

Table 8.   *(continued)*

	Country	Education Index
81	Ireland	0.96
82	Israel	0.94
83	Italy	0.93
84	Jamaica	0.83
85	Japan	0.94
86	Jordan	0.86
87	Kazakhstan	0.93
88	Kenya	0.74
89	Kiribati	0.00
90	Kuwait	0.81
91	Kyrgyzstan	0.92
92	Lao People's Democratic Republic	0.64
93	Latvia	0.95
94	Lebanon	0.84
95	Lesotho	0.76
96	Liberia	0.00
97	Libya	0.87
98	Liechtenstein	0.00
99	Lithuania	0.96
100	Luxembourg	0.91
101	Madagascar	0.60
102	Malawi	0.66
103	Malaysia	0.83
104	Maldives	0.91
105	Mali	0.21
106	Malta	0.87
107	Marshall Islands	0.00
108	Mauritania	0.42
109	Mauritius	0.79
110	Mexico	0.85
111	Micronesia (Federated States of)	0.00
112	Monaco	0.00
113	Mongolia	0.89
114	Morocco	0.53
115	Mozambique	0.45
116	Myanmar	0.73
117	Namibia	0.79
118	Nauru	0.00
119	Nepal	0.50
120	Netherlands	0.99

Table 8.   *(continued)*

	Country	Education Index
121	New Zealand	0.99
122	Nicaragua	0.73
123	Niger	0.18
124	Nigeria	0.59
125	Norway	0.99
126	Oman	0.71
127	Pakistan	0.40
128	Palau	0.00
129	Panama	0.86
130	Papua New Guinea	0.57
131	Paraguay	0.85
132	Peru	0.86
133	Philippines	0.89
134	Poland	0.96
135	Portugal	0.97
136	Qatar	0.83
137	Republic of Korea	0.97
138	Republic of Moldova	0.87
139	Romania	0.88
140	Russian Federation	0.95
141	Rwanda	0.64
142	Saint Kitts and Nevis	0.98
143	Saint Lucia	0.88
144	Saint Vincent and the Grenadines	0.77
145	Samoa	0.89
146	San Marino	0.00
147	São Tomé and Principe	0.76
148	Saudi Arabia	0.71
149	Senegal	0.39
150	Serbia and Montenegro	0.00
151	Seychelles	0.90
152	Sierra Leone	0.39
153	Singapore	0.91
154	Slovakia	0.91
155	Slovenia	0.96
156	Solomon Islands	0.68
157	Somalia	0.00
158	South Africa	0.83
159	Spain	0.97
160	Sri Lanka	0.83

Table 8.   *(continued)*

	Country	Education Index
161	Sudan	0.52
162	Suriname	0.87
163	Swaziland	0.74
164	Sweden	0.99
165	Switzerland	0.95
166	Syrian Arab Republic	0.75
167	Tajikistan	0.90
168	Thailand	0.86
169	T.F.Y.R. Macedonia	0.87
170	Timor-Leste	0.64
171	Togo	0.62
172	Tonga	0.93
173	Trinidad and Tobago	0.87
174	Tunisia	0.74
175	Turkey	0.80
176	Turkmenistan	0.93
177	Tuvalu	0.00
178	Uganda	0.70
179	Ukraine	0.94
180	United Arab Emirates	0.74
181	United Kingdom	0.99
182	United Republic of Tanzania	0.62
183	United States	0.97
184	Uruguay	0.94
185	Uzbekistan	0.91
186	Vanuatu	0.42
187	Venezuela	0.86
188	Viet Nam	0.82
189	Yemen	0.50
190	Zambia	0.68
191	Zimbabwe	0.79

Source: UNDP. http://hdr.undp.org/statistics/data/indic/indic_6_1_1.html.
Accessed 16 August 2005.

Table 9.
Service delivery by stages 2005 (Per cent utilization)

			I	II	III	IV	V	TOTAL
			67–100 % utilization					
1	1	United States	100	99	100	100	76	94.89
2	2	Singapore	100	94	99	100	83	94.53
3	3	United Kingdom	100	99	99	100	76	94.53
4	4	Republic of Korea	100	98	96	90	80	92.70
5	5	Denmark	100	97	98	90	78	92.34
6	6	Chile	100	93	93	85	65	86.50
7	7	Australia	100	95	93	80	61	85.77
8	8	Canada	100	99	90	61	69	84.67
9	9	Sweden	100	99	92	63	52	82.12
10	10	Germany	100	95	100	54	41	79.93
11	11	Finland	100	93	94	73	31	78.47
12	12	Mexico	100	93	86	46	61	77.74
13	13	Japan	100	94	92	37	56	77.37
14	14	New Zealand	100	92	86	46	56	76.28
15	15	Norway	100	99	85	39	48	75.55
16	16	Malta	100	100	90	41	33	75.18
17	17	Brazil	100	90	77	63	33	71.17
18	18	Philippines	100	91	82	44	35	70.44
19	19	Austria	100	94	89	37	24	70.44
20	20	Netherlands	100	90	79	41	41	69.71
21	21	Israel	100	92	81	54	22	69.34
22	22	Ireland	100	90	80	61	13	67.52
23	23	Belgium	100	87	87	29	30	67.52
24	24	Hungary	100	90	73	20	52	66.79
			34–66 % utilization					
25	1	Estonia	100	87	85	27	28	66.06
26	2	Thailand	88	89	76	20	31	63.14
27	3	Argentina	100	83	74	39	24	62.41
28	4	Romania	100	82	79	20	26	60.95
29	5	Mauritius	100	80	83	27	9	59.67
30	6	Italy	100	94	64	15	24	59.49
31	7	Colombia	100	84	70	15	26	58.39
32	8	United Arab Emirates	75	62	79	59	17	58.03
33	9	France	100	90	57	17	33	58.03
34	10	Iceland	100	95	65	7	17	57.66
35	11	Switzerland	88	90	63	12	26	57.30
36	12	Slovenia	75	86	71	17	11	56.20

Table 9.   *(continued)*

			I	II	III	IV	V	TOTAL
37	13	Czech Republic	100	85	65	5	26	55.84
38	14	India	100	77	72	17	17	55.29
39	15	Ukraine	100	87	55	0	39	55.11
40	16	Venezuela	100	76	68	0	35	54.74
41	17	Malaysia	100	69	70	29	20	54.74
42	18	South Africa	100	79	62	17	22	54.01
43	19	China	100	75	71	5	24	54.01
44	20	Peru	100	76	70	0	22	52.92
45	21	Slovakia	100	83	60	0	19	51.09
46	22	Turkey	63	72	64	0	26	49.64
47	23	Lithuania	100	87	51	0	17	49.64
48	24	Bulgaria	88	77	52	2	30	49.27
49	25	Poland	88	76	49	0	35	48.54
50	26	Greece	88	86	44	10	19	48.54
51	27	Jamaica	100	56	64	17	17	46.35
52	28	Panama	100	59	63	20	13	46.35
53	29	Belarus	100	74	43	0	35	46.35
54	30	Latvia	88	82	44	0	20	45.99
55	31	Cyprus	88	79	48	0	7	43.80
56	32	Russian Federation	100	76	39	0	20	43.07
57	33	Uruguay	100	51	67	22	0	42.70
58	34	Kazakhstan	100	74	36	0	28	42.70
59	35	Egypt	88	53	60	22	7	42.34
60	36	Serbia and Montenegro	100	72	48	0	9	42.34
61	37	Croatia	100	71	49	0	7	41.97
62	38	Guatemala	100	63	44	15	13	41.24
63	39	Jordan	88	62	58	0	6	41.24
64	40	El Salvador	88	56	52	0	20	40.51
65	41	Pakistan	100	62	51	0	11	40.51
66	42	Portugal	88	62	43	15	15	40.51
67	43	Bahrain	88	64	44	0	17	39.78
68	44	Nepal	88	49	54	0	17	37.96
69	45	Luxembourg	100	63	42	2	9	37.96
70	46	The Former Yugoslav Republic of Macedonia	75	62	46	0	7	37.59
71	47	Spain	100	66	42	0	4	37.23
72	48	Bhutan	100	51	49	0	13	36.50
73	49	Saudi Arabia	0	62	39	0	20	35.77
74	50	Botswana	75	49	52	0	6	35.04
75	51	Kyrgyzstan	100	56	36	0	15	34.67
76	52	Trinidad and Tobago	88	49	47	0	9	34.49

Table 9. *(continued)*

			I	II	III	IV	V	TOTAL
		0–33 % utilization						
77	1	Lebanon	100	46	43	0	9	32.48
78	2	Seychelles	88	38	51	0	6	31.39
79	3	Qatar	63	36	43	20	9	31.02
80	4	Sri Lanka	100	53	31	0	6	30.29
81	5	Dominican Republic	100	46	35	0	7	29.56
82	6	Maldives	88	48	33	0	7	29.56
83	7	Iran (Islamic Republic of)	0	60	23	0	11	28.10
84	8	Indonesia	100	49	15	0	24	28.10
85	9	Swaziland	88	36	43	0	4	27.74
86	10	Bahamas	100	29	50	0	2	27.74
87	11	Bolivia	75	55	23	0	4	27.37
88	12	Saint Lucia	88	30	47	0	4	27.19
89	13	San Marino	63	40	36	0	7	27.01
90	14	Fiji	75	28	50	0	2	26.64
91	15	Mozambique	75	34	38	0	9	26.46
92	16	United Republic of Tanzania	100	26	48	0	0	26.09
93	17	Uzbekistan	88	44	27	0	6	25.91
94	18	Bosnia and Herzegovina	88	31	44	0	0	25.91
95	19	Samoa	88	23	49	0	2	25.18
96	20	Senegal	88	44	21	0	6	24.09
97	21	Saint Vincent and the Grenadines	88	28	35	0	11	24.09
98	22	Belize	88	17	51	0	2	24.09
99	23	Costa Rica	75	45	24	0	2	24.09
100	24	Andorra	88	43	22	0	6	23.91
101	25	Nicaragua	88	41	21	0	7	23.72
102	26	Ecuador	88	40	21	0	9	23.72
103	27	Kuwait	0	40	26	0	15	23.72
104	28	Algeria	75	36	29	0	6	23.36
105	29	Brunei Darussalam	63	39	24	0	9	23.36
106	30	Morocco	100	37	21	0	7	22.63
107	31	Lesotho	88	29	33	0	4	22.63
108	32	Benin	88	25	37	2	2	22.63
109	33	Burkina Faso	100	32	27	0	4	22.08
110	34	Kenya	75	29	35	0	0	21.90
111	35	Mongolia	100	34	19	0	11	21.90
112	36	Cambodia	100	30	26	0	7	21.90
113	37	Nigeria	100	24	26	5	9	21.17
114	38	Honduras	75	31	23	0	11	21.17
115	39	Viet Nam	0	45	17	0	9	21.17

Table 9.   *(continued)*

			I	II	III	IV	V	TOTAL
116	40	Monaco	63	29	30	0	4	20.80
117	41	Uganda	50	31	27	0	4	20.44
118	42	Barbados	75	20	30	15	4	20.44
119	43	Georgia	0	31	33	0	0	20.07
120	44	Ghana	88	22	24	0	6	17.88
121	45	Madagascar	88	26	15	0	9	17.52
122	46	Guyana	63	13	36	0	4	17.52
123	47	Azerbaijan	0	29	24	0	4	17.15
124	48	Afghanistan	50	23	24	0	4	16.79
125	49	Djibouti	50	26	20	0	2	16.42
126	50	Malawi	75	17	29	0	0	16.42
127	51	Cape Verde	63	33	10	0	6	16.42
128	52	Oman	0	30	19	0	6	16.42
129	53	Liechtenstein	100	16	25	0	4	16.42
130	54	Palau	75	13	32	0	0	16.06
131	55	Zimbabwe	50	24	20	0	2	15.69
132	56	Angola	75	17	25	2	0	15.69
133	57	Namibia	75	20	24	0	0	15.69
134	58	Paraguay	63	24	14	0	9	15.69
135	59	Sudan	63	24	14	0	7	15.33
136	60	Albania	0	30	15	0	6	15.33
137	61	Papua New Guinea	75	21	21	0	0	15.33
138	62	Antigua and Barbuda	63	13	27	2	2	14.96
139	63	Tunisia	88	9	30	0	0	14.60
140	64	Myanmar	88	22	13	2	4	14.60
141	65	Cuba	50	25	11	0	7	14.23
142	66	Congo	88	15	15	0	4	12.77
143	67	Tonga	63	22	10	0	2	12.04
144	68	Rwanda	50	16	14	0	0	10.95
145	69	Timor-Leste	100	9	15	0	2	10.77
146	70	Saint Kitts and Nevis	50	13	13	0	6	10.58
147	71	Armenia	13	17	14	0	2	10.58
148	72	Micronesia (Federated States of)	75	11	14	0	0	10.22
149	73	Solomon Islands	0	13	18	0	0	9.49
150	74	Cameroon	38	13	11	0	4	9.12
151	75	Gambia	38	13	11	0	4	9.12
152	76	Sierra Leone	75	11	7	0	6	9.12
153	77	Yemen	75	17	5	0	0	9.12
154	78	Gabon	0	17	11	0	0	8.76
155	79	Marshall Islands	0	10	17	0	0	8.58

Table 9. *(continued)*

			I	II	III	IV	V	TOTAL
156	80	Grenada	38	16	7	0	0	8.39
157	81	Lao People's Democratic Republic	0	8	16	0	0	7.48
158	82	Bangladesh	88	11	1	0	2	6.93
159	83	Mauritania	63	10	2	0	4	6.57
160	84	Dominica	0	10	8	0	4	6.57
161	85	Syrian Arab Republic	0	13	4	0	6	6.20
162	86	Mali	13	9	8	0	0	5.84
163	87	Tajikistan	0	11	7	0	0	5.84
164	88	Eritrea	0	8	7	0	4	5.47
165	89	Nauru	0	9	8	0	0	5.47
166	90	Comoros	25	8	6	0	0	5.11
167	91	Côte d'Ivoire	50	9	1	0	2	5.11
168	92	Iraq	25	10	2	0	2	5.11
169	93	Republic of Moldova	0	10	6	0	0	5.11
170	94	Suriname	0	8	7	0	0	4.74
171	95	Vanuatu	25	7	6	0	0	4.74
172	96	Burundi	13	7	4	0	0	3.65
173	97	Guinea	25	2	7	0	0	3.65
174	98	Togo	25	7	0	0	0	2.92
175	99	Tuvalu	0	1	7	0	0	2.55
176	100	Ethiopia	0	2	2	0	0	1.46
177	101	São Tomé and Principe	0	0	2	0	2	1.09
178	102	Niger	0	3	0	0	0	1.09
179	103	Chad	13	0	1	0	0	0.73
No online services								
180	1	Somalia	0	0	0	0	0	0.00
181	2	Zambia	0	0	0	0	0	0.00
182	3	Central African Republic	0	0	0	0	0	0.00
183	4	Democratic Republic of the Congo	0	0	0	0	0	0.00
184	5	Equatorial Guinea	0	0	0	0	0	0.00
185	6	Libyan Arab Jamahiriya	0	0	0	0	0	0.00
186	7	Guinea-Bissau	0	0	0	0	0	0.00
187	8	Liberia	0	0	0	0	0	0.00
188	9	Haiti	0	0	0	0	0	0.00
189	10	Democratic People's Republic of Korea	0	0	0	0	0	0.00
190	11	Turkmenistan	0	0	0	0	0	0.00
191	12	Kiribati	0	0	0	0	0	0.00

Table 10.
E-participation Index 2005

	Country	Index	Rank
1	United Kingdom	1.0000	1
2	Singapore	0.9841	2
3	United States	0.9048	3
4	Canada	0.8730	4
5	Republic of Korea	0.8730	4
6	New Zealand	0.7937	5
7	Denmark	0.7619	6
8	Mexico	0.7619	6
9	Australia	0.7143	7
10	Netherlands	0.6984	8
11	Estonia	0.6190	9
12	Chile	0.5873	10
13	Colombia	0.5873	10
14	Sweden	0.5714	11
15	Finland	0.5556	12
16	Germany	0.5556	12
17	Belgium	0.5079	13
18	Brazil	0.4921	14
19	Malta	0.4762	15
20	Philippines	0.4762	15
21	Japan	0.4603	16
22	Switzerland	0.4286	17
23	Venezuela	0.4286	17
24	Austria	0.4127	18
25	France	0.4127	18
26	Norway	0.3968	19
27	Hungary	0.3810	20
28	Ukraine	0.3651	21
29	Poland	0.3492	22
30	Mozambique	0.3333	23
31	Israel	0.3175	24
32	Romania	0.3175	24
33	South Africa	0.3016	25
34	Indonesia	0.2857	26
35	Turkey	0.2857	26
36	Argentina	0.2698	27
37	Belarus	0.2698	27
38	Guatemala	0.2698	27
39	Honduras	0.2698	27
40	Panama	0.2698	27

Table 10. *(continued)*

	Country	Index	Rank
41	Peru	0.2698	27
42	Bulgaria	0.2540	28
43	Mongolia	0.2540	28
44	Thailand	0.2540	28
45	Italy	0.2381	29
46	Slovenia	0.2222	30
47	Czech Republic	0.2063	31
48	Kazakhstan	0.2063	31
49	Portugal	0.2063	31
50	China	0.1905	32
51	Ireland	0.1905	32
52	Cambodia	0.1746	33
53	Croatia	0.1746	33
54	Latvia	0.1746	33
55	Malaysia	0.1746	33
56	Slovakia	0.1746	33
57	El Salvador	0.1587	34
58	Greece	0.1587	34
59	India	0.1587	34
60	Kyrgyzstan	0.1587	34
61	Luxembourg	0.1429	35
62	Russian Federation	0.1429	35
63	Iceland	0.1270	36
64	Mauritius	0.1270	36
65	Pakistan	0.1270	36
66	T.F.Y.R. Macedonia	0.1270	36
67	United Arab Emirates	0.1270	36
68	Viet Nam	0.1270	36
69	Lebanon	0.1111	37
70	Lithuania	0.1111	37
71	Nicaragua	0.1111	37
72	Jamaica	0.0952	38
73	Bolivia	0.0794	39
74	Cape Verde	0.0794	39
75	Cyprus	0.0794	39
76	Egypt	0.0794	39
77	Liechtenstein	0.0794	39
78	Nepal	0.0794	39
79	Nigeria	0.0794	39
80	Saint Vincent and the Grenadines	0.0794	39

Table 10.   *(continued)*

	Country	Index	Rank
81	Spain	0.0794	39
82	Trinidad and Tobago	0.0794	39
83	Armenia	0.0635	40
84	Dominican Republic	0.0635	40
85	Ecuador	0.0635	40
86	Saint Kitts and Nevis	0.0635	40
87	Saudi Arabia	0.0635	40
88	Sierra Leone	0.0635	40
89	Uruguay	0.0635	40
90	Bahrain	0.0476	41
91	Barbados	0.0476	41
92	Bhutan	0.0476	41
93	Botswana	0.0476	41
94	Costa Rica	0.0476	41
95	Gambia	0.0476	41
96	Jordan	0.0476	41
97	Madagascar	0.0476	41
98	Myanmar	0.0476	41
99	Qatar	0.0476	41
100	Saint Lucia	0.0476	41
101	Serbia and Montenegro	0.0476	41
102	Seychelles	0.0476	41
103	Sri Lanka	0.0476	41
104	Uganda	0.0476	41
105	Albania	0.0317	42
106	Algeria	0.0317	42
107	Andorra	0.0317	42
108	Angola	0.0317	42
109	Antigua and Barbuda	0.0317	42
110	Bahamas	0.0317	42
111	Brunei Darussalam	0.0317	42
112	Cameroon	0.0317	42
113	Congo	0.0317	42
114	Eritrea	0.0317	42
115	Ghana	0.0317	42
116	Guyana	0.0317	42
117	Iran (Islamic Republic of)	0.0317	42
118	Kenya	0.0317	42
119	Maldives	0.0317	42
120	Mauritania	0.0317	42

Table 10. *(continued)*

	Country	Index	Rank
121	Monaco	0.0317	42
122	Morocco	0.0317	42
123	Papua New Guinea	0.0317	42
124	Senegal	0.0317	42
125	Sudan	0.0317	42
126	Swaziland	0.0317	42
127	United Republic of Tanzania	0.0317	42
128	Uzbekistan	0.0317	42
129	Afghanistan	0.0159	43
130	Azerbaijan	0.0159	43
131	Belize	0.0159	43
132	Benin	0.0159	43
133	Bosnia and Herzegovina	0.0159	43
134	Burkina Faso	0.0159	43
135	Comoros	0.0159	43
136	Côte d'Ivoire	0.0159	43
137	Cuba	0.0159	43
138	Djibouti	0.0159	43
139	Fiji	0.0159	43
140	Georgia	0.0159	43
141	Lesotho	0.0159	43
142	Malawi	0.0159	43
143	Oman	0.0159	43
144	Paraguay	0.0159	43
145	Rwanda	0.0159	43
146	Samoa	0.0159	43
147	San Marino	0.0159	43
148	Timor-Leste	0.0159	43
149	Tonga	0.0159	43
150	Vanuatu	0.0159	43
151	Bangladesh	0.0000	44
152	Burundi	0.0000	44
153	Central African Republic	0.0000	44
154	Chad	0.0000	44
155	D.P.R. Korea	0.0000	44
156	D.R. Congo	0.0000	44
157	Dominica	0.0000	44
158	Equatorial Guinea	0.0000	44
159	Ethiopia	0.0000	44
160	Gabon	0.0000	44

Table 10.   *(continued)*

	Country	Index	Rank
161	Grenada	0.0000	44
162	Guinea	0.0000	44
163	Guinea-Bissau	0.0000	44
164	Haiti	0.0000	44
165	Iraq	0.0000	44
166	Kiribati	0.0000	44
167	Kuwait	0.0000	44
168	Lao People's Democratic Republic	0.0000	44
169	Liberia	0.0000	44
170	Libyan Arab Jamahiriya	0.0000	44
171	Mali	0.0000	44
172	Marshall Islands	0.0000	44
173	Micronesia (Federated States of)	0.0000	44
174	Namibia	0.0000	44
175	Nauru	0.0000	44
176	Niger	0.0000	44
177	Palau	0.0000	44
178	Republic of Moldova	0.0000	44
179	São Tomé and Principe	0.0000	44
180	Solomon Islands	0.0000	44
181	Somalia	0.0000	44
182	Suriname	0.0000	44
183	Syrian Arab Republic	0.0000	44
184	Tajikistan	0.0000	44
185	Togo	0.0000	44
186	Tunisia	0.0000	44
187	Turkmenistan	0.0000	44
188	Tuvalu	0.0000	44
189	Yemen	0.0000	44
190	Zambia	0.0000	44
191	Zimbabwe	0.0000	44

Annex Two

Technical Notes and Methodology

Technical notes and methodology 2005

Telecommunication infrastructure index

The Telecommunication Infrastructure Index 2003 is a composite weighted average of six primary indicators. These are: PCs/1000 persons; Internet users/1000 persons; Telephone lines/1000 persons; Online population; Mobile phones/1000 persons; and TVs/1000 persons.

Data for UN Member States was taken primarily from the UN International Telecommunication Union (ITU) and UN Statistics Division, supplemented by information from the World Bank. The data was standardized by constructing indices for each of the indicators as follows: Based on the scores of the countries, a maximum and minimum value is selected for each of the six indicators. The country's relative performance is measured by a value between 0 and 1 based on the following:

Indicator value = (Actual value − Minimum value) / (Maximum value − Minimum value). For example, for Singapore, which has 622 PCs per 1000 persons, the PC index = (622 − 0) / (760 − 0) = 0. 818.

Constructing the indices

Indicator (per 1000 persons)	Maximum Value	Minimum Value
PCs	760	0
Internet users	648	0
Telephone lines	1040	0
Online population	698	0
Mobile subscribers	1061	0
TVs	965	0

The Survey deems the prevalence of PCs, Internet users, telephone lines and online population to be of far greater significance than mobile phones and TVs at this point in e-government service delivery worldwide, although it is acknowledged that governments can, and do, use other forms of ICT such as radio and TV to improve knowledge and service delivery to people. Consequently, the Telecommunication Infrastructure Index was constructed as a composite measure that assigns a 20 per cent weight to the first three variables and five per cent to the remaining two.

$$\text{Infrastructure Index} = 1/5 \text{ (PC index)} + 1/5 \text{ (Internet user index)}$$
$$+ 1/5 \text{ (Telephone line index)}$$
$$+ 1/5 \text{ (Online population index)}$$
$$+ 1/10 \text{ (Mobile user index)} + 1/10 \text{ (TV index)}$$

Human capital index

Adult literacy is the percentage of people aged 15 years and above who can, with understanding, both read and write a short simple statement on their everyday life. Combined primary, secondary and tertiary gross enrolment ratio is the total number of students enrolled at the primary, secondary and tertiary level, regardless of age, as a percentage of the population of school age for that level. For country X, with an adult literacy rate of 96.3 per cent and a combined gross enrolment ratio of 81.2 per cent in 2002, the education index would be: Adult literacy index = 0.963; Gross enrolment index = 0.812; Education index = 2/3 (Adult literacy index) + 1/3 (Gross enrolment index) = 2/3 (0.963) + 1/3 (0.812) = 0.913.

Web measure survey methodology

The overarching purpose of the Web measure survey is simply to assess all UN Member States' online presence through their national sites, as well as five pre-determined ministries, along with associated and integrated portals. In order to undertake a thorough review and simultaneously ensure fairness and accuracy, a rigorous methodological framework was developed in 2003. While it has evolved by necessity, the overarching model remains remarkably consistent. The key in conducting such a truly global survey is essentially twofold:

First, for fairness, the assessment utilizes a 60-day survey "window" during which time all country websites are reviewed and also re-evaluated by senior researchers (with the help of translators when necessary). All sites are reviewed during this time frame and no changes are made to the data after the survey collection window is closed. Consequently, the Web measure becomes an instant snapshot of online presence. It is conducted in the shortest amount of time possible for reviewers to evaluate all member states and also give senior researchers the ability to re-review them for consistency purposes.

While the majority of websites provide some if not most of their site content in English, because of the nature of the survey the core research team enlists the assistance of translators or native speakers for the countries surveyed whenever necessary. Every effort is undertaken to review each country in its official language or in the pre-dominant language on its site(s).

Finally, another contributing factor in conducting a consistent global survey is the fact that the senior research team has remained intact; consequently, while a fresh pair of reviewer eyes is evaluating specific sites, supervising senior researchers are there to locate additions, recognize re-modelled sites, verify sameness or identify change, as well as to provide guidance. Every hard copy is stored and all details captured in the online *UN Global E-Government Survey Knowledgebase* for future reference.

General approach

In surveying each site, reviewers are instructed and trained to take the approach and assume the mindset of an average citizen user. While it is possible, although implausible, to search the sites meticulously for all content and features, this approach misses the key point that the average user needs to find information and features quickly and intuitively for a site to be "usable." Even if researchers had the resources to search for hours to locate a specific feature or function at a given site, no average citizen or government website user would expend that kind of time or effort. The actual time spent for any given country review varies widely depending on how extensive the online presence is, and generally how "good" or "bad" the actual websites are, both in terms of design and user-friendliness, as well as in the extent of the content offered. Given the wide variation among sites, it is hard to provide the approximate time needed for reviewing a single country but a researcher typically reviews one or possibly two countries in a full day. As described above, once its review is completed by the original reviewer/translator, a country is subject to complete re-review by a senior researcher (along with a translator when necessary) who re-verifies all answers and, if applicable, compiles outstanding judgment calls that are determined in conjunction with the lead researcher. Through this method, all surveyed sites are thoroughly assessed by at least two people, at least one of whom has years of experience in assessing such government sites.

Selecting the appropriate site/ URL at the national level

One of the baseline decisions for researchers when undertaking this survey was to identify the specific site(s) to review as the national government site for each country. Regardless of where a nation is in its e-government development, a priority should be to provide users a clear indication as to which of the potentially many government sites available is the "official" national government site—in a sense, the gateway or starting point for national users. Not only is this fairly easy to do—a simple, clear statement at the chosen website is sufficient to start—but also an important step toward providing government information and services to the public in an integrated, usable and easy-to-find manner.

The criteria included the following:

1. Is there a distinct national government site or portal?

2. Is there a Presidential or Prime Minister's site (whichever office heads the government of the country in question) that clearly states that it is the national government site?

3. Is there a site operated by another agency, ministry or other government body that is clearly identified as the national government site?

4. If none of the above is present, is there a viable Presidential or Prime Minister's site, even if it is not clearly identified as the national government site (and as long as it is not simply a press or publicity site)? In other words, does it include information about the national government and its services even if there is no clear statement or indication that it is indeed the official national government site?

If no site could be found that clearly met any of the above criteria, then the country received no points for the "Emerging Presence" section of the survey because it was deemed that there was no "true" national site; rather, a substitute national site had to be used. While uncommon, when applicable this typically involved countries that have only one government site online, which usually turns out to be a pure Ministry of Information or Ministry of Tourism site. Tuvalu, for example, has a Ministry of Tourism site, http://www.timelesstuvalu.com, but no other government online presence. Consequently, the Ministry site was reviewed as a substitute national site and received no points for the "Emerging Presence" section.

It should be noted that while sites illustrate some of the problems above, most have in fact engaged in the procedure of actually noting on their national site that it is their "Official" Government site, or "Gateway to Government," or other such statement. A good example of creating and identifying a single government access point is the Malta national site, http://www.gov.mt, whose title bar indicates "Government of Malta Information & Services Online" while the homepage itself, in addition to the "Government Of Malta" header clearly states the site's purpose up front: "Welcome to www.gov.mt where you can access Government services." Such clear user-friendly presentation is not limited to larger, industrialized nations; the Saint Vincent and the Grenadines national site, http://www.gov.vc, for example, includes a visible header simply, but effectively, stating, "The Official Website of the Government of Saint Vincent and the Grenadines" and the footer, at the bottom of the homepage, repeats the message. These types of clear indicators on national sites obviously made the choice for researchers easy, as it would for citizens.

One perhaps ironic dilemma facing researchers is the increasing number of countries that provide more than one apparently legitimate national access point. While some have simply not yet consolidated their government entry points into a single site or portal that can be clearly distinguished, others have actually done this on purpose—offering different access points to different audiences. Since the use of integrated portals or websites is an increasing—and apparently effective—trend in the e-government strategies of states worldwide, when faced with this situation researchers selected as the primary site a National Portal or other portal if it was deemed to be the official homepage of the government; however, to accommodate strategy, more than one site could be scored if it was clearly part of a tightly integrated "network" of national sites. It should be noted, however, that countries for which more than one site was assessed were neither at a disadvantage nor received any benefits from having more than one national entry. A case in point is Norway, which has an official government site for "Information from the Government and the Ministries," http://odin.dep.no/odin/, as well as a site self-described as "your gateway to the public sector in Norway," http://norge.no. Clearly, both are official government sites. The former is, as indicated, informational while the latter provides a guide to the actual services. To accommodate strategy, one site is deemed the primary country national site, in this case Odin, and is assessed as usual; however, since the two entry sites are clearly integrated in that they link to each other, the second, Norge.no, was then evaluated in terms of the services offered there. In this way, the survey was able to assess the basic structure and information offered at the primary site while incorporating the integrated stand-alone services portal without penalizing the country for its strategy.

Some countries have engaged in the convenient practice of organizing and providing their information architecture by audience. This user-friendly "tab" design system enables a country to target different users simultaneously while retaining only one national site gateway. Notable examples of this strategy, found around the world, include the U.S. FirstGov portal, http://www.firstgov.gov, Mauritius, which classifies the audience tabs as "sub-portals," http://www.gov.mu, and Singapore, http://www.gov.sg, as well as the United Arab Emirates, http://www.government.ae.

Despite improvements in consolidation and integration, there are often seemingly overlapping, yet different entry points depending on audience. As noted last year, Australia, for example, has several sites depending on purpose, such as the business entry point, http://www.business.gov.au. Similarly, the U.S. has an "Official Business Link to the U.S. Government" site, http://www.business.gov.

For purposes here, because this survey is concerned mainly with citizens, a site intended for one specific group is too limited to constitute a "national site." While in these instances researchers were able to identify the primary national site and disregard the audience-specific gateways, it illustrates the importance of clearly identifying government sites for what they are and what purpose they achieve. Specifically, in addition to identifying a national site as "official," the emphasis remains on what appears to be the best starting point for citizens. After the starting point is chosen, other national government sites are included and taken into account, provided the main site links to the other access points. Basically therefore, no country is penalized for setting up additional access points as long as they are clearly integrated and identified in an easy to manage fashion.

Selecting the appropriate site/ URL at the ministry level

Finding and selecting the appropriate site(s) at the ministerial level is typically an easy task because most national sites provide links to the ministries, often under a clearly defined header or subsection. Such an approach not only encourages citizen utilization and enhances the delivery of information across government but should, in fact, be considered a standard feature of any national site. Obviously, where this practice was in place, ministerial sites were easily identified by researchers. In instances where this was not the case, researchers consulted the data collection database with ministry URLs from the two previous years' reports. If still unavailable, researchers next attempted to locate the ministerial URLs at other national government sites that might provide them. If unsuccessful the researchers continued by trying to find them through the most common search engines. Finally, independent online collections of government URLs were consulted. If none of these methods resulted in finding the appropriate ministry it was determined to be unavailable. Similarly to locating a national site URL, if a meticulous search by researchers could not locate the site, then it is unlikely a citizen would expend the time and effort to do so.

Selecting the appropriate site/
URL if unavailable at the national level

One obstacle in conducting a truly global survey is the fact that some countries do not offer certain public services at the federal level, but rather at the regional level. It should be made clear that no country is penalized for offering a service at the regional as opposed to the federal level per se. In fact, when this occurs researchers tend to be inclusive in assessing the matter as long as the information and/or service can be found from the national level. For example, motor vehicle services in the United States are handled by states rather than by the federal government. Even so, the federal FirstGov portal clearly re-directs the user where to go by providing links to the specific state URLs where the services can be obtained: http://www.firstgov.gov/Topics/Motor_Vehicles.shtml.

A more difficult problem arises when not only is a specific service located at the local level but entire ministerial functions are altogether missing at the national level. If researchers were unable to locate a ministry as per the above-described method, then the final step was to find out whether the country in question actually had such a ministry at the national level, or whether the function it would fulfil might be locally administrated. While this is a rare occurrence there are some notable examples, such as in Canada, where education is not a federal issue but rather managed at the provincial and territorial level. With no department available to survey at the national level the methodology had to be expanded in order to incorporate structural variation among countries. Again, no country was penalized for administrating services at the local rather than the national level.

In these instances, after much discussion and analysis, it was determined that the best proxy for incorporating structural variation is to survey the specific ministerial function equivalent in the largest local-level entity offering the service. Consequently, in the case of Canada, Ontario's Ministry of Education, http://www.edu.gov.on.ca, was assessed as the substitute site. Similarly, in Switzerland, where labour is a local—not a national—administrative issue, the Department of Labour in the Canton of Zürich was the alternative site surveyed, http://www.awa.zh.ch. While obviously this is not a perfect equivalent, it was concluded to be the fairest alternative in conducting a truly global assessment when taking cultural and structural variation into account. In fact, judging by the numbers, the method was clearly not to anyone's disadvantage as Ontario's site was tied for the highest scoring ministry in Canada while the Zürich site was the second highest scoring one in Switzerland.

Another dilemma, albeit more minor, arises in those countries where one or more ministries are combined into one. Most notably, a fair number of countries have a "Ministry of Health and Social Welfare," such as the Republic of Korea, http://www.mohw.go.kr. In these cases the ministry is assessed as usual and its score simply multiplied by two. Similarly, a very small number of countries have combined three ministries into one, such as Japan, which has a Ministry of Health, Labour and Welfare, http://www.mhlw.go.jp, whose score is then multiplied by three.

E-participation methodology

The e-participation module expands the quantitative survey by emphasizing quality and tracking change mainly, though not exclusively, from the networked presence stage in the survey. The module is segmented into three sections: e-information, e-consultation, and e-decision-making. Specifically then, like previous surveys in 2003 and 2004, the e-participation scoring assesses "how useful" these features were and "how well were they deployed by the government." Focusing primarily on the national site while also considering the ministry sites, the original reviewers—who often had spent many hours reviewing a nation's collective online presence—completed the e-participation module for each country they reviewed. Reviewers were also asked to go back and refine their e-participation scoring after they had completed all of their assigned sites because they occasionally found, for instance, that they may have scored their earlier sites too leniently or too harshly when compared to later sites. Once finalized by reviewers, the e-participation scores were normalized by the lead researcher and one senior researcher who, together, systematically reviewed every national site (with the help of translators when necessary). Sites were compared to other, similar sites, and various sensitivity indexes were created from the quantitative data to help identify clear over or under scoring. Finally, "clusters" of sites that received the same or very close scores were reviewed and compared to each other so that any variations and/or similarities in scoring could be reasonably explained.

The systematic and thorough re-review process reveals that while quantitative scoring may be similar, there are sometimes vast qualitative variations among countries, the identification of which is the purpose of the e-participation module. For example, compare the quality of government information to citizens about the benefits of e-information between Antigua and Barbuda, http://www.ab.gov.ag/gov_v2/government/egov/, which provides a neat but short section on their national site—a first step—to New Zealand's full-fledged e-government portal, http://www.e-government.govt.nz, which is extremely informative, useful and up-to-date. Similarly, the only open-ended discussion forum offered by Botswana on its brand new Ministry of Health site, http://www.moh.gov.bw, again, is an impressive first step, though it pales in comparison with the Republic of Korea's online presence, which incorporates an advanced discussion forum on every one of its surveyed sites (and, for the record, does a great job of promoting them too).

In summary, through the meticulous quantitative assessment of all sites one quickly realizes what qualitative differences are all about. Providing an e-participation module to complement the raw data, therefore, is an important and valuable means to evaluate both the efforts of governments and the actual quality of the information and services they provide. It is not an attempt to single out how things should be done, but rather to offer insight into how things could—or are—being done to provide useful means for interaction between citizen and government, as well as among citizens, to the benefit of all.

Supplemental methodology

The Web measure survey and e-participation module are complemented by additional analysis on UN Member States' online presence in an ongoing effort to evaluate progress. This year, supplemental research focused on disability access, which is a digital divide issue perhaps less apparent than lack of physical infrastructure but enormously important in its own right. The accessibility assessment was undertaken by evaluating all Member State National Site homepages or their equivalent for standard Priority 1 accessibility compliance as defined by the World Wide Web Consortium's (W3C) Web Accessibility Initiative's (WAI) Web Content Accessibility Guidelines (WCAG).[1] The actual test was carried out by entering the applicable URL into Watchfire's free online evaluation tool, WebXACT, to measure the National Sites for their compliance with the current accessibility standards.[2]

Notes

1   More information on the World Wide Web Consortium's (W3C) Web Accessibility Initiative (WAI) can be found at http://www.w3.org/WAI/.

2   Watchfire's WebXACT is available at http://webxact.watchfire.com/.